Sebastian Ringel

Leipzig!

One Thousand Years of History

1015 LEIPZIG 2015

Wir sind die Stadt

Stadtentdeckertouren

Edition Leipzig

Contents

Leipzig, the Livable City at the Crossroads of Europe

Leipzig is located in the heart of Europe, at the crossroads of two ancient roads: The west-east route from Paris to Moscow, and the south-north route from Rome to Stettin (Szczecin) on the Baltic Sea. In 2015, Leipzig turned one thousand years old. During this long period, the city has had its ups and downs: it survived the bubonic plague, the Thirty Years War, Frederick the Great, and Napoleon. The city blossomed during the Renaissance, the era before the March revolution of 1848, and the Gilded Age that ended with the stock market crash of 1873. It was severely bombed during World War II and suffered afterward behind the Iron Curtain. By 1990, its future seemed to be over. "Can Leipzig still be saved?" asked citizens, city planners, and activists, when the Berlin Wall fell.

Under the German Democratic Republic, exceptional buildings were commissioned in the inner city: the Opera in the 1950s and the Gewandhaus in 1981. Also apartments were built in downtown Leipzig, in Grünau, and in Paunsdorf. But the historical parts of the city gradually decayed. Historic buildings were either laboriously preserved by the citizens themselves or else lay gray and empty. Some of those vacant buildings fell prey to large-scale demolition and some areas remained a post-war wasteland—even in the inner city. The rivers were covered with poisonous scum and the sky above Leipzig and its southern suburbs was tinged with coal and chemicals. After the Iron Curtain came down in 1989, the city lost 70,000 industry jobs and 90,000 inhabitants. But Leipzig could still be saved, thanks to many dedicated citizens as well as to politicians like the first mayor after the *Wende* (turning point), Hinrich Lehmann-Grube, who established a competent city administration.

Leipzig became the biggest construction site in the eastern part of Germany. Late-nineteenth-century buildings were renovated, the first gaps in the downtown filled in; also, the renewal of the technical infrastructure began: electrical wiring, streets, sidewalks, and bicycle lanes. The Karstadt department store was rebuilt and extended; Galeria Kaufhof followed; traditional cultural sites like the Gewandhaus found new friends; the Grassi Museum was refurbished; and the Bach Museum newly outfitted. The Museum of Fine Arts was rebuilt and private investors made nineteenth-century cathedrals of industry like Die Spinnerei a new home for artists and other creative folks. Leipzig is now one of the fastest growing cities in Europe, compact but still green, a mecca for flaneurs, the pride of its citizens. In 2000, the city had 490,000 inhabitants; today it has 532,000. Leipzig stands for emergence, innovation, and quality of life, a "city for the people," lively, beautiful, and ready for all things new.

Leipzig is a cultural city par excellence. Artists and philosophers experienced the peak of their creative career here: Martin Luther, who argued with Johannes Eck about the future of Christianity at the university (founded in 1409 and, after Heidelberg, the oldest university in Germany); Johann Sebastian Bach, who led the choir and played the organ in the famous Thomaskirche; Johann Wolfgang von Goethe, who wrote the classic play *Faust* in Leipzig (one scene takes place in Auerbachs Keller, a restaurant in a historic building, where *Faust the Rock Opera* is performed today). Richard Wagner was born here at Brühl, the street where fur coats were manufactured and where the author Karl May also started his career (actually as a fur thief: he began to write in prison).

Felix Mendelssohn Bartholdy rediscovered Bach's greatest works in Leipzig, and Friedrich Nietzsche discovered materialism. Ferdinand Lassalle created the Allgemeiner Deutscher Arbeiterverein (General German Worker's Association). Anton Philipp Reclam founded a publishing house that issued inexpensive classics. Erich Kästner, the author of *Emil and the Detectives,* was a regular customer in Café Felsche on Augustusplatz. Kurt Masur, another supporter of peaceful revolution in 1989, led the Gewandhaus Orchestra before leaving for New York to become music director of the New York Philharmonic. Modern artists such as Neo Rauch and other painters come from the city on the River Pleisse, or have remained in Leipzig after completing their studies at the Leipzig Academy.

The Leipziger Messe, the trade fair, is at least as important for the city as art and literature. The fair dates back to the twelfth century and was authorized by the *Stadtbrief* (city letter) of Margrave Otto the Rich. In 1894, the trade fair became a *Mustermesse* (sample fair). At that time the Renaissance buildings with courtyards for horses and wagons were converted into splendid "fair palaces." During the GDR, East met West in the Interhotel at the train station, one of Europe's largest railway termini, a hub like the Paris Gare du Nord or Grand Central Station in New York. Today, the new *Messegelände* (fairgrounds) have opened their doors with a number of glass halls, designed by the architectural firm of Gerkan, Marg and Partners. Every spring, hundreds of publishing houses from inside and outside Germany meet here for the Leipzig book fair, presenting their authors to their readers. This is accompanied by "Leipzig liest" (Leipzig reads), Europe's largest literature festival.

I have been a city counselor for building and construction for the past year. From my living room, I can see the Neues Rathaus (new city hall). Here, during the Third Reich, Carl Friedrich Goerdeler organized the Kreisau Circle, a resistance group against the Nazi regime. I can see the Thomaskirche, which includes the Bach monument, and the Nikolaikirche, where tens of thousands of citizens demonstrated against the GDR regime before, and also after, the *Wende,* giving Leipzig the name "the city of peaceful revolution." It is a wonderful view, which I enjoy every morning and evening.

But there is still a great deal left to do. Growth has given City Hall new tasks. After years of vacant, abandoned apartment buildings, housing has become scarce. Prices are going up and the city must, with its limited resources, look after those who cannot find affordable housing on their own. For this purpose, we are currently compiling and discussing a new housing concept with everybody who deals with real estate, but also the residents of Leipzig.

The southern and western districts have experienced a recent development, which has turned them into the most popular places to live. But there is still a great need for redevelopment in the eastern part of the city. Some of those eastern districts are developing into multicultural enclaves already. They offer opportunities for self help as well as for sponsored row houses and other innovative projects. We are confident that a colorful mixed quarter will emerge during the next few years.

The prefabricated housing projects from the GDR, still suffering from population flight despite city intervention, are also being newly discovered. These industrialized buildings—remodeled, rebuilt and extended—are again attracting new residents. People's housing needs differ and everyone should find a place in Leipzig to feel comfortable.

Social infrastructure is especially important for a functioning model of the "Stadt der kurzen Wege" (city of short ways): low traffic, pedestrian friendly, short distances between home, work, hospitals, education, and recreational locales. In the coming decades, we need dozens of new schools and kindergartens for the many children who are born here or whose parents have moved to Leipzig recently. Those parents are finding new employment at companies like BMW and Porsche, at new plants built by architects Zaha Hadid and Schlaich Bergermann & Partners. Also universities and scientific and research institutions based in Leipzig offer many new jobs.

For City Hall, it is important to make sure that new housing has a high standard of architectural quality, usability, and sustainability. But public space needs to be improved as well. The city as living space should offer quality public space and guarantee mobility. Commercial traffic needs to flow, but pedestrian and bike lanes as well as public transportation also have to be attractive. The goal is to support local traffic and to make economical use of space, a limited resource after all. The residents of Leipzig participate in all these activities, as they have done for centuries. They make their wishes and ideas heard, and they significantly influence the life and the shape of our city.

In its thousand-year history, Leipzig has survived plagues and bombs, French emperors and Prussian kings. Today it is one of Europe's most desirable and best-loved cities, in which the charm of Prague, the hipness of Berlin, and culture of Vienna are combined: a city in which Leipzigers as well as newcomers live happily. We all hope it may stay that way in the future.

Dorothee Dubrau
Bürgermeisterin und Beigeordnete
für Stadtentwicklung und Bau

Regional map from the 16th century

From Village to City
1015 to 1500

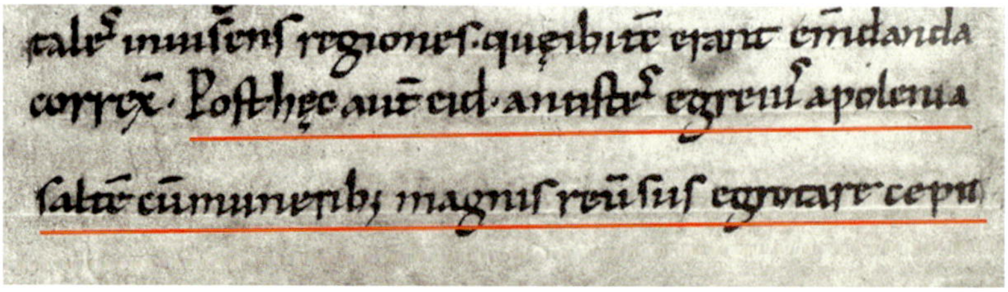

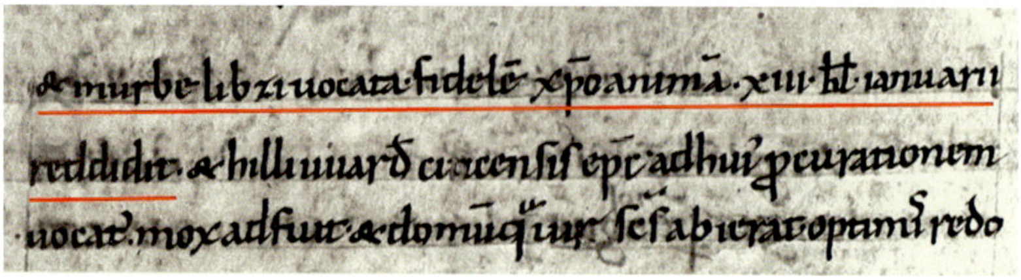

First mentioned in black and white

The Early Bird

December 20, 1015, was probably a rather uncomfortable Wednesday in the middle of the Middle Ages and all in all not much different from most other days at the time. No one likely even suspected the day would become an important one. Thietmar, the bishop of Merseburg recorded the date in his *Chronicle*, however, but not because he wanted to mention Leipzig for the first time. One of his colleagues had died. “Then the valiant Bishop Eido was taken ill after returning from Poland with splendid gifts,” he wrote, “and his faithful spirit returned to Christ in the *urbs Libzi* on December 20.” Granted, the note does not offer much in the way of useful information on the city’s location or for its anniversary. Leipzig is first mentioned more in passing, a topographical addition to an obituary notice. Not exactly a great start in world history.

At the time, however, the little town at the confluence of the Pleisse and Parthe rivers was not the least bit unusual. No urban center à la Merseburg or Erfurt, and definitely no Cologne, which, with about ten thousand inhabitants back then, was less populous than Stötteritz, a Leipzig suburb, is today but was still the largest German city at the time. *Libzi*, on the other hand, was just one of many small Sorbian settlements—one with a German castle, though there were quite a few around at the time. Zwenkau, Schkeuditz, and Taucha had similar fortresses, which served not only to protect but also to Christianize the native Sorbian inhabitants, making up the majority of the population. The Germans had added the region between the Saale and Oder rivers to the realm just eighty years prior, so the Eastern March was no match in structure or status for other regions. Not yet, anyway. *Libzi* was established as a fishing village about two hundred years earlier. Its Sorbian roots are still evident in the name today. It has long been assumed that the name came from *Lipa*—Sorbian for “linden”—and linden (or lime) trees are still the most common trees in the area. A more recent theory suggests that the Sorbian word *lei* or *leibh* formed the root of the name, which means something like “flow,” as in the many flowing streams that were found in the immediate vicinity (the Parthe still flowed then where the ring road runs today), and all the more plausible given that the village was established as a fishing community. Like so many details of early history, this, too, remains just a theory.

The history of the two trade routes that intersected there, however, is well documented, though the roads were not all that important back then. Only after long-distance trade began to flourish in Europe did the village's location on the Via Regia and Via Imperii turn out to be a significant advantage. While the former ran east–west, straight across Europe and along the Brühl (Leipzig's oldest street), the Via Imperii linked the Baltic Sea region in the north to the Mediterranean in the south, running along where Leipzig's Pfaffendorfer, Hain, and Peter streets are today. At that original intersection, located where the Richard-Wagner-Platz is now, there was a market square surrounded by several dozen mud huts with thatched roofs at the time when Leipzig was first mentioned. Most of these housed Sorbian peasants and craftsmen and their families. The first long-distance traders likely also settled near the castle, which was located on a rise (at least by Leipzig standards) just a few yards away, where St. Matthew's Cemetery lies today. Besides the Sorbians, who were becoming increasingly assimilated, German settlers from Thuringia, Franconia, and Flanders began moving into the area, but they had already established a second settlement where the Wilhelm-Leuschner-Platz is currently located. It would take nearly three hundred years for these two settlements to grow together. Bishop Eido was long forgotten by that point—unlike today.

As Bishop of Meissen, he wasn't really responsible for Libzi anyway, which still belonged to the Bishopric of Merseburg. The bishop traveled a great deal, however. In part because Henry II, Holy Roman Emperor of the German Nation, led various campaigns against the recently established Poland in the eleventh century. He was not particularly successfully, so he required a mediator. Eido was the best man for the job not only because his bishopric shared a border with the enemy territory but because he spoke Polish and was considered to be a man of honor and, at sixty years of age, of experience. He visited Poland twice in 1015, traveling back and forth along the Via Regia between Merseburg and Poland's capital, Gniezno. On the second trip, he made it only as far as Libzi. A tragic occurrence for the bishop, to be sure, and yet he died at just the right time in a place that, until then, had escaped mention. The geographic coordinates of his departure from life led, at the very least, to the fact that he is still mentioned a thousand years later, unlike his colleagues.

Selection of Cities' First Mentions

Year	City
19 BC	Cologne
742	Erfurt
765	Aachen
805	Magdeburg
806	Halle
810	Hamburg
1015	Bielefeld
1015	**Leipzig**
1206	Dresden
1237	Berlin

Year	City
880	Merseburg
929	Meissen
961	Eilenburg
974	Zwenkau
974	Taucha
981	Schkeuditz
1004	Wahren

Growth and Revolution

When Frederick II, King of the Romans and future German emperor, stood at the city gate in fall 1217, the people of Leipzig did not expect trouble. They were no strangers to tribulation, but that usually came from their own territorial lord, Dietrich the Oppressed. He was also standing at the gate, and had been for quite some time. He had grown rather angry in the meantime, because his subjects in Leipzig had wrested some significant liberties from him a few months earlier, and so the Oppressed was oppressing them now. Despite the siege, however, the people of Leipzig remained firm. Frederick offered to act as arbiter in the conflict, which seemed like it wouldn't do any harm, so both regents were allowed into the city with a small entourage. The citizens did not realize that it was all part of a treacherous plan that had nothing to do with diplomacy, but that the ostensible offer served as a prelude to subduing the well-secured city.

The population in Libzi had grown to about two thousand, meanwhile, but that was not the only number that had increased. The population density across the entire Margraviate of Meissen was ten times higher than it had been when the region was established 250 years earlier. Additional territo-

Dietrich the Oppressed in the procession of princes in Dresden (detail)

ries had joined the core region around the Elbe and Mulde rivers, such as Lausitz, various Thuringian estates, and the area surrounding Weissenfels. Just as significant was the emergence of the first cities. Dietrich's father, Otto the Rich, had already declared Leipzig a city, though no one knows exactly when because the date is missing on the city charter. It must have been between 1156 and 1170, and so Leipzig was most likely the first place in the Margraviate of Meissen to be chartered. Freiberg came next in 1170, with Görlitz and Bautzen following soon after. The wave of city-founding was just getting started. There were only about 150 cities in Central Europe in 1100, but two hundred years later there were more than 2,500. A city charter did not signify that a certain population had been reached but served more as an opportunity to draw more inhabitants—to generate more size. Legally there was no compulsory labor in cities, an advantage over life in the countryside, hence the popular slogan "Urban Air Makes You Free." Because cities were equipped with rudimentary fortifications, they also offered protection. And the privilege of market rights eliminated unwelcome competition in the immediate vicinity. It was no wonder that merchants settled in the cities. The economic power that developed benefitted the territorial lords, who in turn encouraged the process. Along with the new privileges, the cities developed a new self-confidence, which led to increasing friction between them and their territorial lords.

The "fat cityfolk," as Dietrich called them, did not suspect that he was about to strike back. While he and Frederick pretended to negotiate, more and more of their knights bluffed their way through the city gates, disguised as messengers. They took up quarters in strategic positions and waited for nightfall. When the city was finally asleep, the knights vanquished the innkeepers first, and the guards at the gates soon after, allowing Dietrich's army to pass through. A Trojan strategy—without the horse. Dietrich's men had yet another surprise in store. They removed the clapper from the bell that was to sound the alarm in the event of an emergency. They had an easy job of it then, and the people of Leipzig were defeated before they knew what was happening. As far as Dietrich was concerned, the conflict was settled.

The main reason for the conflict was Dietrich's plan to establish an Augustinian monastery in Leipzig,

List of Territorial Lords in the Margraviate of Meissen, or Saxony (Resp.), until the Division of Leipzig

Name	Reign
Herman I	1009–1038
Eckard II of Meissen	1038–1046
William of Weimar-Orlamünde	1046–1062
Otto I of Weimar-Orlamünde	1062–1067
Egbert I	1067/68
Egbert II	1068–1089
Vratislaus II	1076–1089
Henry I	1089–1103
Henry II	1103–1123
Wigbert II	1123/24
Herman I of Winzenburg	1124–1129
Conrad the Great	1129–1157
Otto the Rich	1157–1190
Albert I, the Proud	1190–1195
Dietrich the Oppressed	1198–1221

Margraves of Meissen (and Landgraves of Thuringia)

Name	Reign
Henry III, the Illustrious	1218–1288
Albert II, the Degenerate	1288–1291
Frederick I, the Brave (the Bitten)	1291–1323
Frederick II, the Serious	1323–1339
Frederick III, the Strict	1349–1381
William I, the One-eyed	1382–1407
William II, the Rich	1407–1425

Electoral Princes Until the Partition of Leipzig

Name	Reign
Frederick I, the Warlike	1423–1428
Frederick II, the Peaceful	1428–1464

which was supposed to have been built where the St. Thomas Church is today. The monastery, holding land and furnished with its own legal jurisdiction, would have had a significant impact on whatever happened in the city, especially because the St. Nicholas and St. Peter's churches were to be subject to its authority. At first the people of Leipzig put up only cautious resistance, by stealing the building materials and scaring off the future abbot. Later they plotted to kill Dietrich but were unsuccessful, which led to the first direct confrontation and was the reason a furious Dietrich rushed to Leipzig and besieged the city.

Because the city was actively supported by the nearby nobility, his efforts were also fruitless, and the situation escalated. The people of Leipzig threatened to terminate their relationship with their territorial lord and were ready to surrender to the bishop of Magdeburg or the emperor. Dietrich was left with no other choice but to negotiate with his citizens, whose demands were many: Only the city was to have legal jurisdiction within the municipality, the bridge and road tolls were to be paid to the town council, and the Margrave would no longer be permitted to build fortifications within city walls. Gritting his teeth, Dietrich agreed, already considering how he might win back control of the city.

Once he did gain back control, Dietrich set some examples. The instigators of the rebellion were imprisoned and the city's fortifications razed. He also had the existing Lipsk Castle on St. Matthew's churchyard converted to a stronghold and two additional fortresses built, so he could subdue his citizens in the future as necessary. While one new castle was built near where St. Paul's Church later stood, the second—Pleissenburg Castle—was built near the new town hall. His efforts would never pay off, however. Dietrich died just four years later, utterly unexpectedly, at least for him. It was suggested that poison might have played a role, supposedly supplied by the people of Leipzig. His fortresses did not fare much better, as Dietrich's successors were unable—or unwilling—to uphold his policies. In 1227, Lipsk Castle and the eastern fortress were torn down again. Only Pleissenburg Castle remained as a margravial palace. And the people of Leipzig were granted all of the privileges they had demanded before.

Construction and Prayer

Heinrich von Morungen was a pious man, which was by no means unusual in the thirteenth century. That he was extremely well known is remarkable, however, considering the dearth of global superstars in the Middle Ages. As a minnesinger he played in the same league as Walther von der Vogelweide, one of his contemporaries, but now in the twenty-first century, Heinrich is more like the best of best-kept secrets. This probably has something to do with the fact that little of his work has survived, and because "of Morungen" has less of a catchy ring to it than Walther's more poetic-sounding "of the Bird Meadow." His past influence can still be felt in Leipzig today, as he was the one who gave the St. Thomas Church its name.

The enormous role that church and faith played during the Middle Ages was already evident in the circumstances under which Leipzig was first mentioned. A prominent cleric had to die there before the site on the Pleisse River found its way onto a map. Even the second mention of Leipzig, just two years later, had a religious basis. Not another death this time, but the occasion when the bishop of Merseburg was given a Leipzig church. It's not clear which one it was, or, consequently, which church is the oldest in the city. There are many theories, but the general assumption is that it was the predecessor of the Church of St. Peter, which apparently was built in the tenth century as a simple wooden building a few yards south of Peter Street, giving the street its name. This was not unusual. Many street names can be traced back to (former) churches. Another example is Jacob Street, reminiscent of the church of the same name built by Iro-Scottish monks in the eleventh century, which once stood west of the first market square (called Richard-Wagner-Platz today). Just as the Church of St. Peter, however, it was not located within the fortified area of the city. A century later, in 1165, construction on the St. Nicholas Church began; a market church that then formed the center of a newly established merchant settlement. Though the historic structure was vastly different in size and form from its current one, its Romanesque origins are still visible on the western side (around the entrance). Another house of worship is thought to have existed within the Lipsk Castle, and the Romanesque predecessor of the St. Thomas Church probably also existed at the time. As described above, it was to play a central role in the new Augustinian monastery planned by Dietrich the Oppressed.

Heinrich von Morungen lived there as well and enjoyed the favor and sponsorship of the Margrave of Meissen. Not an unusual arrangement at the time. Much more remarkable was that von Morungen was said to have traveled to India. There is no

Old building signs in Leipzig's inner city

evidence of this, however, and considering the geopolitical situation at the time—the Mongols controlled vast regions in Asia, and the areas not controlled by them were cordoned off by the Muslims—it seems unlikely that he did. Nevertheless, the name of the St. Thomas Monastery and Church came from a relic of St. Thomas, which von Morungen supposedly brought back from India.

The St. Thomas Monastery would not remain the only abbey in Leipzig, which boasted a population of three thousand by then. Just ten years later, in 1227, the Cistercian convent followed as the next large religious construction project, west of where Wilhelm-Leuschner-Platz is located today, outside of the city wall. And while the Georgian nuns were moving into their new home, the Dominicans started working on their compound near where the university campus lies today, which would be dedicated to the apostle Paul in 1240. As building material, they used what was left of Dietrich's stronghold after it was torn down. Finally, the Franciscans came a few years later and set to work just as pragmatically, using the ruins of the Lipsk Castle to build their monastery where St. Matthew Cemetery is today.

If the religious infrastructure seems overly elaborate, the secular was plagued by many deficiencies. This, for example, was manifest in the choice of building materials used. Unlike the stone church buildings, almost every other building in the city was made of timber frame, clay, or wood, and most of the roofs were thatched with straw. The buildings were much narrower than they are today, usually just three windows wide and two stories tall. The ground floor frequently housed early workshops or businesses, with living quarters above them. Courtyards were also often used for commercial purposes and were usually connected by a passage through the surrounding building to the street. None of that remains today, though the inner-city roads and many street names from that time still exist. The buildings bore no numbers then, and most people would not have been able to read them anyway. A little later and up until the late eighteenth century, people relied on building signs to find their way, some of which are still visible today. The "Golden Hand," the "Blue Pike," and the "Three Riders" are three prominent examples that can still be seen in Nicholas Street.

Not all areas in the town center were developed, however. In the early thirteenth century, there were three separate town centers: one in the northwest, near the former Lipsk Castle; the second in the south, near the old Church of St. Peter; and third in the east, where the newly founded merchant settlement and the St. Nicholas Church were located. Some of the areas between these three cen-

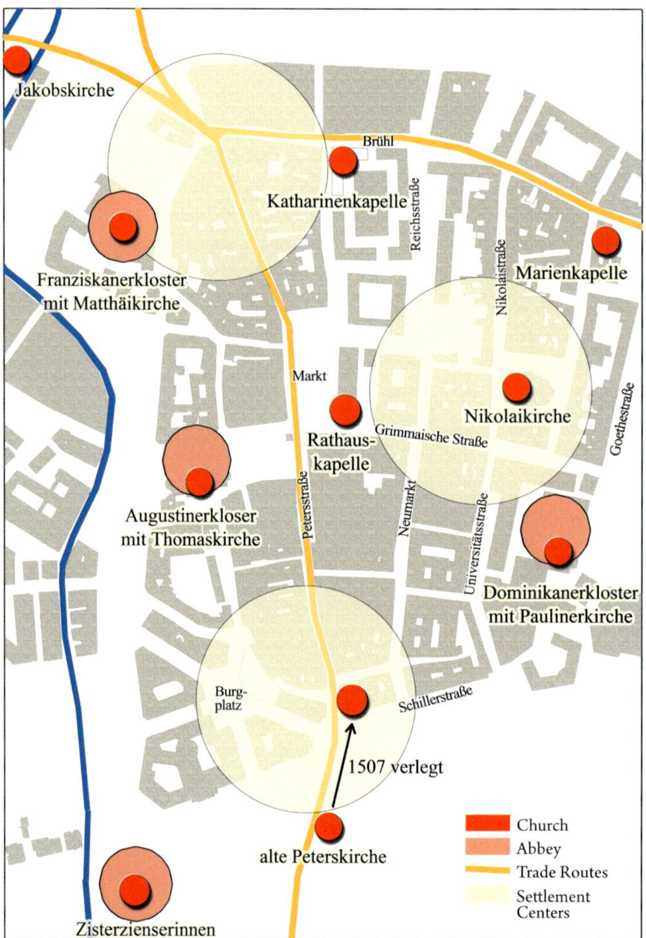

The location of former churches, abbeys, and old settlement centers within the modern city

ters were used for agriculture, and some for building materials. The location where the market square is currently located was once a clay pit in which bricks were made for the St. Thomas Church. It was not until the late thirteenth century that the three areas of settlement grew together and the geographic center of the converging city was elevated to "front parlor" status.

Fortifications existed then as well, including a wide ditch that was partially filled with water, or rather the city's sewage, and formed a natural defensive bulwark that was especially hard to breach for those with a keen sense of smell. Throughout the centuries, the ensuing system of walls was continually reinforced and adapted to the requirements of the time, while the area within—118 acres of security—stayed the same size. The importance of this safety zone is still visible in the word *Bürger* (citizen), which stemmed from the Old German *burga*, which meant "protection." The area outside the wall, however, had only provisional value and was exposed to war, raids, and permanent ruin. It's hard to imagine today what a definitive function an urban island like that really had.

The town center interior was accessible only through four mighty city gates, most of which were named for nearby villages. The Grimmaische Gate was in the east, the Hallische in the north, and the Ranstädter Gate (named for Markranstädt) in the northwest. St. Peter Gate in the south, however, was named for the Church of St. Peter. Pedestrians could gain access to the city by way of smaller doors, the number of which varied over the years from three to six. Besides acting as checkpoints, the gates functioned as a good source of income. Anyone wanting to enter the city after hours (generally after sundown) had to pay a hefty toll, so there was often a mad rush to get through before the gates closed for the night. Leipzig's four city districts at the time bore the same names as the gates. The fact that there were four districts or quarters was no coincidence. This was true of many other cities, as most were founded at the intersection of two roads that divided the settlement into four quarters, which mathematically and historically equals one.

Heinrich von Morungen did not spend much time in his new home at St. Thomas Monastery, however. He died in 1222, one year after its dedication. Because he has been so completely buried in oblivion since then, let's at least let him speak for himself here:

Mîn herze, ir schoene und diu minne

Mîn herze, ir schoene und diu minne habent gesworn
zuo ein ander, des ich waene, ûf mîner vröuden tôt.
zwiu habent diu driu mich einen dar zuo erkorn?
ôwê, minne, gebent ein teil der lieben mîner nôt,
Teilent si ir sô mite, daz sî gedanke ouch machen rôt.
wünsche ich ir senens nû? daz waere bezzer verborn.
lîhte ist ez ir zorn,
sît ir wort mir deheinen kumber gebôt.

My heart, her beauty and Love, it seems,
are intent upon destroying my joy.
Why do these three plague only me?
Love, let my lover share my anguish,
cause her, too, at mere thoughts to blush.
Dare I wish she longed for me? Best not
her ire to provoke,
for my woe no word from her invoked.

The Foundation of a University

In May 1409, when about two thousand students left Charles University in Prague in protest, the largest university in the empire lost 80 percent of its enrollment. A hard blow for Bohemian King Wenceslas, though during his struggle for power and the crown, he maneuvered his educational battleship recklessly and carelessly into turbulent waters. And now it was too late, as the mutinous group was headed for other shores—including Saxony, where the Bohemian demise helped give rise to the university in Liepzig.

The university in Prague had been established more than fifty years earlier, in 1348, the first in the Holy Roman Empire of the German Nation. The nation of writers and thinkers was pretty late in developing its own educational landscape. Throughout Europe, twenty-five universities already existed at the time, the most important in Paris and many in Italy, where the oldest was also located. Prague would not be an isolated occurence, however. Schools were also established in Vienna, Heidelberg, Cologne, Erfurt, and Würzburg, with the seventh finally in Leipzig. The territorial lord of the Meissen March, Frederick the Militant, had long desired his own educational citadel, so offering Leipzig as an educational home to the migrating students from Prague simply made sense. Ultimately only about one tenth switched from the banks of the Moldau to those along the Pleisse, while the others went off to the Rhine, Danube, or Gera.

Yet it was definitely enough for a new beginning, since just about as many newcomers joined the nearly two hundred former students. Suddenly there were four hundred scholars living in the city with a population of four thousand, which must

The Bursa Bavarica, built in the early 15th century, was in the St. Nicholas Churchyard until 1834

have been a shock to some of the Leipzig natives. All in all, however, the university's foundation was beneficial in many ways. Many students were well off, which fueled the local economy, and later they often held important positions. Thus the new educational establishment was not only financially supported by the city and the state but property in Ritter and Peter streets was set aside for it as well. Now, more than six hundred years later, most of those properties are still used by the university. Teaching methods are a little different now than they were back then. Though a PowerPoint presentation would have caused quite a sensation in the fifteenth century—and probably also have led to accusations of witchcraft—even paper, ink, and, especially, books were relatively rare in 1409. This is why classes started a little earlier in the day back then.

At precisely the stroke of five in the morning, Johannes Otto von Münsterberg began the lecture. An apt description, given the lack of books, which the printing press would remedy forty years later. The actual word used was *lectio*, as instruction was exclusively in Latin until the eighteenth century. Not all freshmen were adept at reading or writing yet, as they were often only twelve or thirteen years old and had not necessarily ever been to school before. Von Münsterberg knew the strengths and weaknesses of his protégés. Like most of his colleagues, he had already taught in Prague, and had even been the rector there. Now he would go down in history as the first university rector at the University of Leipzig.

Officially, the university's history began with the papal charter arrival on December 2, 1409, though the first lectures had already started at the beginning of September. In the early years, only the colleges of theology and the arts existed, although assignment to the usual four colleges was anticipated. The arts meant instruction in the seven liberal arts—grammar, rhetoric, dialectics, arithmetic, geometry, astronomy, and music. Mastery of these was a prerequisite for acceptance in the other three colleges, although the medical and law colleges did not start up until 1415 and 1446, respectively. The administration also had four divisions. As was the case at the Charles University in Prague, and most of the older universities, the principle of nations was implemented at Leipzig as well, whereby students were divided into the Bavarian, Saxon, Meissen, and Polish nations. While students from southern Germany and southern Europe belonged to the Bavarian nation, and Polish students to the Polish nation, the northern Germans were put in the Saxon group, as Saxony lay to the north of Leipzig at the time. The inhabitants of the city on the Pleisse, along with those from Chemnitz or Freiberg, belonged to the Meissen nation. By means of this division, as strange as it sounds today, important decisions were voted on, including who became rector.

In addition, the nations operated their own hostels, which were the medieval equivalent of student dormitories. Unlike today, university students were supervised by a magister and had to live in a hostel at first. Most of these hostels were in Ritter Street, where most of the colleges were as well, some of which were residential, and the area soon came to be known as the "Latin Quarter." Residence in

Universities Established

Year	University
1088	Bologna (considered the oldest university)
1348	Prague (divided into a Czech-speaking and a German-speaking university in 1882)
1365	Vienna (earliest remaining university in German-speaking realm)
1379/1389	Erfurt (closed in 1816, re-established in 1994)
1386	Heidelberg
1388	Cologne (closed in 1798, re-established in 1919)
1402	Würzburg (closed in 1413, re-established in 1582)
1409	**Leipzig (second-oldest university in current Federal Republic of Germany)**
1502	Wittenberg (closed in 1813, merged with Halle University in 1817)
1810	Humboldt University of Berlin (oldest university/research institution in Berlin)
1962	Ruhr University of Bochum (first university established in the Federal Republic of Germany)
1992	HTWK Leipzig (University of Applied Sciences, roots extend back to the Academy of Painting, Drawing, and Architecture established by A. F. Oeser in 1764)

the hostels was compulsory until the mid-fifteenth century, after which the student body dispersed into the city and gained new freedoms, as well as life experience. Brawls, duels, and drinking sprees were part of the students' daily lives, along with a deep-seated feud with journeymen. Because university students were subject to collegial law and did not fall under municipal jurisdiction, insignificant crimes could have serious consequences—as happened in 1471, resulting in a cobbler rebellion. The city and the university also fought over various privileges, most passionately over beer, or rather the right to serve it. The city did not like the fact that everyone associated with the university could obtain one hundred kegs of beer and two hundred pails of wine annually, duty-free, which significantly decreased Leipzig's income. The citizens knew that a supply like that couldn't possibly be for personal consumption only, even back in those days.

There was no way freshmen were consuming such quantities. First they had to undergo the deposition: a painful initiation ritual in which they dressed as livestock and their "uncivilized" natures were driven from them by means of humiliation and verbal and physical abuse. For the next four weeks, they held the status of foxes and could wear only shabby clothing, and they were not permitted to approach older students, for whom they had to do favors for several semesters. All of this was strictly forbidden, of course, but such practices remained a part of university life for several centuries.

Urban Disasters

Maria awoke in the middle of the night. She did not know what had awakened her, but she felt something wasn't right. A moment later, she realized what it was. She smelled smoke. Panic gripped her as she rushed through the dark house, the sound of bursting wood confirming that this was no small fire. As she reached the door, someone finally sounded the alarm. Maria had already been through many fires, more than almost anyone else in the city. Big ones and small ones. Twenty years earlier, half of the Brühl had burned down. When she had been born more than seventy years prior, another catastrophe had just begun—the plague.

While the Black Death had taken many human lives in ancient times, the plague had suddenly let up, for six hundred years. Until the specter abruptly arose again in 1347, with no apparent end in sight. The pestilence raged in Leipzig for the first time in 1350, and more than five hundred people died within just a few weeks—one out of every eight inhabitants. Because of the intensity of the Black Death, and because the physicians remained powerless against it, the plague was viewed less as an illness and more as a form of punishment from God. Physicians sprinkled vinegar on their patients, lanced the boils in their armpits and groins to let the blood and puss out, and cleansed the air with fire, yet no matter what they tried, nine out of ten of those afflicted died. So people prayed even more during times of plague, and flogging parades filled the streets. Participants ran through the city half naked and flagelated themselves, striking fear and terror in the hearts of children. Others suspected foreigners, cripples, or Jews of poisoning the wells. So even more died than those claimed by the plague. No

The plague, represented in the Toggenburg Bible, 14th century one had the slightest inkling that it was spread by rat fleas. Nor that people living in close proximity with animals and all of the unappetizing facets of life—such as, chamber pots emptied in the streets, or trash lying around—provided infectious diseases with the perfect breeding ground.

In the Middle Ages, *hygiene* was nothing more than a foreign word in Latin. There were also no scientific or medical structures to speak of. While the city's first apothecary shop, the Löwenapotheke, opened in the wake of the university's foundation, the Löwenapotheke, and the number of educated physicians had increased, they practiced in private. At St. George's Hospital, established in the thirteenth century and operated by the city after 1440, no doctor would be hired until 1520. It primarily served as a refuge for the homeless, pilgrims, and orphans. The medical staff consisted of two infirmary nurses and two pallet carriers. The latter managed medical transportation. With increased demand, the Pestilence House was opened and staffing levels rose a bit. Plague barbers were also employed, but they treated only wounds, unlike educated physicians who treated internal and infectious diseases. Because the sixteenth century alone saw forty years of plague, there were often not enough medical personel available. The plague, however, was just the most dangerous illness around at the time. Typhus, spotted fever, and particularly smallpox were just as feared, though the last raged primarily during the eighteenth century, at a time when the plague had already disappeared from Europe. Leprosy, on the other hand, though less dangerous and less contagious, had more devastating social implications. Characterized by swelling and damaged limbs, the inflicted had to identify themselves by wearing special garments and a rattle, and could speak only downwind of others. They were treated with a salve that contained stork fat, swallow feces, and other strange ingredients. They were wrapped in pigskin or painted with mercury, so the attempts to cure them often caused death instead. In addition, the afflicted lost their possessions and were banished outside the city wall, which is why the disease was also called *Aussatz* (abandoned).

About nineteen thousand leper colonies existed in thirteenth-century Europe, and one of them formed on the eastern outskirts of Leipzig. The society of lepers purchased land on Johannisplatz, which still bears the name of the patron saint, where at first St. John Hospital and Cemetery were built, and later a church. Leprosy would continue to affect societies into the sixteenth century. When the disease suddenly withdrew, it was followed by the "French disease," or syphilis, supposedly imported from America and which, as a sexually transmitted disease, ruined a branch of the hospitality industry. From then on, St. John Hospital treated primarily "Frenchies," as the infected were called. The isolated location outside the city had one advantage: the area was largely spared by catastrophic fires.

Just two minutes after the flames were first noticed, many people had managed to rush out onto the street. Everyone knew that speed was of the utmost importance. Ladders were brought, and buckets dipped in barrels provided as a precaution were sent in a panicked rush toward the source of fire. More and more shadows flickered restlessly in the

European Disasters in the Late Middle Ages and Early Modern Era

Year	Disaster
1315	Heavy rains and flooding result in ruined crops across wide swaths of Europe. Hundreds of thousands die of starvation, mass graves employed.
1338	Locusts swarm across central Europe, causing famine.
1347	The "first" wave of the plague takes an estimated 25 million lives, about one-third of the population of Europe.
1348	Earthquakes (probably rating 6.0 on the scale) devastate upper Italy; Basel is hit ten years later, and Vienna in 1590 (also recorded in Saxony).
1362	Second Marcellus storm tide drowns tens of thousands along the German North Sea Coast—exactly fifty years later, Cecilia flood at the mouth of the Elbe River takes 36,000 human lives.
1437–1440	All of Europe afflicted by severe famine.
1490	Turkish powder storehouse struck by lightning in Constantinople; explosion kills at least 800 people (highest estimates around 4,000).
1494	Syphilis epidemic rages through Europe for about fifty years.
1547	A large fire in Moscow kills 3,000; 80,000 lose their homes. London suffers a similar fate in 1666, when 13,000 houses and 87 churches are destroyed.

increasingly brighter night. Maria, watching what was happening from a distance, knew that it was too late. Strong winds blew over the dry straw rooftops, and while the helpers were doing everything they could to fight the fire at its source, they did not notice that the flames had engulfed two more buildings. Now only prayer would help, preferably from somewhere upwind.

Major fires were not unusual. Open flames were a part of daily living not only in residential areas but in the commercial town center as well. Most buildings were also made of easily combustible materials, so fires quickly grew out of control and spread through the narrow streets. Medieval construction methods contained an additional source of danger, as buildings frequently collapsed. In 1412, for example, the steeple on the St. Thomas Church collapsed due to insufficient upkeep. In other cases, design deficiencies caused collapses, often in combination with weather incidents, which had a more direct effect back then than they do today. Of course, buildings were technologically a far cry from modern standards—it wasn't just radiant floor heating that was missing—but serious damage resulted because hardly any landscape adjustments were made, and this was especially noticeable in flood events. Leipzig's central area was rarely affected, but the inhabitants of the lower lying outskirts to the north and west, who were commercially dependent on the numerous small rivers and canals, were regularly hit by floods. With the advent of the little ice age in the fifteenth century, the effects were even greater. Precipitation rates increased, and shorter growing periods and cold, wet summers decreased agricultural production. Flooding or extremely cold winters often led to famine, partly because regional supply bottlenecks were difficult to overcome before the railway system was created. Cities tried to brace themselves against such occurrences by building granaries.

Just about every life-threatening scenario increased exponentially in times of war, and there was always a little bit of war in those days. The Moorish, Ottoman, or Mongolian adversaries that threatened Europe from abroad, however, played a much smaller role than the countless inner-European conflicts at the time. England and France were at war with each other for one hundred years, beginning in 1337; the Lithuanian campaigns of the German Order led to devastation in the 1410 battle at Tannenberg; while the Hussites laid waste to Bohemia and vast regions of Central Germany. They also showed up outside Leipzig's walls in 1425, but unlike what happened in many other cities in the region, Leipzig's walls withstood that attack.

The city had less luck with that spreading inferno that transformed vast areas of the city into a charred landscape. More than four hundred buildings were destroyed, though there was little loss of life. There was one good thing about the disaster in 1420, however. New buildings would be made of stone and safety precautions increased, including prize money for whoever discovered a fire first. Effective measures, indeed, as the future would show, for Leipzig remained mostly spared from fire disasters from then on, unlike many other European cities.

Ein Sermon geprediget tzu Leipßgk uffm Schloß am tag Petri vñ pau-li ym .xviiij. Jar / durch den wirdigen vater Doctorem Martinū Luther augustiner zu Wittenburgk / mit entschůldigung etzlicher artickel / ßo ym von etzlichen seiner abgůnstigen zugemessen seyn / in der tzeit der Disputacion zu Leipßgk gehalten.

¶ Getruckt zu Leypßgk durch Wolffgang Stöckel im iar. 1519.

Freshly Pressed

The first book verifiably printed in Leipzig was composed by an Italian Dominican monk by the name of Giovanni Nanni, who was more famous for his forgeries of historic documents than for his own writing. His book bore a title that was pretty accurate at the time, but increasisngly less so over the years: *On the Future Victory of Christians over the Saracens—Commentary on the Apocolypse*. When Marcus Brandis proudly pulled the pages from the press in 1481, presumably contract work for the local Dominican monastery, it was more or less routine. The book was Leipzig's first, not Brandis's. As a traveling printer, he had already worked in Magdeburg and in Lübeck, where he learned the trade from his brother Lucas—who had already printed Merseburg's first book eight years earlier.

The new technology had been developed around 1450 by Johannes Gutenberg, who is still considered one of the most famous inventors in history, and his team. Until then, books and, consequently, a great deal of general knowledge had been accessible only to very few people. Books were limited in number because of the work it took to produce them, and because the number of people who could read was extremely low. The illiteracy rate in the Late Middle Ages was more than 90 percent. For a long time, abbeys and private libraries in the hands of wealthy noblemen functioned as exceptional islands of knowledge. Yet even the largest libraries in the High Middle Ages, like the library at St. Gallen Abbey, had only about one thousand books, while libraries in the Islamic world, like the ones in Cordoba and Baghdad, contained up to half a million volumes. Since the thirteenth century, however, scholasticism, the Renaissance, and the founding of universities led to (re)thinking in Christian Europe. Gutenberg's invention proved an accelerant in that process. Just thirty years after the first printing in Mainz, there were already ninety-odd sites where the "black art" was practiced, including Strassburg, Cologne, Augsburg, Nürnberg, Paris, Rome, and Krakow.

Though Leipzig was not among the birthplaces of printing, the trade developed there rapidly in tandom with commerce. The city soon became one of the most important German centers, with nine master printers living there by 1500. The most important and, in fact, the first local to ply the craft was Konrad ("Kunz") Kachelofen. Originally a merchant peddling wares in the old town hall, he sold paper, spices, wine, and finally, beginning in 1484, works by Thomas Aquinas and Albert the Great. An apparently fruitful combination—when he gave the business to his son-in-law, Melchior Lotter, in 1498, he was considered to be the most important printer in the city. About one third of the publications made in Leipzig up to that date was done by Kunz Kachelofen.

The reasons for Leipzig's rise as a center of printing were diverse. For one, the city was home to one of the largest German universities at the time, and this meant a high potential for orders, so many printers set up shop in the Latin Quarter. This was true, for example, of Martin Landsberg, who worked in Ritter Street beginning in 1490; and even F. A. Brockhaus himself chose the seasoned street for his first Leipzig headquarters in the early nineteenth century. Another advantage of locating in Leipzig was the downright lax censorship in the Meissen March, or in Saxony, as it was beginning in 1425. As important was the fact that commerce and trade fairs were developing most dynamically at that time, so the super-regional market was continually growing. Once books were given their own exhibit at the Frankfurt Trade Fair during the last quarter of the fifteenth century, printed materials began to be traded in Leipzig around 1490. Most books were printed in Latin, and they included numerous theological texts. But philosophical texts, grammar and math books, or books on popular themes formed a brisk trade and business boomed. In 1500, there were already presses in 271 locations in Europe, which by then had printed an estimated thirty thousand different texts with a total circulation of ten to twenty million copies. Almost half of these came from the

—— Wolfgang Stöckel printed this first image of Luther in 1519; records show Stöckel was a printer in Leipzig beginning in 1495

German-speaking realm, although the largest publishing center at the time was Venice, with about 150 printers. A short while later, the first municipal libraries opened, whereby most were private collections transferred to cities. Nürnberg's Council Library, which was founded in the fourteenth century, was considered a trailblazer for all of Germany. Relatively late, in 1677, Leipzig's own Council Library was formed from the private collection of a merchant named Huldreich Gross, who donated not only his four thousand books but his entire fortune as well.

It took a long time to get there, though. Around 1500, quite a few printers still owned multiple economic mainstays. Melchior Lotter, for example, not only printed and sold books but traded in fish, soap, and paper—most certainly an intriguing combination! The demand for paper was rising particularly briskly. Paper mills operated on the Elster millrace and the Luppe River, and the business must have been lucrative, as Lotter soon moved to Hain Street (where the Hotel de Pologne is located today) and employed eight journeymen. Twenty years later, he would take a leading roll as a printer and host.

Medieval Market Square

In May 1491, merchant Lorenz Mordeisen the Elder traveled from Hof to Leipzig. It was not his first trip to the Pleisse River; he had been there on business many times before. This time, however, he was not just bringing goods to the people. He intended to stay, because things really seemed to be taking off in Leipzig. He wasn't the only one who thought so. Many found Leipzig to be a city in which business was booming. The location was especially advantageous and made it easy to make new contacts in the East, where there was plenty of potential for him as a cloth merchant. There was also plenty of money circulating, thanks to the economic upswing in the region. Between 1471 and 1550, about three hundred additional merchants would join him in migrating to the city.

Leipzig boasted about eight thousand inhabitants at the time, much less than Cologne or Augsburg, where about forty and thirty thousand lived, respectively. The two Hanseatic cities of Lübeck and Hamburg were more than twice as big, along with Ulm, Nürnberg, and Magdeburg, where trade generally played a larger role. Commerce in Leipzig, however, had developed particularly dynamically during the last few decades. The number of handicrafts had also grown considerably. Even today, street signs in the city center indicate which craftsman once settled there, with alleys named Böttcher (Cooper), Sporer (Spurrier), and Schumacher (Cobbler), though it's not clear whether that was by decree or whether it just happened naturally. Considering the 247 job designations that existed there a few decades later, there weren't just butchers living in Fleischergasse (Butcher Lane). While they, along with cloth-makers, smiths, and bakers, counted among the wealthy, linen-weavers and ropemakers were relatively poor, so they usually lived outside the city gates.

This was the case for many potters, too, most of whom settled east of the city wall. Tanners lived

Replica of the building that preceded today's Old City Hall, at the Saxon-Thuringian Industry and Trade Fair

almost exclusively north of town, as very few inhabitants found the odors associated with tanning even remotely pleasant. The tanners could also use water from the Parthe River, drawn through the area by means of various man-made canals. In the Northwest, in Naundörfchen, was where the fisherfolk lived and fished the Elster and Pleisse millraces. It was no coincidence that the slaughterhouses were located just a few yards upriver. Waste from these served to attract the scaly critters. Dyers and lathe operators were found on the southern outskirts of town. Besides craftsmen, others living outside the city wall—and unable to afford its protection—

Mills

Pleisse Millraces		
Nonnenmühle (Nun Mill)	1287	1890
Thomasmühle (St. Thomas Mill)	c. 1200	1943
Barfussmühle (Barefoot Mill)	c. 10th cent.	1898

Elster Millraces		
Jakobsmühle (St. Jacob's Mill), or *Angermühle* (Common Mill)	1165	1879

(There were additional water mills in former villages, with mills remaining in Gohlis and Dölitz, for example. A mill driven by horses was located on Ritterstrasse until about 1850, and there were also many windmills.)

included beggars, musicians, and day laborers who made deliveries, drove carriages, or swept the markets. Jews were prohibited by law and forbidden to practice most trades. They lived in the Judenburc west of the city center, which they accessed by means of the Jewish gate.

Lorenz Mordeisen, naturally, wanted to build his home in the inner city, which meant that he first had to apply for citizenship. An expensive undertaking, but it was a common practice everywhere. His contact in Leipzig had already found him a suitable property, which was large enough for a substantial compound with a courtyard. It would be made of brick, three stories tall, with retail space and stalls below, an apartment for his family in the middle, and attic storage that would be filled to the brim with trade goods from all over Europe—wax, cloth, wine, silk, and linen. He would sell these to the grocers in Leipzig, who operated as municipal retailers.

Unlike the merchants, the grocers' product lines were regulated, and they were not allowed to do business in private. They presented their wares in stores and booths, and competed with peddlers, hucksters, and hagglers who offered their wares anywhere they pleased. On Tuesdays and Fridays, farmers from around the city came to sell

Angermühle (Common Mill), also known as *Jakobsmühle* (Jacob's Mill), shortly before demolition, c. 1875

their products at the farmer's market, which often resulted in disputes. The merchants, on the other hand, generally did business in larger volumes and made a living from long-distance trade.

In the meantime, Leipzig had good relations not only with other cities in the realm but with England, France, and the Netherlands. In the east, an economically and politically stable Poland and the Baltic provinces had grown in significance, so Leipzig was slowly developing into an important hub between eastern and western Europe. Trade goods included primarily ores, metal products, hides, wool, leather, silk, cloth, and more and more books. Non-local merchants had to pay customs on their goods, along with other levies. In addition, Leipzig became a staple town in 1466, which meant that traders were required to come to Leipzig even if their route brought them only close to the city—a privilege that was especially important for fairs. The term *Messe* (trade show) was not used yet, as Leipzig did not yet have national appeal, and wholesale trade and monetary transactions were still underdeveloped there. Prague, Nürnberg, Breslau, Lübeck, and Gdansk were more important at the time. Nevertheless, there had already been fairs at Easter and Michaelmas for three hundred years and they were even mentioned in the city charter. Towns in close proximity, like Taucha, were not allowed to hold fairs. Since 1268, the margrave also guaranteed protection to merchants traveling in his territory. Eventually, a third fair was established on New Year's 1457. And fourteen years later, something happened that spurred the economy even more: rich deposits of silver, copper, and tin were discovered in the Erz Mountains (renamed the Ore Mountains just a short while later), triggering a big prospecting rush.

As co-owner of a tin mine and outfitter for many other pits, Lorenz Mordeisen profited a great deal from this development. He also had the advantage of his numerous trade contacts in Nürnberg, Frankfurt, Silesia, and Poland, and so was one of the first merchants to gain a foothold in both eastern and western Germany. When he died at the age of sixty in 1510, he left behind a fortune of at least 25,000 guilders, which made him one of the richest men in the city.

Origin of Various Street Names

Inner city	
Naschmarkt	(Sweet Market). Sweet treats were sold here.
Barfussgässchen	(Barefoot Alley). Led to friary of the Franciscans, who were called "barefooters."
Magazingasse	(Depot Alley). Granary that served as a storage house or depot stood here.
Ritterstrasse	(Knight Street). Original location of the royal stables, where municipal horses were kept.
Kupfergasse	(Copper Lane). Named for the armory's copper scale located here.
Salzgasse	(Salt Lane). Named for the salt banks once located here.

Outlying areas	
Johannisplatz	(St. John's Square). Named after the patron saint of lepers, who were original settlers here.
Gerichtsweg	(Court Lane). There was no court here, but people were executed, like at Rabensteinplatz (Ravenstone Square).
Weisse Elster	(White Elster). Like Alster, name originated from Indo-Germanic Al-astra, meaning "to flow."
Brüderstrasse	(Brothers Street). Seven nearly identical houses known as the "seven brothers" gave the street its name.
Egelstrasse	(Leech Street). Named for a leech-filled pond formerly here.
Inselstrasse	(Island Street). Not named for the Insel publishing company, but for a popular destination instead, the Milchinsel (Milk Island) Estate, where milk was produced.

Cabbage Patches and Fishing Towns

June 10, 1488, promised to be a nice day, and that was a good thing. Court Constable Hans von Minckwitz was in town and, together with the steward and three city councilmen, planned an excursion complete with a proper noon meal. That morning, five horses were provided from the municipal stables in Ritter Street and brought to the Grimmaische Gate. When the group mounted and rode through the gate a short while later, they saw the sun rising over the houses in the Grimmaische quarter outside the wall.

The Grimmaische quarter was the largest of the four areas on the outskirts of the city. It consisted of five streets and more than one hundred simple houses, most one story, whose inhabitants often (but not always) counted among those at the bottom of the social ladder. Besides day laborers, beggars, and potters, a few bakers lived there, and their privileges extended to include raising pigs. The animals could be counted on to consume the bakers' waste, and so the street where they lived came to be called Saugasse (Sow Lane). The pigs' grunting blended with the clip-clop of the horses' hooves, the twittering chatter of numerous songbirds, and

Dorfstrasse (main street) in Reudnitz, c. 1880

the city sounds growing softer in the distance. The riders eventually approached St. John's Hospital and its associated cemetery. To prevent the spread of epidemics, the sick as well as the dead were banished from the city, though the deceased had earlier been laid to rest in the St. Nicholas and St. Thomas churchyards, or in one of the many other churchyards.

Passing to the right of St. John's Cemetery, the five men followed the road toward Wurzen, soon leaving behind the Rabensteinplatz surrounded by idyllic fields. Similar to the market square in Leipzig, where only the most prominent of the condemned were allowed to die, justice was dispensed by means of a sword at Rabensteinplatz, too. Still less privileged were those who were hanged or executed by means of the wheel. These were judged, as the name Gerichtsweg (Court Road) still indicates, several hundred yards past town, right on the town line. The five men reached their first destination on their trip to inspect the perimeter of the municipal area, which covered over 5.5 square miles under the authority of the council and the jurisdiction of Leipzig. Besides the developed zone, almost entirely surrounding the area that today is the city center, there were woods, meadows, fields, and swamps.

Criminal Justice in the Middle Ages and Early Modern Era

- Monetary fines for smaller offenses
- Public humiliation for missing church or disturbing the peace, involving the pillory, branks, or rattle stones (4 lbs.), for example
- Corporal punishment for theft or robbery, in accordance with the severity, including flogging and mutilation (cutting off fingers, hands, tongues, ears, or noses)
- Imprisonment for delinquent debts (beginning with the 16th century)
- Exile for fraud or sedition
- Capital punishment
  - Hanging for theft of goods valued over 5 guilders
  - Beheading by sword for murder, adultery, rape, abortions during the latter half of pregnancy
  - Breaking on the wheel for serious deprivation and murder, only used on men
  - The sack, in which the offender is put in a bag with an animal (cat, dog, or even monkey) and drowned in the *Kätztümpel*, for family offenses and murder of one's children, parents, or spouse
  - Death by fire for witchcraft, arson, or counterfeiting coins

From up a slight rise, where the gallows stood, the men gazed all around them. About eleven hundred yards in the distance they could see the low buildings on the eastern outskirts, and the Leipzig fortifications with the towers and rooftops in the city rising above them, perfectly lit by the sun. The scenery was dominated by churches. The Church of St. Paul sat enthroned to the left of the city gate, and the twin steeples of the St. Nicholas Church reached heavenward on the right. In the background, they glimpsed part of the giant nave of the St. Thomas Church, under construction at the time. Turning away from Leipzig, the men looked out in the opposite direction. East of the town line, only a few hundred yards away, lay the village of Reudnitz, which, along with the villages of Volkmarsdorf, Crottendorf, Anger, Sellerhausen, Stünz, and Mölkau beyond it, was a "cabbage village."

All of these places had developed on the banks of the eastern Rietzschke, and while each boasted only a few dozen four-sided courtyard compounds, most still made of clay, they were built so close to each other that they nearly ran together. The infrastructure of each village included a street, usually a pond, sometimes a mill, and occasionally a small church. The soil there, however, was extremely rich, and because the area was not marred by swamps or other geographic inconsistencies, the scene was dominated by fields, vegetable gardens, and grazing pastures that provided the majority of Leipzig's food supply. As purely agricultural villages, they depended on Leipzig since no markets were allowed, due to the city charter three centuries earlier, when a no-competition mile went into effect. Even craft industries were not allowed to start up without permission from the council. Because a Saxon mile was more than nine modern miles long, twenty-seven villages were affected by the regulation—including Schönefeld and Eutritzsch, which were just coming into view as our group of riders turned northward. Each of these villages had a church, and a manor dominated the scene in Schönefeld, where a squire and his family lived, to whom the peasants in Schönefeld were required to pay dues. This was not unusual; there were manors in Lindenau, Grosszschocher, and Wahren as well. If these had not existed, other landlords would have filled the gap: the university, abbeys, independent noblemen, or the Leipzig council, which would become the largest landholder after the Reformation. Eighteen villages would later be required to pay tribute

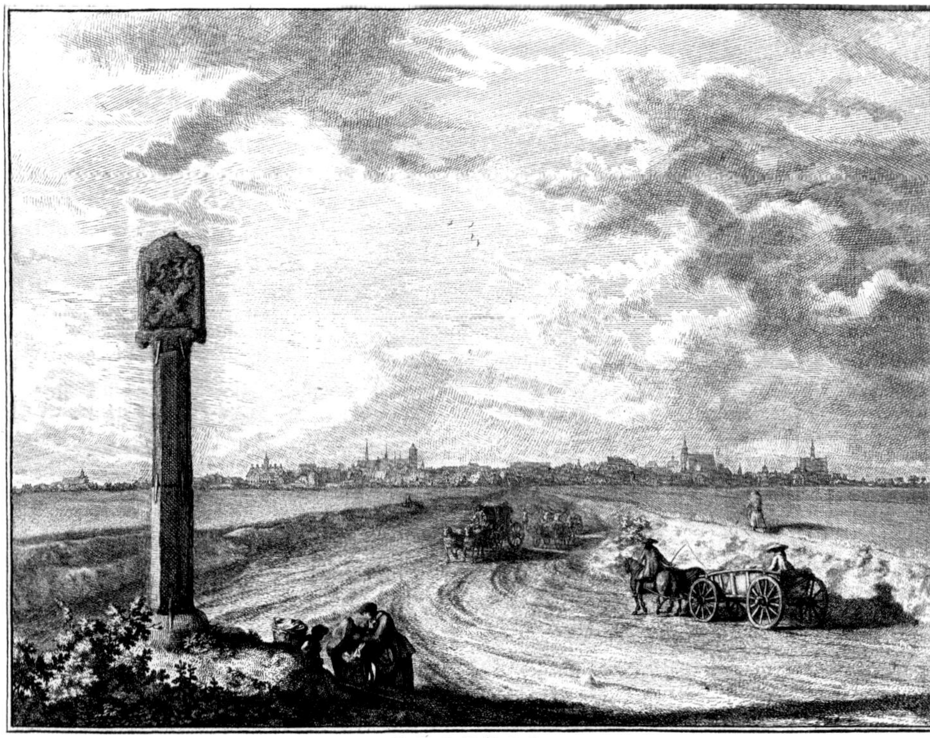

LÉIPZIG
Wie solches auff der Strasse vor dem Hællischen Thor sich Præsentiret
P. Schenk exc: Cum privileg: Regis Polon: et Elect: Sax: et Ord: Holl: et Westfr: Amstelaedami. 1705.

and provide labor to Leipzig. In Eutritzsch, the oldest council village, it happened as early as 1381, and the village would remain dependent until the general repeal of the policy in 1831.

The small pond to the men's left in the Leipzig territory would soon be filled in. For centuries it had served as a place to raise leeches, which is why it was known as the leech puddle. Today the only indication of its former existence is the Egelstrasse (Leech Street), which runs nearby. Several hundred yards farther north, the Rietzschke flows into the Parthe River. Several hundred years later, there is little to be seen of the site, as it lies under the massive track installations at the central train station. For the five men that day, all they observed was the peaceful, rippling waters for a moment, possibly mindful that the Parthe often turned the idyllic hollow into an unappetizing swamp. Following its course, the men soon reached the Hallische quarter, where the tanners lived, which consisted of only a single street, called Gerberstrasse (Tanner Street). As a part of the Via Imperii, the street had national significance and so it was already paved in stone within the municipal area. Paved roads were called Steinweg (cobble stone road), as in: Grimmaischer Steinweg, Ranstädter Steinweg, and Peterssteinweg, names that are still in use today. The name Hallischer Steinweg was used for a long time, before it was called Gerberstrasse.

Now the hardest part of the inspectors' mission stood before them, because unlike in the east, crossing the western region of the municipal area would be a most difficult undertaking. Countless small streams, rivers, brooks, and rivulets dissected the entire area and saw to it that it was constantly flooded. The largest of these little streams was the Weisse Elster, which wound around a little more than half a mile from the city, taking in water from the Pleisse, Parthe, Plaussig, and other tributaries. There were also numerous natural and man-made branches, such as the Kuburger Wasser, Luppe, and Rödel, which functioned as natural borders of the city's territory but also included the Kuhstrang, and the Elster and Pleisse millraces. Besides Schleussig, which consisted of one lonely farm and was therefore considered to be just an outlying estate, the swampy depression had remained undeveloped. Additional towns lay beyond the swamp, such as the relatively large Lindenau, both Zschochers, and the little Plagwitz, which the five men, now on foot, were unable to see through all of the trees. The next evidence of civilization were the houses in Connewitz, several miles to the south. It was there that they met the Via Imperii again, which formed the southern edge of Leipzig's territory. The inspectors planted a wooden cross there, too, which marked the city limits and would be replaced with one made of Rochlitzer porphyry fifty years later. That one is still there today, and even if it serves only as a signpost to the past, it is the basis for the name of one of the most well-known intersections in the city.

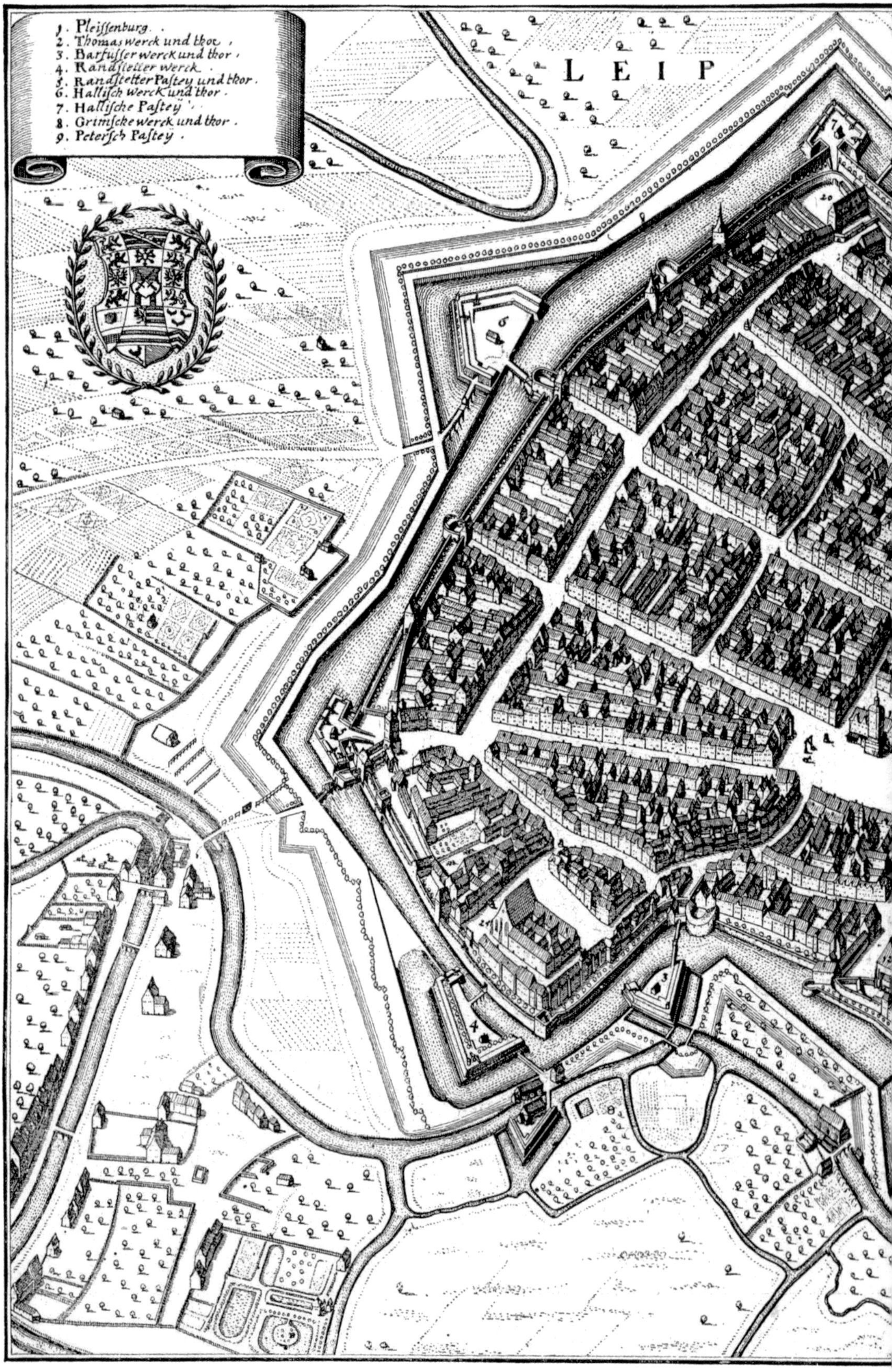

1. Pleiſſenburg.
2. Thomaswerck und thor,
3. Barfuſſer werck und thor,
4. Randſtetter werck.
5. Randſtetter Paſtey und thor.
6. Halliſch werck und thor.
7. Halliſche Paſtey.
8. Grimſche werck und thor.
9. Peterſch Paſtey.
LEIP

Little Paris
1500 to 1789

Leipzig in 1650

Martin Luther

June 24, 1519, was a hot day in a heated time. Two wagons crossed through the Grimmaische Gate around noon, not an uncommon sight. But these were accompanied by about two hundred students armed with axes and spears. The Wittenbergs had arrived, reporting for the battle of the churches, as the Leipzig Disputation was also called. While George the Bearded, Duke of Albertine Saxony, had assured safe conduct to Martin Luther, Phillip Melanchthon, and Andreas Karlstadt, he was not really a fan of the new movement, so the Reformers were taking some precautions of their own.

Martin Luther was no stranger to Leipzig. He had already visited the city four times before, the first time in 1512. That time he had made the round-trip of about ninety-three miles from Wittenberg and back again as a relatively unimportant and lightweight monk on foot, to fetch his stipend for his doctoral dissertation. It was fifty guilders, after all; a sum equivalent to the annual income of a master craftsman, and with which Luther could have acquired fifty letters of indulgence—at least in theory. In practice, the ever more pervasive purchase of redemption from sin seemed to him to be anything but Christian, and he wasn't the only one at the time who thought so. Yet it guaranteed the Pope a steady income, which financed construction of the new St. Peter's Basilica, among other things. Bishops and territorial lords earned a pretty penny as well, and for a long while, subtle theological interpretations did not stand a chance.

Johann Tetzel, who joined the Dominican monastery in Leipzig in 1489, became the most well-known representative of the indulgence trade. Because of this, he was rarely at home and spent most of his time on business trips. With slogans such as, "As soon as a coin in the coffer rings, the soul into heaven springs," he hoofed it across the German lands, and crossed the diocese of Magdeburg in 1517, which bordered Luther's homeland. That same year, Luther took up his quill and hammer, and posted his "95 Theses" on the door of the Wittenberg Castle Church, protesting the indulgence trade. That act alone did not yet turn the world on its head; the road to real change was long, and Luther would need not only plenty of luck and political support along the way but good public relations, most of all.

The Leipzig Disputation, held in the Pleissenburg Castle, was one of the most important PR events of the 35-year-old's life. The initiative, however, came from Luther's challenger, papist Professor Doctor Johannes Mayer, who was not much younger, and who was usually referred to by his opponents as Dr. Eck, after of his birthplace. Eck first debated Luther's colleague Andreas Karlstadt, and both tried to wear the other down with theoretical subtleties of theology. Only when hothead Luther entered the ring several days later did the debate really get going, if only because the five-foot tall and utterly unknown 22-year-old Phillip Melanchthon, a cunning strategist, stood at his side. No one was officially declared the winner of the debate, but the number of Luther's supporters, and enemies, increased by leaps and bounds. Johann Tetzel, however, would not be among them. Just a few days after the delegations left the city, the plague broke out, claiming the lives of Tetzel and 2,300 other Leipzigers. Luther, meanwhile, was excommunicated and ostracized two years later, and his territorial lord and forerunner Frederick the Wise moved him to the Wartburg castle as a precaution, where Luther translated the New Testament into German in just eleven weeks, at Melanchthon's suggestion.

When Luther finally dared to emerge from hiding in early December 1521, disguised as Junker Jörg, with plenty of hair on his head and face, his path led him to Leipzig once again. There he met Heinrich Stromer—Dr. Auerbach. The fact that he was recognized by a whore (who didn't give him away) waiting for a john, bothered him for a long while, and his opinion of Leipzig at the time was not necessarily a good one. Statements like, "Leipzig is like Sodom and Gomorrah. Awash with prostitution and highway robbery. . . . Oh, Leipzig, you are an evil worm, headed for disaster," seemed to indicate the negative impression the city had made on him. He was right, in the long run. Luther's Leipzig really was destroyed, and today only a handful of buildings from that era are still standing.

But Leipzig at the time was not just a den of iniquity. It was also a publishing center that contributed considerably to the dissemination of Luther's ideas. And the fact that the Wittenberg Delegation in 1519 stayed with the most important printer in town, Melchior Lotter, in Hainstrasse, was no coincidence. Lotter was the first to print Luther's "Theses," and another 160 of Luther's texts would follow. The new technology emerged as a weapon that Luther was adept at wielding. Without it, his fate might have been similar to that of Czech reformer John Hus, whose publications were issued in extremely limited editions.

Hus had also criticized the indulgence trade, and translated the Bible on a mountain, though into

Structures Existing in Leipzig During Luther's Lifetime

Building/Complex	Construction Completed	Notes
St. Nicholas Church	1165	Initially built without central spire, which was added in 1555
St. Thomas Church	1212/1496	
Apartment blocks	1511	on Barfussgässchen
St. Nicholas School	1512	
Gazebo at Barthel's Courtyard	1523	On side of the street until 1870, decorating the *Haus Zur goldenen Schlange* (House of the Golden Serpent)
Auerbach's Cellar	1538	Cellar at Auerbach's Courtyard
Community center at 8 Hainstrasse	c. 1545	

Czech. In 1415, Hus was excommunicated in Constance as a heretic. His works, though, were rather influential, especially in Leipzig, indirectly. As spokesman for the Czech nation at the university in Prague, he was not altogether uninvolved with the 1409 emigration of German students, which definitely facilitated the foundation of Leipzig's educational institution. In addition, the unrest that followed his violent death resulted in a shift in trade routes, out of the Bohemian region and into that of Meissen, which strengthened Leipzig's position as a merchant city. Leipzig was also elevated in importance when Margrave of Meissen Frederick the Militant did such a good job fighting off the Hussites that the Meissen Margraviate ultimately earned the status of Electorate of Saxony.

Two years after Luther's birth, in 1483, Saxony was divided between two royal brothers, Ernst and Albert. While Luther's ideas were quickly implemented in Ernestine Saxony, his homeland, they were not in Albertine Saxony, which included Leipzig, until after the death of George the Bearded, a lord who had long resisted any change in his territory. George's brother and successor, Henry the Pious, was open to the new doctrine.

On Pentacost in 1539, shortly after he took office, he paid a visit to Leipzig. The entire court came along, and Luther was also invited. He was to bring about the Reformation in Albertine Saxony. He preached twice during his stay in Leipzig: first at the old battleground, the Pleissenburg Castle, and on Whitmonday in the St. Thomas Church. This officially marked the beginning of the Protestant age in Saxony. Eventually he would preach in the Church of St. Paul one more time and rededicate it as the University Church, in August 1545, six months before his death.

Lotter

"I won't be around to see it happen, but in 1547, Leipzig will experience a great misfortune," Martin Luther once speculated boldly—and he would be right. In the same year that the reformer died, the Schmalkaldic War broke out, and in January 1547, Leipzig was besieged and bombarded for three weeks. Earlier—on Christmas Eve—the buildings on the outskirts of town were destroyed in order to make it easier to defend the city walls. This incident should have ruined Christmas for Hieronymus Lotter, as his house was also affected by the measure, but he did own two others—one on the market square, and one right next to Dr. Auerbach's place.

Lotter was already fifty years old, but he was not a political bigwig just yet. Born in Nürnberg in 1497, Lotter soon moved with his family to Annaberg in the Erz Mountains. They weren't the only ones lured by the big prospecting rush. With a population of about eight thousand, Annaberg was no backward village, but rather one of the largest cities in Central Germany. The Lotters' businesses, however, transferred more and more to Leipzig, which wasn't much larger, and the young Hieronymus ended up there. His debut involved a petty offence. While dancing, he moved his partner so fast that her dress whirled above her knee, normally punishable by a ten-cent fine. After that, however, the money

View from the Old Town Hall to the Old Weigh Station, c. 1880. Lotter was responsible for creating both buildings

began pouring into his pockets. Like his father, he was active in mining and money-lending, but he also worked as a master builder and merchant with contacts as far as Frankfurt am Main and Antwerp. In 1531, he married Katharina Bauer, the daughter of a Leipzig councilman, and with his wife's influence Hieronymus expanded both the family—they brought three sons into the world—and the Lotters' business activities. For the latter, his connection to Saxon Duke Moritz would become important. Since the duke was on the winning side of the war, he managed to grab the electoral land from his Ernestine brother-in-law and increase the size of the Albertine territories. The three-week siege had hit Leipzig hard, however. Damage to numerous buildings was recorded. The entire city fortification had to be refurbished, and the severely damaged old Pleissenburg Castle was to be replaced with a new one. The task was given to the Saxon elector's master builder, whose name was Hieronymus Lotter.

The job was enormous, and the taskmaster, Elector Moritz, was utterly ambitious. The city fortification would not simply be refurbished but be markedly improved. And so fortified ramparts—the Ranstädter, Hallische, and Henker Bastions, called the Moritz Bastion today—were created. In addition, a new Pleissenburg Castle was built, completely modern in form, a triangular citadel surrounded by its own moat. The compound included a 170-foot tower and was completed by 1551, just two years after construction began. Lotter had demonstrated his impressive organizational skills and would continue to do so with additional building projects in subsequent years.

In 1555, Lotter held the office of mayor for the first time, a position that usually lasted one year. Because his successor had died unexpectedly shortly after taking office, Lotter agreed to another term, which was already unusual, and a third term followed in 1558. This unusual cluster was accompanied by an even more unusual period of intense construction. Within just five years, important public buildings were erected, such as the council weigh station, the Rannische bathworks, the butchers' stalls, the dis-

Lotter's house, destroyed in 1943; plans to rebuild were never realized

trict office building, and the (middle) steeple on the St. Nicholas Church. The pièce de résistance, however, was the new city hall, built in 1556, now called the Old City Hall. Since at least the fourteenth century, there has been a city hall on the market square. The Old City Hall's late gothic predecessor would have fit on a much smaller piece of land, though, and was located on Grimmaische Street. Yet with the city's growth, the administrative buildings had to be enlarged as well, so the neighboring properties right up to the Salzgässchen were purchased in the sixteenth century. The existing buildings were not completely torn down, however. The basements and most of the ground floors were integrated into the new building, for which a new shared upper level and roof were built, along with a uniform exterior. This is why there's a slight drop in the façade and why it took only nine months to complete the building—at least the exterior. Still a remarkable achievement.

Lotter was less fortunate when he led the construction of the Augustusburg Castle by order of Elector August the First, beginning in 1568. Disagreements during the ambitious undertaking, executed by 750 workers, turned the project into a debacle. This was true especially for Lotter, who advanced his own money for the project, which was never returned because he and the elector had a falling out in 1571. In 1572, the elector even put Lotter under a construction ban, and a short while later the new situation affected Lotter's relationship with Leipzig as well. Although the council nominated Lotter for another term as mayor in 1574, his ninth, he declined the office, suspecting that the elector would refuse to give his approval anyway. Two years later, Lotter left Leipzig and withdrew to his manor in Geyer, the Lotterhof. His luck in business eventually left him. His businesses performed so poorly that he had to mortgage his Leipzig properties and, a year before he died, the tin mine in Geyer as well. When he died in Geyer in 1580, at the age of eighty-two, there was hardly anything left of his former fortune. And yet, an amazing number of his buildings remain intact.

Structures Built under Hieronymus Lotter's Authority
(Most Built by Paul Speck or Paul Wiedemann.)

Still standing today	
Moritzbastei (Moritz Bastion)	1554
Central spire on St. Nicholas Church	1555
Alte Waage (Old Weigh Station)	Originally built in 1555, rebuilt 1963/64
Renovation of *Alte Rathaus* (Old City Hall)	1556/57
Galleries in the St. Thomas Church	1570

Demolished or destroyed by war		
Granary on the *Brühl*	1546	1702, torn down
Leipzig city fortifications	Beg. 1548	Torn down
Pleissenburg Castle	1549–1567	1897–1899, torn down
Residence Katharinenstr./Brühl	1550	1943, destroyed
Rannisch Bastion Bathhouse	1558	torn down
Fürstenhaus (Royal House, investment)	1558	1943, destroyed
Amtshaus (District Offices)	1559	1900, torn down
Butchers' stalls	1560	1907, torn down
Goldene Fahne, für den Sohn (Golden Flag, for the Son)	1570	1943, destroyed, stair tower remains

Leipzig in 1632, during the Thirty Years War

Thirty Years War

> *"War feeds on war."*
> *—Friedrich Schiller,* Wallenstein

At the beginning of September 1631, Tilly's troops showed up outside Leipzig's city walls—thirty-thousand strong. The war had arrived at Leipzig, and what that might mean was made all too clear by what had happened in Magdeburg four months prior. Over twenty thousand residents had been killed when Magdeburg was sacked, and except for the cathedral, the city practically no longer existed. With Tilly threatening to "Magdeburgize" Leipzig, too, the poorly protected city surrendered without a fight, although the outlying districts had just been dismantled to improve the city's defenses. It was a surprise when the garrison at Pleissenburg Castle also gave up, as not a single shot was fired at the specially secured fortress. When the arrival of the Swedes was announced several hours later, the surrender suddenly seemed premature and questionable. The Swedes beat Tilly at Breitenfeld, nearly four miles north of Leipzig, and the city was soon liberated again. The captain at Pleissenburg, Hans Vopelius, faced ridicule from Leipzigers as well as the wrath of his superiors in Dresden for his lack of combat initiative.

The war was actually a series of conflicts and was by no means over yet. It all began with three light casualties at the second Defenestration of Prague in 1618. An incident that at first involved only Protestant Bohemians and their Catholic Habsburg king, it quickly turned into a super-regional conflict pitting the Catholic League against the Protestant Union. Soon other European powers got involved as well—Spain, France, and Denmark—and the conflict expanded beyond religious supremacy to include the secular realm. Saxon Elector Johann Georg joined the Habsburgs, who promised him control over Upper and Lower Lusatia in return, which until then had been Bohemian territory. The territorial gain came at a high price, however. Though Saxony had been spared the kind of devastation seen in other areas, the cost of the war had been enormous, and the elector simply minted the money he did not have, leading to high inflation. Even trade and mining, the pillars of Leipzig's economy, collapsed, forcing the city to declare bankruptcy in 1626 and endure six years of subsequent receivership to the elector. Peace was maintained in Saxony, though, until the Swedes got involved in the conflict in 1630. The Swedes did not declare war on Electoral Saxony but declared them allies, which had the same effect. After the Battle of Breitenfeld, the fighting moved to the southern region of the empire.

On October 23, 1632, however, a good year after the first victory over Leipzig, an imperial detachment about two thousand strong suddenly stood at the gates, led by Heinrich Holk. The one-eyed mercenary leader was not adverse to drink and had already developed a considerable reputation as a butcher of men. He would likely have conquered the nearly defenseless city without much effort, so it surrendered a second time and was plundered. But this time Pleissenburg Castle, still commanded by Vopelius, would not fall so easily. Seven cannon shots were fired before the white flag was raised.

Two weeks later, the largest battle in the war took place at Lützen, just over six miles west of Leipzig. The battle decided nothing, though nearly ten thousand people were killed. One of them was the Swedish king Gustavus Adolphus. Like many times before, the northern luminary led the troops, but this time the results were fatal. Separated from his troops in the fog and gunsmoke, the king was struck down by multiple shots, and his corpse was plundered and left naked on the battlefield. While the body was transported to Sweden a short while later, hundreds of Leipzigers died from the plague and starvation. In 1632 alone, 1,390 fell victim to the plague, followed by another wave just one year later. The disease also claimed troops, laying waste to the city again under Holk. The captain left the city in a hurry, but the plague was faster. Holk died a short time later—one scourge wiping out another. Wallenstein, on the other hand, supreme commander of the imperial troops, was assassinated one year later.

The political situation grew more and more difficult. In 1635, Saxon Elector Johann Georg renounced his alliance with Sweden and continued to fight for the Catholic cause. Electoral Saxony remained a war zone. The Swedes conquered Leipzig three times, with similar consequences as in the previous sacks. Meanwhile, the war had become so radicalized and the area so bled to death that entire regions were depopulated. Villages and unfortified cities were especially vulnerable to murder and pillaging. The peasants who remained were either violently forced into the army or decided to join voluntarily to increase their chance of survival. This meant that armies were comprised of soldiers from very different areas, and the maxim from Schiller's *Wallenstein*—"War feeds on war"—took on a double meaning. Anything that did not serve the war was destroyed. In 1637, forty-two hundred people starved in Leipzig alone, and another four thousand became victims of the latest outbreak of the plague.

When the drama finally came to an official end with the Peace Treaty of Westfalia in 1648, the destructive consequences were so huge, especially in Central Europe, that the landscape looked like something from the Apocalypse. The Holy Roman Empire of the German Nation, in which about sixteen million people had lived at the beginning of the war, lost more than a third of its population. Saxony lost half, with its western region hit especially hard. There were only about fourteen thousand inhabitants left in Leipzig, and they would feel the economic effects of the war for a long, long time. Frankfurt, hit less hard than Leipzig, surpassed Leipzig as a city of books and trade fairs for the time being. In addition, the Prussians, besides Sweden and France, clearly established themselves as winners in the conflict.

Hans Vopelius's fate, on the other hand, had already been determined by 1633. In a large trial it was decided that he was guilty of treason, even though neither Pleissenburg nor its garrison had been fit for war. He was sentenced to lose three fingers from his right hand before being killed by means of a sword, and his head was to be hung from the fortress as an admonition. His wife, however, begged desperately for mercy, with some success. In the end, he was simply beheaded.

Old Drugs—New Drugs

"He who has no beer, has nothing to drink."
—Martin Luther

When Christian Reuter moved to Leipzig to study law in 1688, he was just twenty-three years old. That he dedicated twenty semesters to his studies had less to do with his passion for the administration of justice and more to do with his fondness of theater and self-indulgent visits to the ale house. He soon developed quite a reputation, as some of his drinking bouts led to brawls and similar acts of excess.

The consumption of alcohol, even to excess, was not an unusual phenomenon—neither in those days nor at others times, with only the means changing. Mead, for example, a 15 percent brew made from honey and water, was very popular in the Middle Ages, but its price jumped in the late seventeenth century because bees were practically decimated during the Thirty Years War. As a result, brandy took over—at first made from grain and fruit, but later from imported sugar cane. Because of its higher transportation costs, wine was mostly consumed among wealthy circles. Wine was often thinned with ingredients like mustard, ash, ginger, or salt. Beer, on the other hand, was pretty cheap and healthy, compared to the even cheaper water, which was often contaminated. Beer was considered not only a preventative of disease but a nutritious dietary supplement as well. Adults at the time consumed on average half a gallon per day, and even children drank beer. Most types back then contained less alcohol than today's varieties. Pilsner did not exist yet, and Gose-style beer, top-fermented with salt and coriander and originally from Goslar, would first gain a foothold in Leipzig in the mid-eighteenth century, when it would become the

Richter's Coffeehouse on the third floor of the Romanus House, 1794

city's best-loved brew, celebrated in hymns, ceremonies, and by other means of homage. Until then, amber beer was the kind most often served, though for quite some time there was no getting around Leipzig's local beer, Rastrum.

Although it did not taste very good, Rastrum was a success because the sale of nonlocal beer was regulated by the city-run Burgkeller (Castle Cellar). Only the university was allowed to serve its own beer, which often led to passionate disputes, because the amber nectar was not just used for nutrition and enjoyment but was becoming a profoundly significant source of income. For a long time, the beer tax was the most substantial excise tax. There were about a hundred taverns and inns in the city at the time, including one famous for its wine bar—Auerbachs Keller. That a certain Dr. Faustus was said to have ridden out of the preceding establishment on a keg in 1525 was rather unlikely, despite the already advanced state of keg technology, though it did make quite an impression on many a future guest. The establishment was operated by Heinrich Stromer, originally from Auerbach, who expanded it in 1530 to become the largest wine bar in the empire. There were also a great many taverns on the Brühl.

In the Gasthof zum roten und zum weißen Löwen (Red and White Lion Inn), proprietress Anna Rosine Müller was not particularly excited about her new guest, Christian Reuter. A few weeks later she threw him out, but that did not make matters any better. On the contrary, Reuter found a way to retaliate. When his first comedy *Die ehrliche Frau zu Plißine* (*The Honest Woman in Plissine*), debuted in October 1695, the tavern mentioned in the play was called Zum göldenen Maulaffen (The Golden Gawker), but it was owned by a Mrs. Schlampampe (a folksy term for slut), and everyone knew who was meant by that. Further action would follow, and

Leipzig's first coffeehouse was located at Petersstrasse in the market. The Café National followed later. Photo 1876

not even the death of the proprietress, lawsuits, censorship, detention, or expulsion from the university would diminish Reuter's efforts. Another text published in Leipzig in 1695, *Die Heut zutage gebräuchliche und wohlbewehrte Koche-Kunst* (*Today's Common and Treasured Cookery*), was comparatively much more peaceable.

That book presented all kinds of contemporary culinary dishes. Almonds were popular, and expensive. With bread, the lighter it was, the grander, and in times of fasting, hemp, lentils, and aquatic animals were allowed—not only fish but beaver as well. Most Leipzig specialties were not yet known. *Allasch*, a caraway liqueur imported from the Baltic region would first come to Leipzig in 1830, and *Leipziger Allerlei* is just slightly older, and was originally made with morels, crab, and spring vegetables. With the draining of swamps, water pollution, and the East German economy of scarcity, nearly all of the important ingredients went by the wayside, so that now it is known simply as a mixed-vegetable stew. No other German dish has ever suffered a more pronounced erosion of assets. Leipziger lark, meanwhile, has undergone a complete transformation. Now a marzipan pastry, it really was once made with a bacon-filled songbird, a culinary hit exported as far as Moscow. Besides lark, goose, and quail, the entire palette of avian foodstuffs landed on the plate in those days, including eagle, swan, woodpecker, blackbird, thrush, finch, and starling. Imported fowl from abroad or the Orient added to the variety available.

Exactly who discovered the stimulating effect of the coffee bean is still disputed. One theory, however, is that a bleary-eyed Ethiopian shepherd suffering from the effects of his goat herd's incessant wide-awake behavior first stumbled upon the stimulating property of the bush's fruit. The bean had definitely reached Arabia by the fifteenth century, in Mocha, among other places, where it was roasted, ground, and steeped in water. The result was first called *qahwa* (stimulating drink). The first coffeehouse opened in Venice in 1647, followed by London (of all places!), Amsterdam, and other centers of trade. By 1670, a package of these new beans also reached a Leipzig merchant, though without any instructions on how to prepare them, so the cook in the house added them to the meat broth of a soup, which presumably did not taste very good.

There is no evidence to support this story, but suffice it to say that the new drug did not have an easy time of it at first. It was outrageously expensive to acquire and transport, and its complicated processing had to be completed on site, as packaging that could retain the beans' aromatic properties had not been invented yet. So it took nearly twenty years for coffee (without meat broth) to be served in Leipzig, after Bremen (1673), Hamburg (1677), and Vienna (1685). Royal chocolatier Johann Schmidt opened the first Leipzig coffeehouse on the market square in 1694. It became better known through his fellow coffee-carrier, Johann Lehmann, who soon ran the Lehmannsche Kaffeehaus (Lehman's Coffeehouse) alone. It did not take long for competition to appear. The Café Geswein welcomed its first guests on the Brühl just two years later. Documentation shows that the Coffe Baum (Coffee Tree) has been serving coffee since 1720, where August the Great, Johann Sebastian Bach, Christian Fürchtegott Gellert, Gotthold Ephraim Lessing, Johann Wolfgang von Goethe, Napoleon, Robert Schumann, and Richard Wagner have each enjoyed a cup.

Ten years later, there were already eight coffeehouses in Leipzig, although the initial reputation of the newfangled brew was downright awful. The rector of the university even posted notices to his

Coffeehouses in the 18th Century

Coffehouse	Location	Established in
Lehmann's Coffeehouse	Markt/Petersstrasse	1694
Café Gesswein	In the Golden Apple	1697
The Arabic Coffee Tree	Kleine Fleischergasse 4	1720
Klassig's Coffeehouse	In the Golden Anchor, Hainstr. 11	1723
Zimmermann's Coffeehouse	Katharinenstrasse 14	1723
Schrepfer's Coffeehouse	Zill's Tunnel today	1770
Richter's Coffeehouse	Katharinenstrasse 23	1772
Jägersches (Hunter's) Coffeehouse	In Amtmann's Courtyard, Reichsstrasse 10	
Venoni Wine- and Coffeehouse	At Pleissenburg Castle	

students, warning them off constant visits to coffeehouses and tearooms, and the "wenches who consorted there." The coffeehouses were also infamous for fronting card and billiard games, for money, of course, and tax-free to boot. It didn't take long for rules to appear: By 1697, Germany's first coffeehouse regulation was issued in Leipzig, and during the New Year's trade fair six months later, enforcement took effect. Despite a ban, "all sorts of common wenches and other loose riffraff" were found in the establishments, and were publicly flogged and sentenced to prison, subject to fines, or chased out of town. Coffee maids or chocolate girls were part of the service at many coffee bars, where a cup of coffee was at least twice as expensive as the accompanying sexual favors. For three weeks, three times a year, the trade center hosted wealthy male travelers, the perfect market for prostitution, which grew just as fast as the trade fairs themselves.

Soon it was not just businessmen but whores as well who were flocking to Leipzig from all directions, although it is speculation, at best, to say that hot beverages were the cause of this. Especially in Baroque times, prostitutes were ubiquitous at the trade fairs, and in some wine bars, on inner-city streets, and especially on the newly built promenade between the St. Thomas and St. Matthew's churches, where the offerings were not all that Christian. Some public gardens established a similar reputation. There—and we come full circle—more and more coffee was served, along with cake, which was also just making its debut.

An important ingredient had been missing before: sugar. The sweet confection was so expensive for so long, that it was called "white gold." It was not until sugarcane was grown in large quantities on South American plantations that the middle class could afford this luxury, and so coffee and cake soon became associated. Other products had already found their way to Europe but not onto European plates. Potatoes are one example, and tomatoes, which young women were forbidden from eating because the Church was afraid that the consumption of this vegetable would lead to delusions of love. For a long time, religious sensibilities also kept people from using forks, which were thought to be a symbol of the devil. Cups and plates had it better, especially those made of porcelain. In 1708, alchemist Johann Friedrich Böttger invented the European version in Meissen, which was immediately applied to the new forms of eating and drinking. In August of that year, the heavy coffee drinker found these to be the perfect ambassadors. Coffee Easter eggs and the manufacturers of cooking implements gained economic relevance. Leipzig quickly took a leading role, particularly in the production of coffee grinders. In addition, many significant societal institutions developed out of the new circumstances. Because women were forbidden from entering coffeehouses, they celebrated the "black hour" by holding their own coffee parties.

Along with all of the culinary novelties, tobacco use came on the scene, and had an equally a rough start. The first time English pioneer Sir Walter Raleigh was smoking away in the privacy of his own home, his maid prudently put him out by dumping a bucket of water over his head. Aside from initial irritations such as this, smoking became unexpectedly popular. The downright deadly Thirty Years War saw to it that smoking spread quickly—a perfect story for a no-smoking campaign. Except that smoking was first employed as a general medicine and was often used to fight the plague, pox, and all kinds of other illnesses. (The fact that these diseases have been eliminated, meanwhile, should not lead to the wrong conclusion!) The village of Stötteritz, southeast of Leipzig, was long considered to be the center of German tobacco production. Tobacco thrived there and was processed in the Quandt tobacco mill. In 1813, Napoleon chose the mill for his command center, and it was destroyed during

Gasthaus zum Roten und zum Weißen Löwen (Red and White Lion Inn) was home not only to Christian Reuter, but would also be the birthplace of Richard Wagner in 1813. Demolished in 1886, three years after Wagner's death. Photo 1884

the fighting. Because business was dwindling, the mill was not rebuilt.

Four years later, Christian Reuter was rediscovered, after remaining forgotten for over a hundred years. Forced to leave Leipzig in 1700, he had soon found employment as a court poet in Prussia. He did not become famous for his writings there or for those from his time in Leipzig. The date and circumstances of his death are not clear. In the late eighteenth century, however, his Schelmuffsky novels served as the model for Gottfried August Bürger's Münchhausen stories. Several years later, Clemens Brentano and the Brothers Grimm also became fans, and the latter produced the first reprint of Reuter's complete works in 1817.

On the Long Death of a Misunderstood Genius

"There are a lot of Bachs."
—Gravediggers at Old St. John's Cemetery

On October 22, 1894, there was a lot of digging going on at Old St. John's Cemetery. The reason for this was not a mass exodus, but rather an attempt to find an immortal. According to tax notices, the grave of Johann Sebastian Bach and his wife, Anna Magdalena, were supposed to be about six steps from the southern portal of St. John's Church. There was no tombstone, however, which made the task challenging. The fact that Bach was buried in an oak casket, however, as the tax files revealed, indicated that he did not die without financial means. The detail also narrowed the search for the Messiah considerably. Only after two oak caskets were found, opened, and the contents determined not to match the person they were looking for, was a third finally found. There was tense silence all

"Study Bach; you'll find everything there." (Johannes Brahms)

Old St. Thomas School, where Bach's family lived for 27 years, torn down in 1902. Photo c. 1870

around as that casket was opened. It contained the skeleton of an older man.

That Bach's career would someday include being a tourist attraction was inconceivable for quite a long while. He was appreciated as an accomplished musician, not only in Leipzig but at the Saxon and Prussian courts as well. Yet he was not considered that eternal genius as we think of him now during his own lifetime. Just a few years after his passing, the Baroque era ended. *Sturm und Drang* and Viennese classicism made their predecessors sound not only old but outdated. Although Bach had performed his *St. Matthew Passion* in Berlin and Frankfurt am Main outside of Leipzig for the first time when he was twenty, it was not until the Berlin Sing-Academy, directed by Felix Mendelssohn Bartholdy, presented Bach's work to the public eighty years after his death that the Eisenach native and Leipzig's great son experienced a real breakthrough.

"Bach's name should not be 'Bach' [stream], but 'Meer' [sea] instead." (Ludwig van Beethoven)

Yet as famous as Bach became, his grave was still nowhere to be found. It was embarrassing, especially because the magnificent gravesite of George Frideric Handel, who had also made a comeback, was a wonderful site of pilgrimage in London's Westminster Abbey. On the other hand, Handel had already enjoyed cult status during his lifetime. Even more popular at the time was Georg Philipp Telemann, who was the candidate that the Leipzig Council really wanted to fill the position of *Thomaskantor* (director of the St. Thomas choir), after Johann Kuhnaus's death in 1722. Telemann had demonstrated his talent along the Pleisse River during his legal studies, as director of the Leipzig Opera, for example, established in 1693. He also initiated the establishment of the Collegium Musicum in 1701. After Hamburg countered with a small increase in salary, however, Telemann declined the position in Leipzig, and candidate number two, Christoph Graupner, declined as well. The council decided, "If we cannot have the best, we will take the mediocre," and so it was that the 37-year-old conductor from Köthen came into play. After Bach passed all of the tests for acceptance, the search for a director was finally concluded.

"Compared to him, we are all incompetent." (Robert Schumann)

But 170 years later, the case of Bach's grave was not even close to being settled. In order to determine whether the mortal remains found in the oak casket were really the right ones, they were subject to an elaborate combination of science and art. Leipzig professor of anatomy Wilhelm His, one of the most accomplished physicians of his time, reconstructed the facial features of the dead man, with the help of budding legendary sculptor Carl Seffner and some brand-new technology. When the result was compared to a portrait painted by Elias Gottlob Haussmann in 1746—the only portrait of Bach that exists—the verdict was, "highly probable." A short while later, the remains of the man who was most likely Bach were transferred to the new St. John's Church, where he was laid to rest in a crypt with Christian Fürchtegott Gellert and the latter's brother. At just about the same time, Bach's residence and workplace, the Old St. Thomas School, was torn down.

When the Bach family had moved into the director's apartment in 1723, it had just been completely renovated. The school building, however, had been in desolate condition, not having been refurbished since its construction in 1553. Rats and mice scurried throughout the derelict rooms, and Bach's predecessor, Kuhnau, had complained that the scratches the choirboys suffered impaired the choir's musical quality. Aside from choral instruction, one of the director's duties was to instruct the fifty-six boarding schoolboys in Latin. He also functioned in the capacity of municipal minister of music, presenting a new cantata each Sunday in one of the four large municipal churches and responsible for the musical accompaniment for baptism, weddings, funerals, or celebrations of council members. The full-time job included weekends. Bach handed the tedious Latin instruction over to his deputy rector, along with half of his salary, so he was not particularly well paid, considering all of his duties. He was able to augment his salary with many private compositions, though. While there was enough money for the Bach household, the director's apartment soon grew too small. Bach became a father twenty times, though only half of his children lived to adulthood.

His second wife, Anne Magdalena, bore him thirteen children.

In 1732, St. Thomas School was finally renovated, expanded, and updated in the Baroque style, which significantly improved Bach's living situation as well as that of the St. Thomas boys. Bach's reputation among the municipal administrators, however, went in the opposite direction. Everyone was angry with the new director, who was constantly demanding improvements, according to the council's estimation, and his salary was educed in a disciplinary response. Even musically he rarely scored any points among the city's elite. When the *St. Matthew Passion* debuted in 1727, its length—two hundred minutes!—caused a scandal. But Bach, who was well respected in the city's music scene, would not be deterred. His regimented church music took more and more shape, with Christiana Mariana von Ziegler, daughter of Franz Conrad Romanus and a well-known author, contributing to the texts. For the musical execution of his works, initially Bach had only the municipal wait (two wind and three stringed instruments) and the St. Thomas Choir at his disposal, whose musical talent was limited, as he often complained. In 1729, he eventually took over the directorship of the Collegium Musicum, which gave him access to a large number of accomplished musicians. With these he performed in the city's coffeehouses, like Telemann had before him, especially at Zimmerman's on Katharinenstrasse.

"Now that's something you can learn from! Bach is the father, we are the children. If any of us are doing anything right, we learned it from him." (Wolfgang Amadeus Mozart)

Other musical concepts emerged in the city at that time as well. In 1741, the concerto grosso debuted at the tavern of the Drey Schwanen (Three Swans) on the Brühl. For Bach, that address was less acoustically than visually portentous. It was there that oculist John Taylor, a cataract surgeon to whom Bach turned, showed up nine years later. But for Bach, instead of seeing better, complications arose, and he died several weeks later, on July 28, 1750. The official record read, "One man, age 67, Mr. Johann Sebastian Bach, Director and Cantor of the Schools at St. Thomas, at the St. Thomas School, died. male. 4 underage children, hearse free of charge." George Frideric Handel was also treated by John Taylor, but he lost only his eyesight.

While Handel still lay buried in his old place in Westminster Abbey, Bach's remains were moved yet again. When St. John's Church was destroyed during World War II, Bach and the brothers Gellert went missing once more. The crypt remained intact and was found again, however, and after some back and forth, it was decided that they would be moved to the St. Thomas Church. Master-mason Malecki was said to have accomplished the feat by hauling an open zinc coffin through the city, saying, *"Tach, wir bring 'n Bach'n"* ("G'day, Bach's underway"). The brothers Gellert, meanwhile, were laid in state in the choir at the Church of St. Paul, and in 1968, endured an additional, fourth move—this time, hopefully, to their final resting place in the Southern Cemetery.

"Let's look to Bach, the dear god of music to whom composers should turn before getting to work, so that he might protect them from mediocrity" (Claude Debussy)

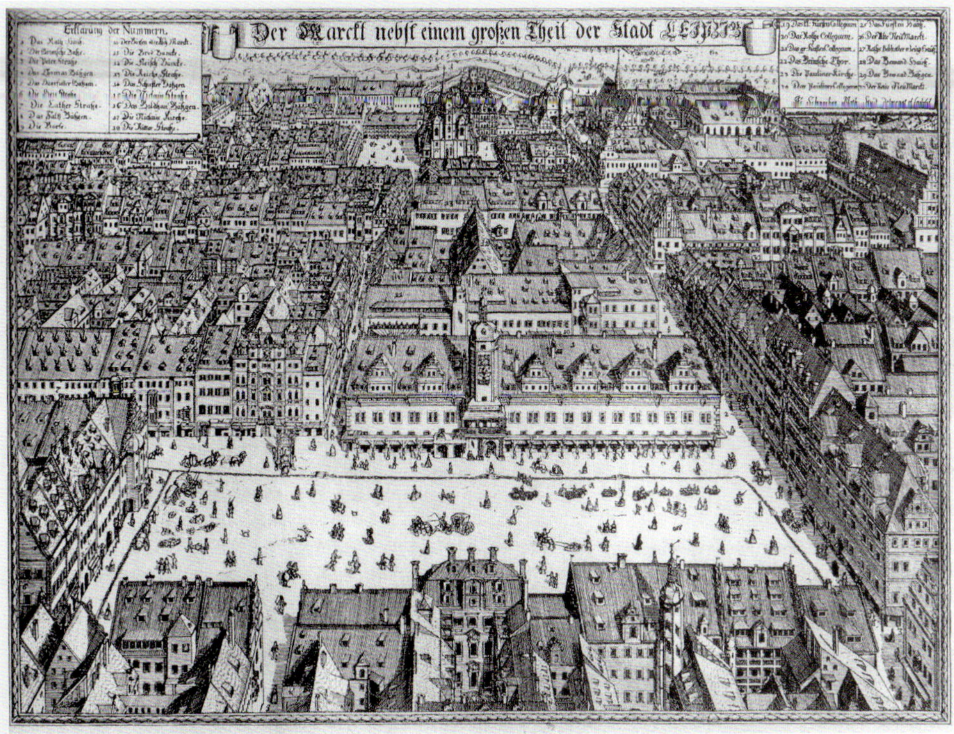

Europe's Marketplace

When Johann Martin Haugk built his mercantile on the corner of Sporergässchen and Petersstrasse in 1750, numerous new homes and businesses were already lining the city streets. Katharinenstrasse had become the most genteel boulevard in Leipzig, but the area around the market and along Klostergasse and Petersstrasse gleamed as well. Overall, one out of every three buildings in Leipzig had been built during the last fifty years, or had at least undergone massive restoration—in the Baroque style, of course. The new buildings were much larger and more ostentatious than the older ones, as their construction was funded by lucrative businesses. Wealth from trade served as the representation of, or even the possibility of creating, cultural value—in the form of a house, for example. Buildings were made to last forever. Johann Martin Haugk thought so, too, and he was fortunate. Today, 265 years later, his residence is still admired, and is now the oldest house on the street. Business continues there as well—manufacturing shoes.

In the middle of the eighteenth century, Leipzig was one of the leading trade and trade-fair cities on the continent and was described as Europe's marketplace, despite the fact that the city was tiny, compared to metropolises like London, Paris, and Constantinople, where there were already half a million people. With a population of thirty-five thousand, Leipzig barely ranked fifteenth on the list of most

Market Square, 1740

populated cities in the empire, which included Prague, Brussels, Breslau, and Königsberg at the time. Frankfurt am Main was right behind Electoral Saxony. Population development in both trade-fair cities along the Via Regia was characteristically nearly identical. Leipzig's densely populated inner city was a little smaller, however; at times more than twenty thousand people lived on just about sixty-two acres there. And their apartments were not the only buildings—as nearly every municipal institution was there as well, including countless craftsmen's workshops.

Craftsmanship had developed extraordinarily well in Electoral Saxony, where innovation contributed heavily to prosperity. In Leipzig alone, there were many master craftsmen in the mid-eighteenth century, including two hundred tailors, thirty button-makers, one hundred and fifty cobblers, and nearly fifty wigmakers, and twice as many just twenty-five years later. There were also 40 distillers, 52 booksellers, and 264 grocers registered. The number of bakers and master butchers, however, was not as high, at just thirty each, probably due to competition in the outlying villages. In addition to craftsmen's workshops, there were also a great many manufacturers (mostly in the outlying areas), where hundreds were employed. Silk and cloth goods, gold- and silverwork, wallpapers, and tobacco and snuff, among other things, were all produced there. The owners of the manufacturing sites were often also the salesmen, the number of which had grown to nearly 250. Numerous merchants had moved to the city from other places, including many from abroad. So the expulsion of the Huguenots in 1685 strengthened France, but among Italian merchants, for example, Leipzig had come to be considered an exceedingly attractive center of trade. Last but not least, Leipzig traders had established a European-wide network of business contacts, which would increasingly expand to other continents.

Trade Courtyards

Name	Built	Location	Today	Demolished/Lost
Auerbach's Courtyard	1538	Grimmaische Strasse/ New Market	Mädler Passage	1913
Kleines Joachimsthal (Little Jachymov)	1606	Hainstrasse/Fleischergasse	Pieces remaining	1908/1943
Deutrich's Courtyard	1655	Reichsstrasse/Nikolai-strasse	Motel One parking lot	1896/1968
Amtmann's courtyard	1700	Reichsstrasse/Nikolai-strasse	Motel One parking lot	1943
Peter Richter's Courtyard	1709	Reichsstrasse/Katharinen-strasse	Art Museum	1943
Grosse Feuerkugel (Big Fireball)	1711	New Market/Universitäts-strasse	*Kaufhof* (Dept. Store)	1870=original building torn down; 1943=destroyed
Aeckerlein's Courtyard	1714	Markt/Klostergasse	Market Gallery	1943
Hohmann's Courtyard	1731	Petersstrasse/New Market	*Messehof* (Trade-show Courtyard)	1943
Stieglitzen's Courtyard	1733	Markt/Klostergasse	Market Gallery	1894
Lattermann's Courtyard	1735	Brühl/Richard Wagner Str.	*Höfe am Brühl* (Courtyards on the Brühl)	1943
Koch's Courtyard	1739	Markt/Reichsstrasse	Penguin Milk Bar	1943
Quandt's Courtyard	1749	Nikolaistrasse/Ritter-strasse	Oelssner's Courtyard	1907

Barthel's Hof, built in 1750, is the only remaining trade courtyard from the trade-fair era in which goods were sold; originally there were about 30.

And so merchant Haugk and his family traded goods from Spain, England, Portugal, and, beginning in 1770, even Greenland. Whale meat, boning, blubber, and furs came from Greenland and sold for large profits in Europe. The trips were made at great risk, as the grandchild of homebuilder Johann Martin Haugk would learn in 1790. Storms damaged his ship and pushed it off course, and although the coast was close by, fog and ice floes made reaching it impossible. The crew thought all was lost, when suddenly a Greenlander appeared in a kayak and guided the ship to the treacherous shore. The rescuer was invited to spend his golden years in Leipzig.

Though most Leipzig traders first made direct contact with America or countries in the Far East in the eighteenth century, advantageous constellations had already emerged for the city from the new transoceanic routes. Though the Mediterranean region, especially the Italian city-states and also the Hanseatic League, had decreased in significance, the new transoceanic ports on the Atlantic and North Sea coasts had become more important. Hamburg and Amsterdam, in particular, became vital landing sites and chose Leipzig as the prime inland location for stock turnover. At the same time, the intensity of east–west trade was increasing, though it was phasing out over the Via Regia, whose offshoots, meanwhile, stretched much farther east. Just twelve years before the discovery of America, cities in the Rus had broken free of Mongol domination and had since developed into an empire ruled from Moscow, which stretched all the way to the Pacific.

Besides Leipzig's favorable location, clever maneuvering also played a decisive role—aided by privileges gained especially for the trade fair. The crucial breakthrough came in 1497, or rather 1507. The staple and market rights were extended to fifteen Saxon miles (sixty-eight miles), and every merchant trading in Central Germany had to offer his wares in Leipzig first, for three days. Failure to do so resulted in a fine. Because no other annual markets were allowed in this area, Leipzig's rise led directly to the decline of competing trade cities. Erfurt, in particular, dwindled in importance in the sixteenth century. Other developments led to the closure of trade-fair locations, such that two hundred years later, Braunschweig, Naumburg, and Frankfurt (Oder) were the only places still hold-

St. Peter's Gate, 1723, rebuilt by Matthäus Daniel Pöppelmann and last city gate to be demolished; photo taken shortly before demolition in 1860

ing trade fairs—and, of course, Frankfurt am Main, which at the beginning of the eighteenth century had been the leading location. But Leipzig had surpassed Frankfurt am Main continued to increase its lead. By 1871, Leipzig would be the only international trade-fair city in the newly established German empire.

The lifesaver from Greenland, meanwhile, did move to Europe, though he never actually made it to Leipzig. He became ill during the crossing and died in Lübeck, barely making it onto German soil. In the municipal cemetery there he found eternal peace, alone but for the Holsteins. His boat, nearly six yards long, was sent down to the Pleisse, though it would never be used on that river. Instead, the exotic vessel and a wooden figure with the face of the Greenlander carved on it, was placed in Haugk's home, a curiosity that drew countless visitors.

There was an abundance of unusual things on Petersstrasse in those days, especially during the trade fairs. Many businesses, with goods from around the world, were established there because the street was an inner-city section of the Via Imperii, and it was wide, well lit, and attractive. All kinds of customers passed through as well. Peter Hohmann, one of the richest merchant princes in Leipzig, built a business structure there, too, and Johann Friedrich Böttger presented European porcelain to the public for the first time during the Easter trade fair in 1710, in the house Zum Blauen Engel (Blue Angel), just a few paces from the future Haugk residence. All manner of wares were peddled in the streets, markets, and courtyards for the three-week fair every Easter, Michaelmas, and New Year's. Merchants from all over the world accompanied the wares. About three thousand fairgoers plus their attendants attended the Easter fair at the time, which was generally the best-attended one. While most of the visitors came from Electoral Saxony, Prussians, Transylvanians, English, Poles, and Dutchmen flocked there, too. Because of the many Russians and Greeks that came in 1741, an Orthodox community was established, the first in the German-speaking realm.

Eighty years later, the first Brazilians, Argentineans, and Americans attended. These were joined by Indians, Persians, Armenians, and later Chinese, Arabs, and Africans. An assembly of international guests, the likes of which was rarely found anywhere else at the time. The foreigners dispersed among the city in accordance with the range of goods. The cloth merchants were located in Hainstrasse, Fleischergasse, and the front area of the Brühl, for example, while the eastern side was home to the fur traders. A highly diverse assortment of merchants could also be found in Peterstrasse and Reichsstrasse, as well as the Grimmaische and Nasch Markets. Most of the buildings used were designed with courtyard throughways specifically for the fair. One advantage of this design was that carriages could be driven out the other side, once the goods had been unloaded in the courtyard, without blocking each other's way. This also conserved space normally required for turning vehicles. Space that could be rented to stands instead.

Auerbach's Hof, the largest of the thirty-odd courtyard areas, could hold up to a hundred different stands. Barthel's courtyard is the only one that remains. Today's passages in the sample fair palaces often lead through the blocks of the inner city where the courtyards once stood at fair time. Products were stored in their deep cellars and remarkably high attics, complete with catheads for hauling wares—the fairs then were an opportunity not just to present all of the goods assembled but to sell them, too. Just as challenging as finding space for all of the wares was finding space for all of the visitors. The 120 inns at the time were hopelessly overcrowded, and there were not enough apartments vacated by the students and employees for the fair. Attendants and carriages were usually sent to the outlying areas or to villages along the Via Regia and Via Imperii, which generated income in those places. This was true in Leipzig, too, where the fair mark-up made everything—literally everything—much more expensive than normal.

Trade Show Attractions

Year	Attraction
1692	Elephant exhibition
1701	Man ate rocks, live cats, dogs, and sheep with pelts
1704	Wax figures displayed
1706	English ladder acrobat
1706	Philipp Hoetten exhibited hippopotamus, tiger, three lions
1717	Strongman show
1747	Rhinoceros exhibition

During the era of the sample fair, the house *Zum Grönländer* (The Greenlander) served as a fair building for the German lighting industry. The Greenlander's boat was declared public property during the GDR-era, and later its fluid, dynamic properties were researched by the *Deutsche Hochschule für Körperkultur* (German Academy for Sports) before it finally landed in its current location in 1974: the Ethnography Museum at the Grassi Museum complex. A little worse for the wear, the boat still awaits curious visitors, though its rudder, weapons, and wooden figure have disappeared.

On Prussia and Saxony

"The Prussian monarchy is not a country that has an army, but an army that has a country."
—Comte de Mirabeau

At the end of August 1756, Prussian King Frederick the Great), was in Saxony again and had brought his entire army with him. What a surprise! While he had neither issued a declaration of war nor said anything else about it, he probably assumed that those under attack would notice that they were being attacked. This was not unusual, however. Frederick was famous for taking control of everything his army held in its sights. So he conquered Leipzig and Dresden and surrounded the Saxon army, which surrendered a short while later. The soldiers had to go right on fighting for Frederick, then. This did not work particularly well, and soldiers deserted in droves.

Actually, Prussia was once a completely normal country. Formed from estates of the Teutonic Order, it was far, far away from Saxony, in Eastern Europe, with a capital city in Königsberg, now known as Kaliningrad and located in Russia. Even the March of Brandenburg behaved inconspicuously for a long while. Its martial activities seldom exceeded normal medieval standards, and even when the Margrave of Meissen pledged Leipzig to his northern neighbor in 1312, the city was returned a short time later in decent condition. In 1486, Berlin became the royal capital and remained so when Brandenburg merged with Prussia, located until then in the Baltic region, to form a super-state in the seventeenth century.

While the Prussians heralded from the Baltics, the history of the Saxons, who originally settled around the mouth of the Weser River, was a bit more complicated. At the peak of their power in the twelfth century, the Saxons ruled an empire that encompassed broad regions of northern and western Germany, but clashed with Emperor Barbarossa, who split off the most significant federate state at the time, along with the coveted title "Saxon," and handed it off to distant Wittenberg. In 1423, the ruling nobility there died out, and Wittenberg-Saxony became part of the Margraviate of Meissen. The Saxon title migrated farther up the Elbe River, and the Wettins, elevated to the status of electoral princes, bore the name with pride from then on. As time went by, their subjects, originally called Meisseners, became Saxons. At the same time, the descendants of the true Saxons lived primarily in northern Germany or in England, where they had migrated with the Angles as Anglo-Saxons back in the fifth century. The question of where in those three regions Saxon is spoken best is simply not asked.

But coming back to 1423, the Wettins achieved electoral status and saw the territory they commanded expand considerably and become large enough to be divided. At least that's what the co-

Lost Wars—Victorious Battles

Great Nordic War (1700–1721)
Instead of adding territory: Swedish King Karl XII destroyed Electoral Saxony, Polish crown lost.

1st Silesian War (1740–1742)
Allied with Prussia and Bavaria against Austria, nothing gained.

2nd Silesian War (1744/45)
Despite alliance with Austria, England, and the Netherlands, Prussia prevails.

Seven Years War/3rd Silesian War (1756–1763)
Major defeat and extortion of Electoral Saxony, which is administered by Prussia during the war.

Fourth Coalition War (1806/07)
Defeat of Prussia in the Battle of Jena and Auerstadt, upon which Saxony joins the Rhenish Confederation and is elevated to a kingdom.

Wars of Liberation (1813–1815)
After Napoleon's disastrous Russian Campaign, the French are defeated in the Battle of Nations, during which some members of the Saxon Army switch sides.

Saxony and Prussia in rare pose—left: Augustus the Strong; right: Frederick William, the Soldier King. Painting by Louis de Silvestre prior to 1730

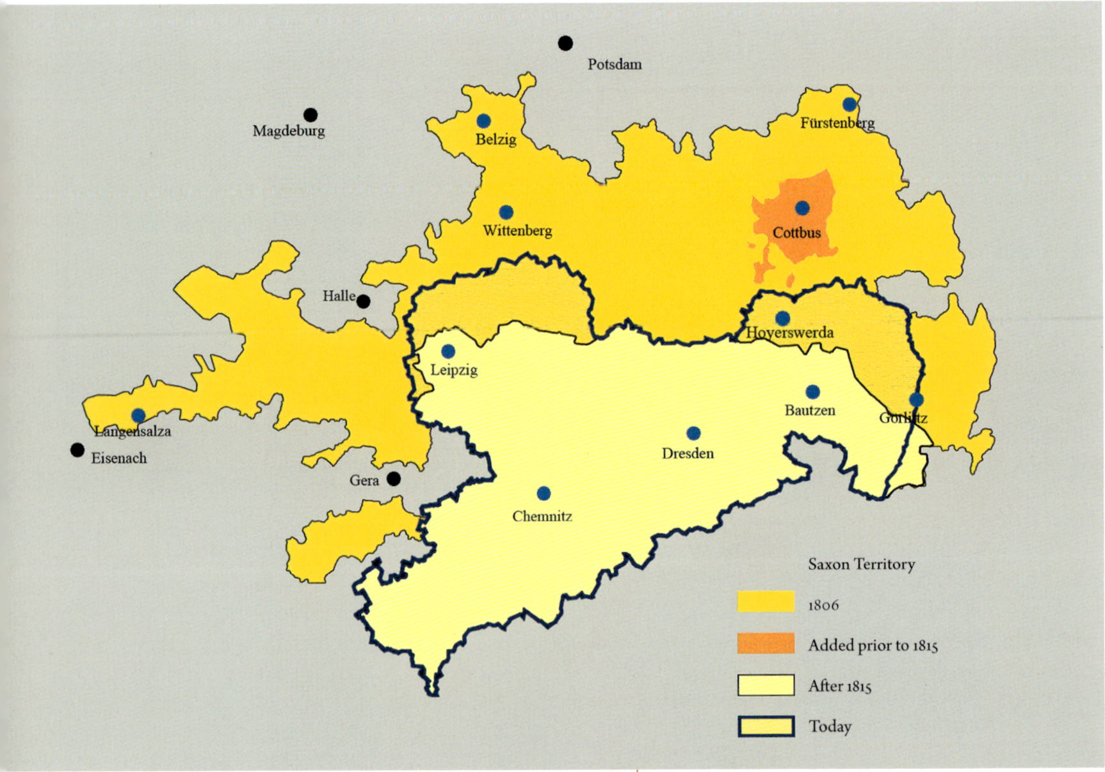

The territory of the state of Saxony, from the 18th century until today

ruling brothers, Ernst and Albert, thought at the time, who made the division in Leipzig in 1485. And so it came to pass that two Saxon states existed in a region in which not a single Saxon lived. As countless other divisions followed in the Ernestine region, whose capital was in Wittenberg, many other states were added. Albertine Saxony, meanwhile, centered in Leipzig, Chemnitz, and Dresden (elevated to the status of royal capital in 1485), was able to strengthen its position. In 1547, the Ernestines' electoral status was revoked, and they expanded mightily, territorially and economically. Militarily, however, it soon went downhill.

That Saxon soldiers were not fighting machines but wired for comfort was something that Frederick knew well when he tried to integrate them into his army. Their reputation for passionately indulging in coffee and cake during lulls in the action preceded them. This tendency must have exasperated the Prussian King. One day, when his Saxon soldiers did not report for battle, he reportedly asked why they had refused. "We can't fight without coffee!" was supposedly their reply. Even if the story is anecdote, the very un-Prussian behavior of his forcibly recruited neighbors must have been frustrating at times.

These different mentalities evolved around the beginning of the eighteenth century. In 1713, Frederick's father, Frederick William I, ascended to the throne of Brandenburg-Prussia. Yet while the average European regent, powdered and perfectly wigged, pulled all-nighters at one ball after another and consorted with concubines, the soldier king spent 73 percent of his state resources on his army. Had Prussia been around two thousand years earlier, even the Spartans might have been frightened.

The Saxon ruler at the time, Frederick Augustus, better known as August the Strong, on the other hand, was Frederick William I purely opposite. He had been elector of Saxony since 1694, and would become king of Poland three years later. Though he liked to wage war now and then, he was not all that interested in the army, as no women were enlisted back then. Women were by far August's favorite hobby, and so his nickname referred not to his military might but to his sexual vigor. The fact that he

organized porcelain workshops and covered his provincial capital with pompous, architectural folly merely completed his utterly un-Prussian image. He was beloved nevertheless, or perhaps even because of it. His son succeeded him in 1733, Elector Frederick Augustus II, while the soldier king was succeeded by his son, Frederick the Great, in 1740. The latter pushed his army to its capacity.

That same year, Frederick the Great declared war on Austria and wrested Silesia's economic might from them. The second Silesian war followed in 1744–45, in which the Austrians tried to reverse the previous annexation. They were allied with the Saxons at the time, for whom positive military results were the exception, not the rule. And so the status quo was maintained, though the Saxons got to bear the cost of the war. Frederick was peaceful for the next eleven years, although he did formulate his first political testament, in which he described control of Saxony as an advantageous and highly likely expansion. He followed through on this in the Seven Years War that began in 1756. He occupied and exploited Leipzig as well as Dresden, which suffered considerable damage and whose population dropped from sixty-three thousand to forty thousand. Alhough the destruction in the city on the Pleisse was minimal, the population was significantly reduced by assault, humiliation, dysentery, and smallpox. In 1763 there were twenty-eight thousand inhabitants, five thousand less than before the war began. In that battle alone, forty-three million thalers flowed from Saxony to Prussia, with more than ten million from Leipzig itself. Entire cartloads of gold left the city for Berlin. "You can always raise a little more dust if you hit hard enough," the insatiable Frederick explained smugly.

Saxon Dukes and (after 1547) Electoral Princes

Name	Reign
Albert the Bold	1485–1500
George the Bearded	1500–1539
Henry the Pious	1539–1541
Maurice	1541–1547/1553
Augustus I	1553–1586
Christian I	1586–1591
Christian II	1591–1611
John George I	1611–1656
John George II	1656–1680
John George III	1680–1691
John George IV	1691–1694
Frederick Augustus I, "the Strong"	1694–1733
Frederick Augustus II	1733–1763
Frederick Christian	1763
Frederick Augustus III, "the Just"	1763–1806

Moritzdamm, called Schillerstrasse today, was once part of the city fortification, which did not work very well

Goethe

"Good night, I'm as drunk as a beast."
–Johann Wolfgang Goethe

Sixteen-year-old Johann Wolfgang traveled by stagecoach for four days to get from his hometown of Frankfurt am Main to Leipzig. Four days for forty miles through various lands—passing through Hanau, Fulda, Eisenach, Erfurt, and Naumburg. An arduous undertaking, and a bit adventurous; heavy autumn rains made the bad roads even worse, and the travelers had to pull the carriage out of the mud in Thuringia. Finally, though, on October 3, 1765, the destination came into view. From Lindenau, the last town they passed through, Leipzig's steeples were visible, and the coach drove in through the Ranstädter Gate soon after.

Actually, Goethe wanted neither to go to Leipzig nor to become a lawyer. He dreamed of studying the liberal arts in Göttingen. That was not his father's dream, however. Thirty years prior, Goethe's father had studied law on the Pleisse River, at the best college of law in the realm, in his opinion. In addi-

The Old Theater (left), whose opening in 1766 was attended by Goethe, and the Riding Arena (center), where the young poet Traben practiced; photo 1868

tion, his son was to take on the habit of speaking proper German in Saxony. While these reasons did not really convice Johann Wolfgang, the generous financial support his father offered did. His annual allowance of 1,200 Rhenish guilders was more than most of his professors earned. With an easy and eager mind, he turned toward his new place of residence, where the Michaelis fair was just taking place—an event with which he already knew from Frankfurt. He was also familiar with mulberry trees for silk production, many of which were planted in Leipzig as well.

Leipzig's architecture impressed him with its innovation. "The huge buildings suited me just fine, facing two streets, towering high and surrounding courtyards containing a bourgeois world, giant fortresses like demi-cities," he is said to have written later in *Dichtung und Wahrheit* (*Fiction and Fact*). As winter approached, the public gardens made a great impression on the sixteen-year-old, who had never been anywhere outside of Frankfurt before. Compared to the fair city on the Main River, Leipzig seemed very modern and more sophisticated, complete with a promenade, a dozen coffeehouses, a gallant sheen, and, since 1701, seven hundred oil-fueled streetlights. Only three European cities had that innovation earlier. One was Paris, which generally served as an example for others. The latter's fashion standards were actively imitated in Leipzig, and besides German, French was often spoken there. Leipzig's nickname, Little Paris, was no accident—not even the *Little*, as the population of the real Paris was twenty times that of Leipzig.

Yet as nice as the Baroque splendor looked, the domiciles and their inhabitants did not smell so nice. While water supply had advanced to include waterworks near Pleissenburg Castle in the form of a dozen public and private wells, apartments with bathrooms would remain the exception until the late nineteenth century. People bathed and showered away from home—at bathhouses, usually on Saturdays, because on Sundays they went to church. There were toilets in most residential buildings, though they emptied directly into cesspits. Plumbing systems, like the ones the Romans had good experience with, would not be installed in European cities for another hundred years. Sewage, including the content of chamber pots, was dumped into flat pits in the middle of the street, some of which at least were covered with boards. The fact that the elegant populace took summer vacations when temperatures rose was not some fashionable trend but an act of self-defense. Other problems arose in the search for a public toilet,

"Leipzig Educates Its People"—
Johann Wolfgang von Goethe and Co.

Name	Birth and Death Dates	In Leipzig for
Thomas Müntzer	c. 1490–1525	Univ. studies: beg. 1506
Tycho Brahe	1546–1601	Univ. studies: 1562–1565
Gottfried Wilhelm Leibniz	1646–1716	Univ. studies: 1661–1666
Christian Thomasius	1655–1728	Univ. studies: beg. 1669
Johann Christoph Gottsched	1700–1766	Professor and Dean
Christian Fürchtegott Gellert	1715–1769	Univ. studies: 1734–1738 and 1740–1744
Gotthold Ephraim Lessing	1729–1781	Univ. studies: 1746–1748
Johann Wolfgang von Goethe	1749–1832	Univ. studies: 1765–1768
Johann Gottfried Seume	1763–1810	Univ. studies: 1780/81 and 1789–1792
Jean Paul	1763–1825	Univ. studies: 1781–1784
Novalis	1772–1801	Univ. studies: 1791–1794
Robert Schumann	1810–1856	Univ. studies: 1828–1830
Richard Wagner	1813–1883,	Univ. studies: beg. 1831

which really was much more difficult then than in Leipzig today. Privy vendors would address this supply gap in the late eighteenth century. Equipped with a bucket and a wide cloak (behind which customers needing to relieve themselves could hide), these vendors walked the streets in which the litter-bearers were just phasing out the short-range traffic trade. These ran parallel operations outside their offices on the ground floor of the Alte Börse (Old Trading Floor), offering extremely reasonable haircuts and homemade bandages for sail. Meanwhile, the *Stadtmeisen* (town titmice), as the blue-and-yellow-uniformed city soldiers were lampooned, provided security.

Young Goethe was mocked for his clothing, which was so old-fashioned, according to his new female acquaintances, including Friederike Oeser, that he looked like he'd dropped in from another planet. Goethe wasted no time trading his entire wardrobe for modern clothing better suited to his new location. His makeover was so profound that an acquaintance from Frankfurt observed, "His pride has made him such a dandy... he has adopted a gait that is utterly obnoxious."

The room Goethe rented for the next three years was in a Baroque building with a courtyard throughway called the Große Feuerkugel (Big Fireball). Gotthold Ephraim Lessing and Ewald Christian von Kleist had both lived in the same building just a few years before; later, Novalis and Friedrich Schlegel would live on the same block, though along the Grimmaische Gasse, at the same time as

After 1913, all that remained of Auerbach's Courtyard (not far from Goethe's room) was the cellar. Photo 1905

when engraver Johann Friedrich Bause would live in the Feuerkugel. The location was good, right between the university and Auerbach's Keller. Goethe dropped option one relatively quickly. His classes in the college of law were in the far distant Petersstrasse, after all. In February 1766, he turned his back on his studies and followed his passion.

First he was into the fresh doughnuts he bought in the St. Thomas Churchyard. Not long after, it was Kätchen Schönkopf. That too began with a culinary basis—the sixteen-year-old ate his noon meal at Schönkopf's pub, where the nineteen-year-old served him—the infatuation proved to be much more complicated. They met in early April. In late April, he professed his love for her. At first the pretty platter bearer played hard to get, but eventually she surrendered. The relationship lasted two years, until Kätchen ended it because Goethe's jealousy cast an ever darker cloud over it. At the same time, his closest confidant, Ernst Wolfgang Behrisch, eleven years Goethe's senior, left Leipzig, which affected Goethe deeply. His attempt to drown his sorrow in alcohol and poetry ended unsuccessfully. *Annette*, a collection of poems, appeared in 1896, and he was banned from Auerbach's Keller, even though he had not been a bad customer.

He preferred to drink champagne, but was not adverse to wine and beer, and especially liked Merseburger—"The first time makes you shudder, but after drinking it for a week, you simply can't stay away from it," he told his sister. This was not the only reason his Leipzig years were informative. He learned to ride and fence there as well, incurring a black eye and cut lip. He demonstrated more talent, however, to Adam Friedrich Oeser, director of the Art Academy founded in Pleissenburg Castle in 1764. A critic of Baroque ornamentation and shellwork, he gave Goethe a considerable appreciation for the classical world. The Cicero lectures by Johann August Ernesti impressed Goethe a great deal, and he completed practical training in diction with Christian Fürchtegott Gellert, who was a professor of poetry and oratory in Leipzig.

The best-read author of his time warned Goethe, however, of the malady of poetry. Johann Christoph Gottsched, the second leading literary pundit in Leipzig, had earned a great deal from literature and theater but was considered more of a relic than a pioneer. When Mrs. Gottsched, also a writer, died, the 65-year-old married again. His bride was nineteen years old, just like Goethe's maiden, though Goethe was fifty years younger. The same year that Gottsched died, in 1766, his great bastion, theater, found a new home on the Rannische bullwar. Merchant Benedikt Zehmisch had a comedy house built there, the first fixed theater in the city. Goethe attended its opening on October 7. Lessing, Christoph Martin Wieland, William Shakespeare, and Jean-Jaques Rousseau were performed there, and Goethe continued his musical studies by attending the concerto grosso, where he saw the singer Corona Schröter, who he later guided to the Weimar court.

"One night I awoke with a severe hemorrhage and hovered for several days between life and death," Goethe recorded in *Dichtung und Wahrheit*. Though historians doubt his life was really in danger, the incident definitely resulted in his departure from Leipzig. After his acquaintances in Leipzig nursed him for a month, he left on August 28, 1768, his nineteenth birthday. It would take him two years to recover after Leipzig. It was also then that Goethe was published for the first time. The title of the book was *Neue Lieder in Melodien gesetzt* (*New Songs Set to Melody*), and was published by Breitkopf-Verlag in 1769. The book contained twenty poems set to music, composed by Goethe. Because the score was the crucial element, however, his name was not mentioned. He first became famous four years later, with *Götz von Berlichingen* (*Götz of Berlichingen*), and *Die Leiden des jungen Werthers* (*The Sorrows of Young Werther*). By 1823, he was already an institution. At the age of seventy-four, he would fall in love one last time—with a nineteen-year-old woman from Leipzig, Ulrike von Levetzow. He would die in Weimar in 1832.

Goethe's family died out in Leipzig. Wolfgang Maximilian died at 29 Humboldtstrasse in 1883, followed two years later by the last grandchild, Walther Wolfgang, at the Norddeutscher Hof hotel, of a hemorrhage, of all things.

Pleasure Gardens and Promenades

With satisfaction, Mayor Wilhelm Müller and municipal master builder Johann Carl Friedrich Dauthe gazed up at the peak of their brand-new mountain—built in 1785. It was about sixty feet tall, practically a Matterhorn, by Leipzig standards. Because of the spiral paths winding up the hill, it came to be called the *Schneckenberg* (Snail Mountain). The two men moved slowly, inspecting every detail on their way to the top. Both knew that it had looked much different here just a few years ago. They remembered all too well the "cat," as the battery was called, now buried inside the hill. Time had caught up with the bastion named for an animal, as it had with all of the city's fortifications, which had already been completely redone here

The reason behind this was the continual advances in weapons technology, which even the thickest walls could no longer withstand. The Leipzigers could thank the Prussians, among others, for their liberation from their custom-built embrace, who showed them during the Seven Years War just how useless all of those entrenchments, ditches, and bastions had really become. So the elector decided after the Peace Treaty of Hubertusburg, to turn the area over to the city for the benefit of the public. It took some time to clear the ground, because of the tough financial situation, but work finally began on razing the ancient, idle bulwarks and filling the ditches in 1777. Lawns and trees were planted and idyllic paths made, a floristic initial spark of inestimable value.

Water-jousting was held from 1714 to 1938, patterned after Venetian events

The population of Leipzig was still heaped together in the city center, where the only green was on people's plates, in the courtyard at the royal house, or in the botanical garden. Until then, the locals had been cut off from the blooming landscape outside the gates, even though a first section of a promenade existed between the St. Thomas and Barefoot churches, where people had been strolling as much as they could since 1725. There only the glacis—the open area against the walls—was transformed. Between the Hallische and Grimmaische Gates, however, the entire ensemble was removed, including the town moat, which people might recall when they saw the swan lake. There really were swans there at one time, and several Leipzigers were so taken by the idyllic, English style that they found themselves some nightingales and moved them there. The birds likely disappeared when cruising in motor vehicles came into style. But besides driving the fauna away, the ever-increasing automobile traffic had a protective effect similar to that of the former city walls. Carelessly setting foot in the area had fatal consequences, just like it did five hundred years ago, though the bereaved were not shot anymore, just run over.

Misters Müller and Dauthe could hardly see that coming, back then. Reaching the top, they cheer-

Leipzig's public gardens in the late 18th century

ing year, bullion-dealer Caspar Bose created the first Baroque garden, the Grossbosischen Garten (Big Bose Garden). While this developed southeast of the Rossplatz, Bose's little brother, George, satisfied his own need for prestige with the Kleinbosischer Garten (Small Bose Garden) beginning in 1692, west of the wall, in which he expressed his ideas in green.

By the mid-eighteenth century, the number of public gardens had reached nearly fifty. The gardens were usually open to the public many times each week. The largest and most well-known ensemble was created by merchant Andreas Dietrich Apel. The large gem gleamed with opulent sculpture groups—replicas of Juno and Jupiter still grace Dorotheenplatz today—and countless exotic plants. Apel also built a manufacturing site there, where luxury goods were produced. In addition, water jousting, imported from Venice in 1714, was held on the artificial ponds, where Leipzig rivals dueled in Venetian garb. The proud owner of the garden regularly informed visitors of various botanical sensations, like blooming aloes, orchids, and coffee trees. The gardens also served as summer venues for concerts and plays, or as Gose-beer or cake destinations, and were famous far beyond city limits.

Given all of that bourgeois splendor, August the Strong could not resist getting into the electoral act. He wanted a little house surrounded by green, too—or, more specifically, in Rosental. There were neither roses nor hills in that place , which are really need for a valley in order to exist, but Leipzig's oldest park was always lovely. August furnished it with the necessary infrastructure, created eleven absolutely straight avenues through the forest, and forced the undergrowth to grow symmetrically. The citizens talked him out of the palace itself, however, because they would have had to foot the bill. They claimed, truthfully, that the mosquitoes at the potential construction site would be extreme in both number and size. And that there were wild animals, which was also true at the time, if hedgehogs and squirrels were counted. In addition, the locals mentioned there were shady characters living there—which they organized themselves by sending riffraff from the city into the countryside whenever the elector announced he might visit. In view of these varied scare tactics, August decided he would rather build a little more in Dresden, instead of Leipzig, so the Leipzigers had some peace and quiet.

fully observed the waterfall burbling away into the pond below, and then their gazes moved to the landscape spread before them. While the hill would have been declared flat even in a subalpine region, in the Leipzig area it facilitated excellent visibility into the distance, though the view to the west was blocked by city rooftops that stood just as tall as the "mountain." To the east, north, and south, however, they could see numerous little villages in the region beyond the flat houses on the outskirts of town—and lots of green.

Exactly one hundred years earlier, Leipzig's first Baroque gardens took shape outside the city walls. The results of the Thirty Years War had been assimilated as much as possible, and a new era ushered in new prosperity—the Baroque. With it came not just its own new architecture, seen for the first time in Leipzig in the Alte Börse in 1679; and the follow-

Japanese House in Richter's (later Gerhard's) Garden, decorated with 16,000 tiles of Meissen porcelain, shortly before demolition in 1870

Public Gardens

Name	Garden Created	Garden Redeveloped	Notes
Grossbosischer (Big Bose) Garden	1680	1824	Pleasure House, Vivarium, Aviaries, Concerts, Cabinet of Natural History, Library
Kleinbosischer (Little Bose) Garden (later Lehmann's Garden)	1692	1835/1890	Pleasure Garden, Orangery
Apel's Garden (later Reichel's Garten)	1701	1787	Fountains, Water jousting, Bathhouse, Orangeries, Summer concerts
Heinsberg Garden (later Jöcher's Garden, then Lurgenstein's Garden)	First half of 18th century	1837	Part Baroque, part meadow garden design
Krumbhaar Garden (later Schimmel Estate)	First half of 18th century	1880	Several large ponds and *Buen Retiro* Pleasure Island
Trier Garden	First half of 18th century	1880	Two large ponds, Botanical Garden (beg. 1806), Midwifery Institute (1810)
Richter's Garden (later Reichenbach's Garden, then Gerhard's Garden)	1740	1866	Japanese House, Summer Theater, Bathhouse
Löhr's Garten (later Keil's Garden)	1770	1870	Garden House of current Royal Courtyard, large pond, English style
Rudolph's Garden (later Riedel's Garden)	1780s	1845	Originally part of Apel's Garden, known as a coffee garden

Several decades later, many poets would also find some peace and quiet on the Schneckenberg, which was often a place where people went to find their muse. Theodor Körner wrote Lützow's wild and reckless hunt there. The Schneckenberg was not meant to last forever, though. It crowned the swan pond for only eighty years, until it was demolished and the significantly taller New Theater was built on the same spot. The theater was destroyed another eighty years later, during World War II. Its ruins were replaced fifty-five years ago by the Opera House.

The New Theater, opened in 1868, along with the university, post office, and art museum built in earlier decades, characterized Augustus Square. Photo 1889

New Era
1789 to 1870

Classicists

In May 1796, a young man—let's call him Lothar—moved into his new apartment and workplace, and a few things changed for him—first of all, his view. He was an assistant watchman in a tower now, and, as such, he lived in a small apartment in the steeple of the St. Nicholas Church. There was only one person farther up: his boss, Friedrich. While the occupation of tower watchman was not a common one, with only two of them in the city, at the St. Thomas Church the task was nevertheless of enormous importance. At least when danger threatened. Unlike in the past, warning of an approaching army was no longer so important, but when fires broke out, sounding the alarm really was. If a fire was not seen immediately, it could mean catastrophe for a population of thirty thousand over which Lothar kept watch.

In 1796, that population lived in 1,332 buildings, 765 of which were located in the city center. Most had four floors and tall rooftops, but Lothar's new home, at 246 feet tall, towered high above its stony surroundings. The St. Thomas Church would remain the tallest building in the city until 1905. An abode like that is not exactly suited to those who do not like climbing stairs. Luckily there was a winch that made it easier to bring everyday objects up to the top. Even the watchmen's bathwater was hauled

Schneckenberg (Snail Mountain)—a hill without a future. Torn down in 1864 to make way for the New Theater

up that way, and sent back down through the gutters. Inside the church there was a lot of construction going on. After twelve years, the project was nearly complete.

Mayor Wilhelm Müller and municipal master builder Johann Carl Friedrich Dauthe had set the reconstruction in motion, and had also paved the way for Leipzig's promenade. As with that project, however, they were no longer adhering to the French model of Baroque but trying some completely new ideas. For several decades, the ideas of the Enlightenment had been creating quite a stir, and in Classicism they resulted in a new direction of architectural expression. The period when this radical change was taking place was not an easy one for the city, which was still grappling with the fallout from the Seven Years War. Additionally, Leipzig had gone through two severe famines and economic setbacks. Not much was built then, but it was a time of great achievements. The wealthy bourgeoisie was especially committed to generously supporting culture and education.

So fur trader Benedict Zehmisch built the Old Theater on the foundations of the Ranstädter bastion in 1766, for example, and the *concerto grosso* established in 1743 also got a permanent venue. In 1781, a five-hundred-seat concert hall was inaugurated on the intermediate floor of the cloth-manufacturing building, which, in light of the goods traded there, was called the *Gewandhaus* (garment building). And so a phrase normally associated with textiles took on a musical imprint, as people began to use the term to describe a *Gewandhauskonzert* (concert at the *Gewandhaus*) or a *Gewandhausorchester* (orchestra at the *Gewandhaus*). Long financed by Leipzig merchants, it is recognized as the oldest civic orchestra in the German-speaking world. The *Stadtpfeifer* (waits, or town pipers' guild), a musical institution employed by the city since 1479, were also associated with it. Beginning in 1599, they played daily on a balcony they built themselves on the tower at City Hall. They did not have to live there, though.

The watchers in the tower, on the other hand, had no choice. Their duties were so varied and spread throughout the entire day that it made no sense for them to move back and forth between their homes and workplace. Besides keeping watch, their responsibilities included ringing the bells and blowing a horn to mark the time. Despite the burdensome nature of the work, they were poorly compensated. Nevertheless, Lothar was happy. Especially when the raucous clamor of the city slowly stilled as twilight settled in and people settled into their parlors and eventually snuffed out the lights, and the entire city below went peacefully to sleep. Then only the night watchmen's lanterns bobbed along through the tangled alleys.

In one of those alleys, the Gewandgässchen (Garment Alley), the new city library was built in 1755, a sure sign of the growing interest in education developing at the time. The general trend would only increase in the coming decades, manifested in the large number of schools established. For a long time, there were only a few small private schools in the city, besides the St. Thomas School and the St. Nicholas School founded in 1512. The cost–benefit ratio in those small schools left much to be desired, however. In the late-eighteenth century that changed. Although the population increased only slightly, several privately funded schools opened, like the Hohenthalsche Frey- und Armenschule (Hohenthal Free and Charity School) or another free school founded by bookseller Johann Wendler, each providing instruction to sixty children. In 1792, the *Ratsfreischule* (council free school) was finally established as a site for cost-free public education. Its former location is still marked by Ratsfreischulstrasse. Construction began, meanwhile, on the first public secondary school, the first nondenominational public secondary school in Germany, which was located on the walls of the Moritz bastion. As with nearly every other initiative, Müller and Dauthe were in charge of this one, too. Both men belonged to the same Masonic Lodge, the Minerva Lodge of the Three Palms.

While the masons today are often thought of as an association of secretive global conspirators, they played a much different role in the second half of the eighteenth and throughout the nineteenth centuries. Committed to the ideals of the Enlightenment, the lodges particularly influenced intellectual and cultural life. Since the members represented a who's who of society—politicians, bankers, publishers, scientists, teachers, and artists—demand and capital came together in a specific manner. Established in 1741, Minerva Lodge was the oldest in Leipzig and the most significant. But it was by no means the only lodge. After World War I, the masons, who institutionally refused to be co-opted, were discredited and accused of being unpatriotic. After the Nazis seized power, the masons were pressured to disband. But later several lodges in Leipzig became active again, though with far less influence. The Minerva Lodge of the Three Palms came back, too.

There are no more tower watchmen in Leipzig these days, despite the fact that they held out amazingly long, with the tenacity of meerkats. The last tower watchman at St. Nicholas Church, Karl Pospich, died in 1932, and his assistant bell-ringer, Ernst Robert Schurich, moved to a nursing home three years later, right across the street from the tower.

Donated Buildings

Building	Completed	Purpose	Benefactor
Second Gewandhaus	1884	Cultural	Franz Dominic Grassi
Art Museum	1858	Cultural	Adolf Heinrich Schletter
Old Grassi Museum		Cultural	Franz Dominic Grassi
Mende Fountain	1886	Cultural	Pauline Mende
Frege Houses	1864	Social residential (first)	Christian Gottlob Frege
Meyer Houses	Beg. 1888	Social residential (2,700 total)	Herrmann Julius Meyer
Salomon Foundation	1890	Social residential	Arwed Rossbach

Battle of Nations

In mid-December 1812, the men finally reached Vilnius. During the preceding weeks, they had fought their way westward and were now wounded and utterly exhausted, and winter had finally caught up with them. Nighttime temperatures fell to −35 °F. Toes, fingers, and ears froze first, and dead bodies froze as hard as rock within minutes, including the horsemeat that had been their only source of food for weeks. To keep from starving, they had to cut the flesh from the live animals, before it froze. Prince Józef Poniatowski recalled with sorrow how the Grande Armée had set out from Vilnius half a year earlier. Now it no longer existed.

Unlike the Germans, who waged their battle for independence against Napoleon, the Poles waged theirs *with* the French. Twenty years earlier, Prussia, Austria, and Russia had divided up Poland among themselves. After Napoleon established the Duchy of Warsaw, a Polish rump state, and finally marched on Russia, the Poles euphorically supported him. Poniatowski put thirty thousand soldiers at the Grande Armée's disposal, which included nearly three hundred thousand French and many others from other nations, mostly recruited by force. And so half of Europe, and even a North African cavalry unit, crossed the Russian border on June 24—six hundred thousand soldiers in all. Yet when the giant army marched on Moscow, it had shrunk to one hundred thousand, due to plagues, starvation, and desertion. Those that remained, after the Russian capital burned for two days—"the grandest, most sublime, and most fearsome sight the world ever saw," as Napoleon wrote later—had no wintering ground. So they had to pull back. Of thirty thousand Poles, only four hundred returned to their homeland, and of twenty thousand Saxons, only fifty-five. This gave Napoleon's numerous enemies hope. But as they were they putting their armies in order, Napoleon was able to raise new troops himself. After various small skirmishes, the French and their allies finally met on October 16, 1813, at the

Death of Josef Poniatowski, depicted by January Suchodolski

gates of Leipzig. What started as a massive cavalry campaign turned into the largest battle in European history to date.

Napoleon put the majority of his 190,000 troops into position south of the city. Poniatowski's corps had also settled in near Dölitz, on the opposite bank of the Pleisse River. Because it had rained nearly every day since the beginning of September, the river was swollen and presented a barrier that would be difficult to cross, considering that the bridges had been destroyed or blockaded. Under constant fire, an Austrian contingent led by General Merveldt tried to create an artificial ford, and after four hours and heavy casualties, it worked. When the troops reached the other shore, however, a French guard arrived, attacked the exhausted Austrians, and took Merveldt captive. A glorious victory, although it would have no bearing on the outcome of the larger battle.

There was hope for Napoleon at the beginning of the battle. Led by Karl Philipp Fürst Schwarzenberg, the coalition had begun the onslaught at nine o'clock in the morning. But since not all contingents were able to be deployed, their superior numbers were insignificant, and initially they were not successful. While the Prussian general Ludwig Yorck von Wartenburg won some victories in the north, the troops in the south were unable to take the French positions or had to give them up again after heavy counterattacks. The assault lines were weakened so much that Napoleon switched to counterstrike mode around three in the afternoon. He attacked the opposing force's center with eight thousand cavalry, and it was only with massive effort that the attack was halted before it reached the coalition's command post, later known as Monarchs' Hill. When a second sortie by Napoleon was also unsuccessful, the situation seemed almost unchanged as darkness fell, at least from a strategic point of view. By that time, forty thousand soldiers had already lost their lives, and the villages along the battle lines were pretty much destroyed.

The next day was relatively quiet. Reinforcements were called in, almost exclusively by the Coalition, which sent more than one hundred thousand new soldiers into the field. They did not bother to dignify Napoleon's peace offer with a reply. Faced with these new superior numbers, he was forced to give up his old positions. On October 18, at two o'clock in the morning, he pulled 150,000 soldiers closer to Leipzig. The Coalition forces, meanwhile, numbered nearly three hundred thousand, and additional reinforcements arrived—a hopeless situation, even for Napoleon. Though his army managed to put up a good defense, win skirmishes, and claim many positions on the eighteenth, the Coalition in the north marched into Gohlis and Eutritzsch by evening and captured the villages of Zuckelhausen, Holzhausen, and Paunsdorf in the east, aided by several thousand Saxon soldiers who switched sides there. Napoleon pulled back to Leipzig during the night, intending to slip through the only remaining channel of escape to the west. But while his withdrawal was still underway, the Coalition charged toward the city.

Poniatowski was covering the retreat of a baggage train. It moved slowly over the Elster Bridge on its way out of the city. Because Napoleon was afraid they would be followed, the bridge had been prepped for detonation. Three barrels of powder on a boat were to move into position if the enemy tried to take the bridge. Riflemen from a scattered enemy corps finally approached, and Corporal La Fontaine wasted no time. Without waiting to clear the bridge, he gave the command to detonate it, killing several dozen of his own soldiers and cutting off the retreat for twenty thousand of his men.

Quandt Tobacco Mill, served as Napoleon's command center on October 18, 1813; destroyed during battle

While most were captured, some tried to swim to the other side of the flooded river, including Poniatowski, who was gravely wounded. On October 19, the French marshal drowned on the back of his horse, having been given the rank by Napoleon just a few days earlier.

When the battle ended, the misery in Leipzig was just getting started. Looting and pillaging were forbidden by those at the top and not much was destroyed, save for a few buildings on the outskirts of town. But out of nearly six hundred thousand soldiers, ninety thousand were left lying on the battlefield. Graver still was the fact that the city of 33,000 now had to deal with just as many severely injured people. Besides the St. Nicholas Church, every house of worship and nearly every public building was converted to a military hospital, yet countless lay dying in the streets and squares. All over the city, limbs were amputated every minute—the only effective means of fighting gangrene—and the only anesthetic available for the procedures was a big gulp of hard liquor.

A horrific scene, only made worse by the outbreak of pestilence that naturally followed. By spring, one out of every ten Leipzigers would fall victim to disease, most to typhus. It would take many years for the city to overcome the ordeal and bury the dead from the battlefields. Napoleon, meanwhile, suffered defeat at Waterloo, and Saxony, his ally, though well rehearsed in the art of losing wars, had to pay tribute once more at the Congress of Vienna. For real this time. On the new map of Europe published by Misters Metternich and Co. in 1815, Saxony's territory comprised only a third of its original area, and nearly half of all Saxons became citizens of Prussia. As the northern and western regions were primarily affected, Leipzig was no longer in the middle of the state but was suddenly on its upper-left edge.

War Participants and Numbers of Soldiers

Napoleon	c. 206,000	Coalition	c. 355,000
France	165,000	Russia	150,000
Poland	13,500	Austria	118,000
Italy	5,500	Prussia	70,000
Naples	1,500	Sweden	17,000
Holland	800	Mecklenburg	320
Spain	600	England (rocket brigade)	150
Illyria	500		
Rhenish Confederation of which:	c. 19,000 Saxony: 6,500 Baden: 4,600 Hessen-Darmstadt: 2,500 Württemberg: 2,000 Westphalia: 2,000 Others: c. 1,000		

The Soul on Horseback

When Saxon King Frederick Augustus II and his court made their way to Leipzig on the morning of April 8, 1839, it was as if they were starting off in a new era. It was not his first visit to the trade-fair city, of course, and what distinguished this trip from others was not the destination but the path he took to get there. The road led the royal carriage and his entourage first to the east, which seemed unusual enough, given the geographic position of their destination. Nevertheless, hundreds of curious onlookers were already assembled on the Augustusbrücke (Augustus Bridge) and along the streets of the new town. Even more cheered for their majesty just beyond the city limit, where a brand-new

The Dresden and Magdeburg train stations, the two oldest stations in the city

building was about to be officially dedicated in the middle of the idyllic rural landscape.

In general, the rural areas of Saxony had hardly changed during the past few centuries, and until just a few years earlier, the lives of those living in the villages was about the same as that of their medieval ancestors. In an edict on March 17, 1832, however, the Saxon government had abolished compulsory labor once and for all, and lifted the countless medieval privileges enjoyed by cities, under the disdainful name of municipal territory reform. Individual craftsmen had been able to move to the villages since the mid-eighteenth century, but there was no real commercial freedom until this new reform. The locals were not the only ones to profit from this. Coupled with new agricultural methods, agrarian production would increase greatly in the coming decades, which led to better supply of the entire population. Industrialization was also getting started and leaving its mark, first visible in the immediate vicinity of larger cities.

In just a few decades, fields, ponds, kitchen gardens, and small village greens that had been there for hundreds of years were turned into industrial cities, with countless factories and dense workers' quarters. Saxony was not the only place to receive a completely new face and experience a new pace—all of Germany and half of Europe would also change fundamentally. The mobility required for this process pushed technological development even further, which would have an effect at least as far-reaching as the industrialization itself.

Until then, locomotion had been accomplished almost exclusively on foot, and most people never traveled farther than thirty miles beyond their birthplace. The only form of public transportation available were the ponderous stagecoaches lumbering across the landscape, whose passengers were squeezed together in a jumble at every pothole. And then there were the coachmen, whose pasts were sometimes as sketchy as the bandits who robbed them. Travel speed was a leisurely five to six miles per hour, but that could not be maintained at night since headlights had not yet been invented. It took thirteen hours to get from Leipzig to Dresden—if the weather cooperated—twenty-two to Berlin, three days to Munich, and thirteen to Madrid. In terms of travel time, Dresden was farther away from Leipzig then than North America and South Korea are today, and the costs corresponded to the duration of the trip. Soon all of these obstacles would be a thing of the past, and that change would be celebrated as a symbolic entry into a new era of mobility.

Saxon Kings after Saxony Elevated to Kingdom in 1806

King	Ruled
Frederick Augustus I, the Just	1806–1827
Anthony the Kind	1827–1836
Frederick Augustus II	1836–1854
John	1854–1873
Albert the Good	1873–1902
George	1902–1904
Frederick Augustus III	1904–1918

Despite all fears, every passenger on the maiden voyage survived unharmed

Finally the royal carriage reached the Leipzig train station in Dresden, where thousands were gathered to watch. Frederick Augustus climbed out of the carriage to fanfare and the cheers of his subjects, and, after a few grand speeches, he climbed into an open train car. A completely unspectacular event in and of itself, yet it became a symbol of the changing times. The maiden voyage had already taken place on the day before, without any royal celebrities. Twenty-four hours earlier, Leipzigers had celebrated the transportation of the future with civic pomp at the train station in Dresden. There were already three railway routes operating in Germany alone, but the seventy-two-mile stretch from Leipzig to Dresden was considered to be the first long-distance railway line in Continental Europe.

There were already trains in the United States, and in England, too, of course, where the first train ever rolled between Stockton and Darlington in 1825. Ten years later, Germany's first train traveled between Nürnberg and Fürth. While the iron horse traveled the four-mile stretch every four days, regular horses made the trip much more frequently, because the coal from distant Zwickau had to be hauled in by horse cart. In May 1835, twelve citizens of Leipzig founded the Leipzig-Dresdner Eisenbahn-Compagnie (Leipzig–Dresden Railway Company), and construction began half a year later. Because Leipzig merchants did not have a large river at their disposal on which to send their wares out into the world, they tried to correct this shortcoming using new technology. South German economist Friedrich List led the effort, after gaining experience in planning such an undertaking during a sojourn in America. After these merchants purchased the property required, they cut swaths through forests, drained swamps, and built bridges over the Elbe and Mulde rivers, without any subsidies. They even cut a tunnel through a mountain near Oberau, the first railway tunnel in Europe, though they figured out later that it had really not been necessary. It no longer exists today. Three years and one month later, the last track was finally laid. While their conventional contemporaries were still wondering what eight thousand workers could possibly be doing in the middle of the Saxon prairie, the great minds of the time were debating the pros and cons of this new technology, the dangers of speed, and the destruction of the environment.

Meanwhile, the king crossed the newly constructed bridge over the Elbe River near Riesa completely unharmed, which would not collapse until 1876. The train he was in was traveling on the left, of course, as this new technology was an English creation. The two locomotives from England, the Robert Stephenson and the Elephant, made their presence known as they flew by at speeds up to thirty miles per hour, while the first German locomotive, the Saxonia, brought up the rear. Although in the near future that train would stop at forty-five stations along the way, its pioneer voyage took only three hours and forty minutes for the seventy-two-mile trip—one third of the time it took a stagecoach to travel the same distance. This new technology developed quickly. Twenty years later, there would be five long-distance train stations in the Leipzig area, and the German railway system would grow to cover more than 6,835 miles. King Frederick Augustus II would not live to see that. He died in August 1854, after a carriage accident in Tyrol, where there were no railway tracks yet. Development continued without him, with progress seeking new methods and means. And so it is that distances that only globetrotters traveled 180 years ago have shrunk to today's common commutes.

Romance

Disillusioned, Robert Schumann took off the band he had fastened on the fourth finger of his right hand. Long practices lay behind him—seven hours today alone. A session he had completed nearly every day for the last four years. "Though I want to, I cannot be weak. Where there's a will, there's a way," he told himself. But instead of improving, he felt more and more as if that finger in particular obeyed him less and less. Even the device he had designed himself, which he called cigar mechanics, increasingly less. On June 14, 1832, the twenty-two-year-old noted in his journal, "My finger is completely stiff." And it would stay that way. After one single acclaimed public concert, the fate of his lofty dreams of being a pianist was sealed. Neither dieting nor electrical treatments nor bathing his hand in animal blood resulted in any improvement.

Twelve-year-old Clara Wieck, meanwhile, had achieved long ago what Robert Schumann had dreamed of. Born in 1819, the child prodigy had debuted at the Leipziger Gewandhaus five years earlier, was touring Europe with her father, Friedrich, and was even celebrated in pampered Paris. Robert and Clara had met through Father Wieck. Both had lived in a building on the corner of Grimmaische Strasse and Reichsstrasse, and Robert was also a student of Friedrich, a piano guru. Clara, however, ranked somewhat higher than Robert in Friedrich's plan to create the world's greatest pianist. But these

Robert and Clara Schumann in a romantic pose, 1847

two were not the only musical geniuses in Leipzig at the time. On Gerberstrasse in Pinchof lived Leipzig native Richard Wagner, who was studying music at the university.

When Wagner left Leipzig for Magdeburg in 1833, Albert Lortzing was just moving in. Eleven years later, Lortzing would be working at the Old Theater and composing world-renown operettas in his apartment in a courtyard building at the Grosser Funkenburg, like *Zar und Zimmermann* (*Tsar and Carpenter*) and *Der Wildschütz* (*The Poacher*). Two years later, Felix Mendelssohn Bartholdy also

Musicians

Musicians	Birth and Death Dates	Lived in Leipzig	Notes
Georg Philipp Telemann	1681–1767	4 years	
Johann Sebastian Bach	1685–1750	27 years	(died in Leipzig)
Ignaz Moscheles	1794–1870	25 years	(died in Leipzig)
Heinrich Marschner	1795–1861	3 years	
Carl Friedrich Zöllner	1800–1860	40 years	(died in Leipzig)
Albert Lortzing	1801–1851	12 years	
Felix Mendelssohn Bartholdy	1809–1847	12 years, non-continuous	(died in Leipzig)
Clara Schumann, née Wieck	1819–1896	25 years	(born in Leipzig)
Robert Schumann	1810–1856	about 15 years	
Richard Wagner	1813–1883	about 7 years	(born in Leipzig)
Edvard Grieg	1843–1907	4 years	
Arthur Nikisch	1855–1922	44 years	(died in Leipzig)
Gustav Mahler	1860–1911	2 years	
Max Reger	1873–1916	about 7 years	(died in Leipzig)
Hanns Eisler	1898–1962	3 years	(born in Leipzig)
Kurt Masur	1927	31 years	

Grosse Funkenburg; Albert Lorzing lived in one of the courtyard buildings

became a Leipziger, and in October 1835 he took the position of Gewandhaus conductor. The grandchild of the famous philosopher Moses Mendelssohn, who was memorialized by Gotthold Ephraim Lessing in *Nathan der Weise* (*Nathan the Wise*), was enjoying at least as much popularity. His father, Abraham, commented, "I used to be my father's son, but now I'm my son's father."

The twenty-five-year-old Schumann was lauded not only for rediscovering Bach, but for his own work, which was getting a lot of attention throughout Europe, especially in England. Yet he swept Leipzigers off their feet by combining progress with tradition. He was one of the first conductors to lead the orchestra with a baton instead of the harpsichord. The founding of the Leipzig Conservatory in 1843, the second institution of its kind in the German-speaking world, was also due to his initiative, as was erecting the world's first monument for Johann Sebastian Bach, which occurred that same year, on the Promenade, near the St. Thomas Church. Schumann's second apartment in Leipzig, in Lurgenstein's Garden, looked out on Bach's domain. There, he met not only the music scene in Little Paris but virtuosos from Big Paris, like Franz Liszt. Years earlier, in 1835, Schumann had met Frédéric Chopin when he was still living in his bachelor pad in Reichel's Garden. This was also where he arranged a meeting between Chopin and the sixteen-year-old Clara Wieck. Friedrich, as her piano teacher, hoped for musical synergies, but as her father, he hoped for emotional indifference. He carefully corrected a too-positive passage in her diary after her meeting with Chopin. His concern was completely unfounded. A composer he knew even better had already won his daughter's heart, though the way to her hand would be blocked for five long years.

Until the morning of September 12, 1840. At nine o'clock, the thirty-year-old Robert Schumann and the twenty-one-year-old prodigy took a carriage to the Schönefeld Church. One hour later, Clara's name would no longer be Wieck, and just one year later, she would bear a child. Their wedding was the culmination of a mutual rebellion. Against the will of one of the most supreme institutions of the time—a bride's father—a marriage for love par excellence took place. Pure romance in the Romantic Age.

Nearly a thousand people lived in the village of Schönefeld at the time, a rural idyll recently dissected by the newly established railway line to Dresden. Twenty-four thousand people lived in nearby Leipzig, about twice as many as live in the Schönefeld district today. Although there were many much larger German cities at the time, which also served as royal capitals for ambitious regents, Leipzig had become the most important musical metropolis in northern Germany—Vienna being the one in southern Germany, of course. And Leipzig would

Felix Mendelssohn Bartholdy lived in a new building in Lurgenstein's Garden before moving with his family to the apartment still on Goldschmidtstrasse today. Right: Café Merkur (Mercury Café), often frequented by Erich Kästner

retain this position throughout the nineteenth century, for many reasons. For one, the city's own musical history provided a rather solid foundation, even though some of its power had not really been discovered until recently. Bach and the Thomanerchor (St. Thomas choir) were widely acclaimed, as were the Gewandhaus Orchestra and the Leipzig Stadttheater (municipal theater). In addition, there was much to be heard in the public gardens, trade halls, and coffeehouses. The wealthy and culturally assiduous bourgeoisie at the time financed much of this active intellectual life. The city profited from the trade fairs, too, which not only drew many concert attendants for three weeks three times a year and was constantly providing new stimuli.

Leipzig also had a good reputation for the manufacture of musical instruments, especially pianos. At times there were twenty different piano factories, one of which was owned by Friedrich Wieck. Much more renowned was Julius Blüthner, who first debuted on stage a good ten years later, and whose works, like those of Hupfeld, were counted as some of the world's best in the early twentieth century. Leipzig had even more influence as a center of music printing, with Breitkopf and Härtel leading the way. The latter published the music journal *Allgemeine musikalische Zeitschrift* (*General Musical Journal*). Because that European market leader was downright conservative, the more rebellious *Neue Zeitschrift für Musik* (*New Journal of Music*) was established in 1834. Cofounder Robert Schumann was editor until 1845, winning much acclaim. In 1850, Richard Wagner published in the journal under the pseudonym Karl Freigedank (Carl Free-thought), though much less prestigiously. In his essay, "*Judentum in der Musik*" ("Judaism in Music"), Wagner vilified Jewish music in general and Mendelssohn in particular, who had converted to Christianity in early childhood. Mendelssohn had died three years earlier in his apartment on what today is Goldschmidtstrasse.

The Schumanns had also left the city. The young family grew to four in number and lived on Inselstrasse for four and a half years, before moving to Dresden in late 1844, where Robert hoped for a new beginning. He would not get one until six years later, when he was hired as the municipal director of music in Düsseldorf. The mood swings that plagued him more and more in Dresden did not get any better in faraway Rhineland. On the contrary, they took on entirely new characteristics. Because of the harmonies and dissonances bottled up inside his head, which developed a wild and uncontrollable life of their own, he tried to commit suicide in 1854. A short while later, he checked into a private psychiatric clinic near Bonn. Clara was not to visit him for two long years. Two days before his death, on July 29, 1856, they would see each other one last time.

Clara Wieck became Mrs. Schumann in the Schönefeld town church on September 12, 1840

Revolutions Big and Small

"Vienna is magnificent, glorious, the kindest city I have ever seen; yet revolutionary in flesh and blood. The people revolt politely but thoroughly. Their defense systems are terrible, their desire to fight infinite. Everything vying for sacrifice, effort, and valor. When Vienna is not victorious, it's as if only a heap of rubble and corpses remain, beneath which I would gladly and proudly wish to be buried." When Robert Blum, the man with the big, bushy beard, arrived in Vienna in mid-October 1848, he wrote these words to his wife. He was filled with optimism: Vienna was rising up against Kaiser Ferdinand for the third time, and Blum was there to lend his support, as a representative and vice president of the Frankfurt Parliament.

In 1848–49, nearly all of Europe was in a state of emergency. It began in France again in February, when the Second Republic was declared. In early March, the rebellions spilled over into German territory, where the princes were pressured to appoint liberal governments, guarantee freedom of the press, and pave the way for Germany unity—elections for parliament were held. An unprecedented departure. To date, only the nobility had ruled over the thirty-nine German federate states and their nearly thirty million inhabitants, which, while united in the German Federation after the dissolution of the Holy Roman Empire of the German Nation, were barely competent in the face of Prussia's and Austria's might.

Rejection of the existing order was nothing new, however. Earlier, in 1830—again the revolt began in France—liberal adjustments were imposed in several German principalities. One such center was Saxony, where King Frederick Augustus I died three years earlier after sixty-four years on the throne. The Saxon people's hope for a fresh regent were set back when his old brother Anton was named successor. The latter's conservative politics led to increasing tension, which spontaneously erupted on September 2, 1830, in Leipzig's Brühl—in the wake of the eve of a wedding party. A little clash with the peacekeeping force escalated to an outraged attack that lasted several days in which the windowpanes of disagreeable councillors and officials were destroyed all over town. Besides the broken glass, entire buildings and apartments were damaged.

When the protests finally spread to Dresden, the king had no choice but to leave the city and make

The Execution of Robert Blum. Painting attributed to Carl Steffeck

compromises. One year after the little revolution, Saxony became a constitutional monarchy, complete with its first constitution and parliament. In addition, Leipzig chose a city council in free elections, although only two thousand of Leipzig's forty-one thousand residents were allowed to vote. Just a few years later, however, King Frederick Augustus II tried to reverse the democratic successes achieved. In 1843, he swapped the liberal cabinet for a conservative one. Two years later, heir-apparent Prince John's trip to Leipzig resulted in protests in which eight people were shot and the nation and the court were completely divided. This climate brought new participants onto the political stage. One of them was Robert Blum, who had been living in Leipzig since 1832. As chairman of numerous associations, publicist, and publisher, he was well connected and also, as a man of a lower class, extremely well liked. His immense popularity grew throughout Germany.

His luck ran out in Vienna, though. After a bloody battle—some even died in St. Stephen's Cathedral—the city was initially taken by the rebels. The minister of war was subsequently lynched, and the kaiser was on the run again. Yet on October 28, the supreme commander of the imperial troops called for an attack on Vienna, which was not brought under control until three days later, under artillery fire. Although two thousand people lost their lives during the fighting, the uprising was not a success. Countless arrests ensued during the next few days, including that of Robert Blum and Julius Fröbel, another German politician of the 1848 March revolution. Blum was by no means unknown, as leader of the democratic faction in the St. Paul's Church parliament, and as a delegate he enjoyed immunity as well. But it would not end well for him.

It was not only in Vienna that the revolution came under increasing pressure, for in nearly every Ger-

Men declared "enemies of the state" in the 1860s met at the "villains' table" in the Gute Quelle restaurant on the Brühl

man principality, the hard-won rights were defused or repealed. When Prussian King Frederick William IV refused the crown offered to him by parliament on April 3, 1849, collapse was inevitable. While the subsequent protests increased in intensity, the aristocracy had consolidated and was able to regain control by force. Even the last rebellion, the May Uprising in Dresden, ended in a bloodbath. While the twelve thousand rebels were initially unable to drive the king out of the city, the Prussian army offered him aid, resulting in two hundred dead. With the dissolution of the Frankfurt Parliament in May, the revolution ended. Countless participants subsequently left Germany or were apprehended.

The fate of Carl Rudolph Bromme was particularly remarkable. Born near Leipzig in the village of Anger in 1804, and named supreme commander of the newly established imperial navy in March, he immediately built a small armada, which lost its country and employer when parliament was dissolved. When all of Bromme's attempts to come up with a new purpose for his fleet failed, he retreated with a heavy heart. Yet the defeat of the bourgeoisie brought with it not just an end but many beginnings as well.

In the pre-March era, women began to find their political voice—for example, in the *Frauen-Zeitung* (*Women's Newspaper*), first published in 1843 by Leipziger Louise Otto-Peters. In 1865, she founded the Women's Education Association and the General German Women's Association, together with Auguste Schmidt. Afterward, Leipzig remained a stronghold for women's issues. The same was true for workers' issues and unions, whose influence increased in the 1830s. In 1863, the General German Workers' Association would be established in the Pantheon on Dresden Street, from which the Social Democratic Party of Germany would later emerge.

Meanwhile, Robert Blum was hung in Vienna on November 9, 1848, one day before his forty-first birthday—either despite or because of the fact that he had been a delegate in the St. Paul's Church Parliament. Decades later he would be venerated as the most prominent victim of the revolution, especially in Rhineland and Saxony, where his portrait hung in countless homes. A plaque on the Old City Hall commemorates his work.

Taming the West

In 1842, Karl Heine, "Leipzig's most beautiful student," as Theodor Götz described him later, had a lot to do. His mother had appointed the twenty-two-year-old as general agent of the family's 314-acre property, and he was energetically expediting its cultivation. After his father became ill, Karl also led his estate in Neuscherbitz. At the same time, the future lawyer obtained a doctoral degree with a dissertation on the subject of water rights and tried with it to win the heart of his beloved Doris Trinius—or, more precisely, the blessing of her father. He was successful on all fronts, and his responsibilities would only grow.

Today, Karl Heine is considered to be a pioneer of Leipzig's western region, for leading the small villages of Plagwitz and Lindenau into the industrial age. His involvement in transforming the landscape and as an entrepreneur and developer did not begin in the distant west, however, but in the city's near west, at Reichels Garten (Reichel's Garden). Formerly known as Apels Garten, the well-known area had lost its once Baroque character and, after changing hands several times, had come to be owned by Heine's mother's family. Meanwhile, nearly two thousand people had come to live there. Vast parts of the area, filled with ditches and small streams, were prone to frequent flooding and thus not usable. The same was true of the neighboring properties. Heine acquired most of them in the subsequent months, until he owned an area that extended from the pastures across from Pleissenburg Castle to Lindenauer Chaussee, today's Jahnallee.

After making extensive changes to the landscape, he parceled the area to sell as building plots. Before the Leipzig Council officially approved his plan in

The little village of Plagwitz became one of the densest industrial areas of the world in the 1920s

fall 1844, the first property had already changed hands. He transferred it free of charge to a municipal minority, the Catholics. Yet altruism played only a minor role. With God's help, a scenic site with a new 177-foot-tall city landmark was completed in 1847, right in the middle of the potential building sites: the Holy Trinity Church. The adjacent parcels along West and Rudolph streets practically sold themselves and proved popular among wealthy citizens. The development of the surrounding area progressed as well. Nearly two million cubic feet of dirt were brought to raise the terrain. Five floodgates and two bridges over the Pleisse and Elster rivers were built, along with many new streets, maintaining the fan-shaped arrangement of Kolonnaden, Moritz, und Erdmann streets following the old garden lanes. Heine functioned as a builder as well, and was involved with constructing the Hufeisen (horseshoe). The giant building was equipped with the latest features and was one of the first in the city to have running water, though building employees had to pump the water into a reservoir in the attic each morning. Despite or possibly because of his numerous enterprises, Heine was initially plagued by financial difficulties, which were soon forgotten as development of the western annex progressed. Soon he was able to devote himself to new plans.

In these, the Ritterwerder, a small wooded area between Leipzig and Plagwitz, played a particular role. It was idyllic, presumably, but to Heine it was just a wooded obstacle standing in the way of a direct connection between the two communities. Many times he sought the council's permission to cut a swath through it, but the council kept putting him off. Botanical sensitivities were not the deciding factor, however. The city was more afraid of the neighboring communities circumventing customs restrictions. In the winter of 1857–58, Heine finally lost patience. He moved in with a band of workers and bore down on the little forest—the road was his goal. He dutifully paid the thirty-thaler fine, knowing full well how much more he had gained.

Unlike in Leipzig or the adjacent communities to the east, there was barely any trace of modern times in Plagwitz. When Heine began buying property there in 1854, the small village on the swamp had a population of about 350, living in several farmsteads along today's Alte Street. One of the first buildings that Heine built in 1856, the Steinerne Haus (Stone House) on Zschochersch Street, still remains today. He also built a steam sawmill and a brickyard that same year (near where a traffic roundabout is today), but neither remain.

During the following year, the first factory moved in nearby, a mechanical weaving mill. Through 1862, additional industrial facilities settled between Nonnenstrasse and the Elster River, including a petroleum refinery and two iron foundries. The first res-

View of the Catholic Church and Weststrasse, as seen from New City Hall

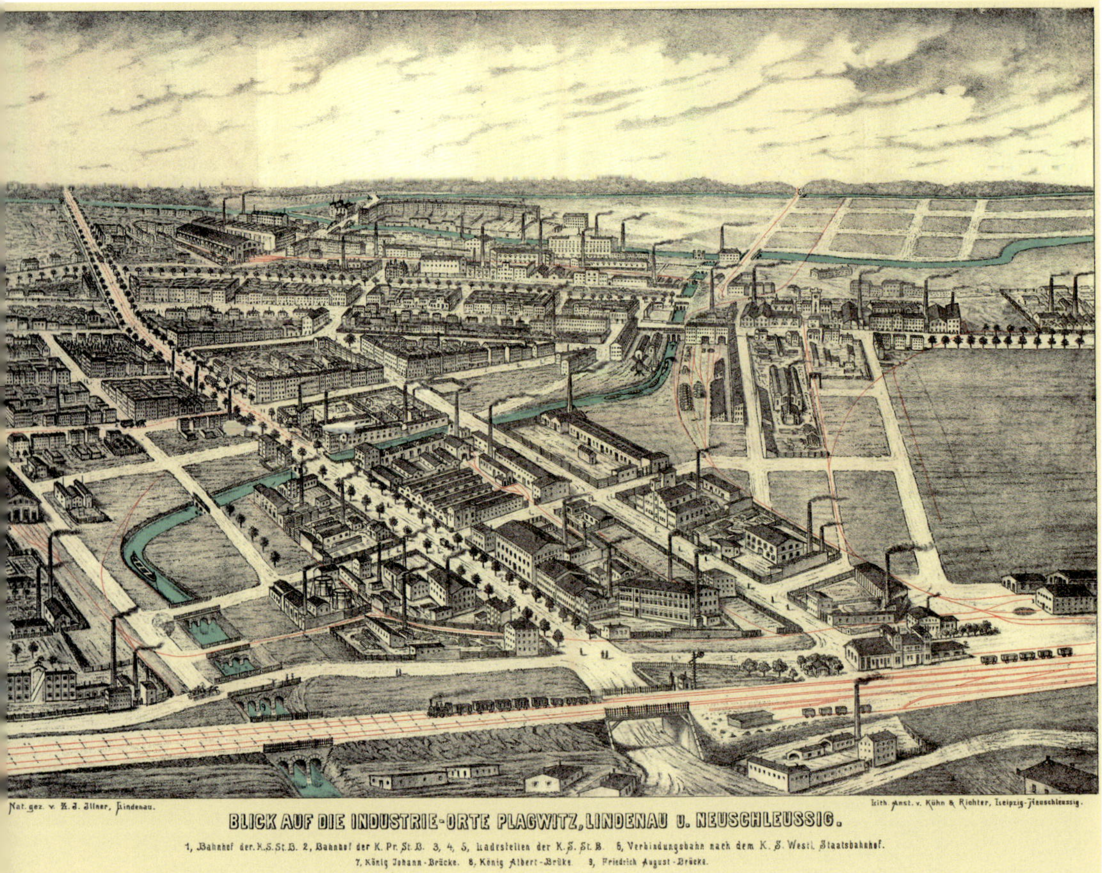

idential buildings rose up next door. Within just three years, the population of the village doubled, and its thirty-four houses became seventy. Plagwitz also transformed into one of the most modern villages in Saxony, with gaslights, mail service, and public transportation to Leipzig. The horse-drawn bus service that Heine established in 1860 for that purpose connected Plagwitz and other surrounding communities to Leipzig as well. Just twelve years later, one of the first horse tramways took over the task.

Plagwitz was also accessible to Leipzig by water. From the Leipzig train station (the *Hauptbahnhof*, or main train station today), the waterway led over the Parthe River, the Pleisse millrace, an old steamboat canal, the Elster millrace, the Elster and Luppe River, and the Karl-Heine-Canal into the heart of the continually growing industrial area. At its peak, sixteen steamboats traveled the route, with fine-sounding names like "Neptune" and "Columbus." They carried passengers only on Sundays and transported building and raw materials to Plagwitz on weekdays, along with finished products to the train stations. Thanks to Heine, the graywacke from construction of the Karl-Heine-Canal was moved to the west of Leipzig, where it was used to raise the ground. Because of this, the parts of the city built there, such as the Bachstrassen Quarter, the Waldstrassen Quarter, and the Music Quarter, are standing completely on Plagwitz ground.

The dedication of the Plagwitz train station meant an abrupt decrease in ship traffic to Leipzig, and yet the trains provided a stimulus for industrial growth. Commercial transportation was simplified by the railway network, as Heine laid industrial lines directly connecting the factories to the train station. By 1886, thirty-seven companies in Leipzig's western region had their own access lines. With the railway connection to Connewitz that opened two years later, whose former embankment

Aerial view of Plagwitz in the late 18th century

on Könneritzstrasse helped it achieve "hill" status, there was now direct access to the southern track network that lasted until 1925.

Besides Heine's role as creator of infrastructure, the all-around entrepreneur operated his own flavor factory, where Schreberstrasse is today, cultivated his estate on Lützner Street, and devoted himself to establishing a telephone exchange agency. As a representative in the Saxon State Parliament—and later the Reichstag (the Imperial Parliament in Berlin)—he also had considerable political influence. His vision of Leipzig with its own shipping access to the sea, however, fell flat, like so many other attempts before and after his time. In 1898, work on the Karl-Heine-Canal was finally halted, after it had reached a length of 1.6 miles and required fifteen bridges to be built. Ten years earlier, on August 25, 1888, Heine had died in his villa on Könneritzstrasse at the age of sixty-nine.

Leipzigers were uncommonly moved by his death. Residents from all social strata rode in an extraordinarily long funeral procession, leading the deceased's casket straight through the city to the New St. John's Cemetery (after that was deconsecrated, he was moved to Old St. John's Cemetery). Obituaries in all the newspapers honored his life's work. In 1897, a monument created by Carl Seffner was dedicated to Heine at the beginning of the street known today as Karl-Heine-Street. It was originally located on the other side of the street, where Heine had once had a view looking out over Plagwitz. In 1936, however, his monument was relocated. In 1942, Heine had no more view at all, as his monument fell victim to the Nazi armament effort, when bronze monuments were turned into weaponry. Sixty years later, with financial backing from the city and Heine's descendants, a replica was made that has adorned the border of his former empire since 2001.

View of the city from the west, c. 1850. The land between Leipzig and Plagwitz did not belong to the city yet and was largely covered by water

Garden Plots and Green Spaces

The history of Leipzig's green spaces is much more exciting than the title might convey. It includes two tragic father–son relationships, one death by excessive infatuation, insanity at the highest level, and, of course, all kinds of geraniums—hard to believe that Hollywood has not pursued movie rights yet.

One of the main characters in this green melodrama was Johanna Seyfferth. In 1856, still a delicate little sprout of nineteen years, she married (at her father's behest) banker Dr. Gustav Schulz. The fact that her heart actually belonged to estate owner Wilhelm von Minckwitz did not matter, as he did not work in her father's financial institution. When she died of a broken heart two years later, her father, Wilhelm Seyfferth, was profoundly shocked, and his reaction unusual. Not only did he acknowledge both men as his sons-in-law, but he appointed von Minckwitz as sole heir to his daughter's wealth. Of even more significance, however, was Seyfferth's decision to donate a park—one that would bring as much joy as his daughter had brought him. For that purpose, he bought up several fields west of the Alte Pleisse River, also known as cattle pastures, and engaged Prussian horticultural legend Peter Joseph Lenné, who had created

Ice skating pond in Johanna Park

the Sanssouci gardens in Potsdam, and a section of the Promenade along Leipzig's Schillerstrasse one year earlier.

Lenné saw to it that the area was enlarged through the purchase of additional properties. He created a pond and used the dirt from the pond's excavation to raise the level of an area that had regularly flooded before. He added a network of paths that still exists today, along with many exotic trees and shrubs, and all kinds of geraniums. For five years after Johanna's death, her father expressed his guilty conscience completely in botanic form. In 1863, Johannapark was opened to the public. Because the Alte Pleisse River carved a wide path around it, it was originally surrounded by water on three sides, and the peninsula was accessible only from Leipzig over the old Heubrücke (Hay Bridge). In those days, the whole neighborhood was green. On the southern border lay partially overgrown public gardens, the Botanical Garden, and a few ponds that were formerly gravel pits. The areas to the north and west were also characterized by various shades of green.

In 1881, Wilhelm Seyfferth died and Johannapark was transferred to city ownership, subject to the conditions that it would always bear Johanna's name and nothing would ever be built on it. The city expanded the property to where Ferdinand-Lasalle-Street is today and equipped the pond with fountains. Since then the area surrounding the park has been almost completely transformed. The Alte Pleisse River was filled in after the Pleisse flood channel was completed, and the Botanical Garden, where the Supreme Court would be built, was moved in 1877 to what would be its fourth location, on Linnéstrasse. The neighboring ponds and public gardens to the south made way for construction of the Music Quarter, while the first buildings in the Bachstrassen Quarter were built on the fields to the north. There were also plans to develop the area to the west of the park, but initiatives by Seyfferth and Council Gardner Wittenberg blocked them. Both advocated for a green corridor connecting the city center with the lowland woods, and, amazingly enough, they were able to convince the council members to agree to their request. And so Clara-

Parks and Green Spaces

Name	Created	Location	Notes
Rosental	1318 first documented	Northwest	Publicly owned since 1663
Johanna Park	1863	West	Renamed Clara Zetkin Park for a time
Scheibenholz Park	1877	West	King Albert Park merged with Clara Zetkin Park in 1955
Karl Heine Square	1890	West	Former cemetery, still called Bone Square
Schönau Park	1890	West	Former Schönau Manor
King Albert Park	1897	West	Exhibition grounds 1897
Volkshain Stünz	1898	East	Not part of Leipzig until Stünz incorporated in 1910
Palm Garden/Klingerhain	1899	West	Admission charged originally
Eutritzsch Park	1904/1914	North	Arthur Bretschneider Park today
Marianne Park	1928	East	With sledding hill
Kleinzschoch Public Park	1928	Southwest	With a grove of trees of the year
Peace Park	1983	Southeast	Formerly New St. John Cemetery (beg. 1846)
Güntz Park	1920s	Southeast	Formerly belonged to a private sanatorium

Zetkin-Park is in that same location today, named for the Saxonia-born leader of the Communist Party in the Reichstag during the Weimar Republic.

In 1865, a playground was built on the brand-new Johannapark's northern border. Nothing special, one might say, but in the mid-nineteenth century, playgrounds were extremely unusual. Ernst Innozenz Hauschild, a Leipzig school principal, who had also introduced girls' gymnastics to the city came up with the idea. He was inspired by the ideas of Moritz Schreber, a pedagogue and orthopedist who died in 1861, and who researched disturbances in children's psychological development resulting from industrialization. Because the workers' quarters did not offer many suitable opportunities for play, Schreber advocated for creating new spaces. And so the site that 250 citizens helped create was named Schreberplatz. There were no gardens there, however, as gardens had not played any role in Schreber's plans. Supervised by a teacher, the first activities offered there were footraces, sack races, and tug-of-war contests.

Three years later, when a teacher named Heinrich Karl Gesell started several children's garden plots, the gardens finally arrived. Despite the original plans, the parents occupied the green island and made themselves at home among the geraniums, while their little sprouts played. Because the area was still largely unused, the portion of botanically purposed plots increased rapidly. Watering cans were brought, which required sheds in which to store them, which were converted to garden houses in no time at all. Just one year later, the grounds had already yielded about a hundred neatly divided plots and an initial Schreber Garden Charter. Garden plots had already been around for a long time. By 1830, more than twenty German cities had them, and this primarily enabled poor people to plant fruits and vegetables.

There had even been garden plots in Leipzig's Johannistal as early as 1832. While those are still in the same location, if not in a smaller place, the first Schreber garden had to move ten years after it was established. Coincidentally, the association moved right next door to the Schreberbad (Schreber pool), which opened in 1867 and was just as much not invented by Moritz Schreber as the gardens named after him. The things Schreber actually did invent, on the other hand, have long since been forgotten, fortunately. His five children, however, really struggled with their combination pedagogue/inventor father, from time to time. He was constantly fitting them with new devices, like the straightener, which forced them to sit up straight; orthopedic chin straps, designed to prevent underbites; and mechanical devices that prevented masturbation.

While such inventions might seem strange today, in the mid-nineteenth century they were viewed merely as tools that aided with educational methods that were generally accepted. Whether and in what ways Schreber's methods would affect his children later in life became topics of discussion for leading psychologists, since their development was so unusual. While Schreber's eldest son, Daniel Gustav, committed suicide, Daniel Paul began a successful career as a lawyer and was named senate president in Dresden's regional court of appeals in 1893. That same year, however, he became ill and struggled with insomnia and severe depression for weeks at a time. Despite medical treatment, his condition worsened to include delusions and paranoia. Ten years later, after stints in many psychiatric facilities, he described his condition in the book, *Denkwürdigkeiten eines Nervenkranken* (*Memoirs of a Neuropath*), which served to corroborate the theories of Sigmund Freud, Carl Gustav Jung, and Elias Canetti, among others.

From Furs to Peace Pipes

During Karl May's sojourn in Leipzig in March 1865, no one knew that he would one day bear the title of most-read author in Germany—indeed, at the time, the twenty-three-year-old had not yet published a single word. He was already using pseudonyms, however, though his motives were not all that poetic in nature—serving only in the illegal acquisition of others' property. And so it was that he stepped into Erler's fur shop on the corner of the Brühl and Reichsstrasse on March 20, 1865, under the illustrious name of Hermes Kupferstecher, chose a beaver fur, and arranged to have it delivered to his rented room at the St. Thomas Churchyard.

May's beaver coat was not the only dead fur animal on the Brühl at that time, which was teeming with *Rauchwaren*. The root of the word *Rauchwaren* is the Old German word *rauh*, meaning "hairy" or "shaggy." The fact that Leipzig, of all places, developed as the center of the fur trade had something to do with the significance of the trade fairs and with the city's location in the heart of Europe, where it connected fur suppliers in the east with markets in the west. Though at first Leipzig really was just more of an industrial meeting place and would not have its own fur industry for quite some time.

Right after the Napoleonic Wars, 1814 saw a particular low point, when there were only two fur traders in the city. One hundred years later, there would be 267, and by 1928, as many as 794. At times, one third of the global fur trade passed through Leipzig. The city's tax receipts from the fur industry in the late 1920s were correspondingly high. The fur trade was concentrated almost exclusively in the northern part of the city center, on Ritter Street, Reichsstreet, and Nikolai Street, and par-

The Brühl where it meets Ritterstrasse, c. 1850

The Brühl all decked out, to the disadvantage of the animal kingdom

ticularly in the eastern section of the Brühl. For a long time, it was impossible to imagine the Brühl without furs. Countless reports described the international fur street in the most brilliant colors. The extent of international fame that this Leipzig street once enjoyed is best illustrated in a letter from a Canadian fur trapper, who had a falling out with his local buyers in 1928 and was looking to connect directly with the global market. It was not the letter's content that was remarkable but the way it was addressed. *Brühl* was the only word on the envelope, but the note traveled via Montreal and Bremen to its intended destination just the same.

Karl May had no inkling of any of this in 1865, but he did have other concerns of his own. His formidable beaver coat, which he stole under a pretense on his way to the pawn shop, got him four years in jail in Zwickau a short while later, which would not be May's only prison sentence. While he wrote his novels after his sojourns in prison, the ideas for them came to him while he was behind bars, so one might conclude that the compelling workmanship of a bunch of dead rodents indirectly led to the birth of Winnetou, the famed, albeit fictional, Apache chief from the Wild West, who fought side by side with his white brother Old Shatterhand, both known to every man, woman, and child in Germany.

While Karl May's road through the 1860s and 1870s initially ran downhill, the Brühl's quick rise to the top of the fur trade was just beginning. A series of decisions and events in the mid-nineteenth century, like Saxony joining the German customs union, the creation of the first railway lines, and the introduction of free trade, contributed to a huge increase in economic activity that affected much more than the fur industry. The latter profited especially from the gradually expanding equality of Jewish merchants, which allowed the Jewish-dominated fur trade in Eastern Europe, where Jews struggled with increasing restrictions, to move closer to Leipzig. Countless Russian and Polish Jews settled in the city as merchants. At the same time, the fur industry severed its ties to the trade-fair calendar. The original three-week trading period was slowly extended until finally trade-fair time on the Brühl lasted all year long. Most of the buildings were centuries old and not suited for year-round trade, and the proud Leipzig merchants did not feel represented in the least by the ramshackle courtyard structures of the past. New buildings were required.

And so it was that the Brühl became more and more of a modern business street, transformed not only architecturally but structurally as well. For the street on which Karl May's criminal ambitions led him to a dead end had long been just that. Appropriately, the Georgenhaus (George's House), which functioned as both a jail and orphanage, blocked the street at the east end, by the swan pond. Once the building was demolished in 1869, the Brühl became a throughway, and soon after was used for one of

Mid-19th Century—Value of Leipzig Imports in 1863 (in Thalers):

Import Type	Value in Thalers
from America	2,622,500
from Central Europe	2,128,000
from Russia	1,382,000

(In 1863/64, Leipzig bought a total of 35.2 percent of the global harvest, which amounted to 17 million thalers or 32 million pelts.)

the first horse tramways. There was still plenty of room on what was once the widest street in the inner city, though, for traders, who at fair times sold their furs right on the street or covered entire building facades with them. The buzz on the Brühl was especially active, with traders haggling in all sorts of languages—an immutable constant, as more and more old buildings were replaced with new ones. Construction finally reached its peak shortly before World War I, when adjacent streets were increasingly swallowed up in the building boom. Nikolaiststrasse, in particular, got an almost complete facelift in the early twentieth century. Originally ending at the Brühl, in 1911 it punched its way through to the central train station under construction at the time and experienced rapid development as a new commercial street.

Today's Brühl, meanwhile, has lost most of its ambience and has little in common with the street Karl May knew. Only two buildings from the time of his first visit are still standing, the Romanushaus and the Haus zur alten Heuwaage (House of the Old Hay Scale), which had just been completed. After a global economic crisis, the Nazis, air raids, and Soviet occupation, its old flair is gone. No furs have been peddled here for a long, long time, which should make the hairy representatives of the animal kingdom happy, but does not exactly fuel hopes for a Winnetou 2000.

The Brühl in 1862, with the Georgenhaus (George's House, left), the Pelzdom with Zur Guten Quelle (Fur Dome, Good Spring Tavern, center), and Erler's fur shop (right)

The Emperor's New Clothes
1871 to 1918

Europe's Literary Emporium

For centuries, professions identified themselves with a true hodgepodge of patron saints and icons from antiquity, the Bible, and other sources. Many symbols have been used in the book trade—geese, for example. The role that common fowl plays can be attributed to the inventor of the printing press, who was born at the court of Gutenberg and later assumed the name of his birthplace. Most have forgotten that Johannes Gutenberg actually came into the world as "Johannes Gensfleisch" (Goosemeat), or "Henne Gensfleisch," as he's called in his obituary. Geese can still be found on the facades of old book-industry buildings in the Graphic District. Even more prevalent is the image of Henne Gensfleisch. Whether the bushy-bearded young man depicted looked anything like the real Gutenberg is highly questionable, as no portraits exist of his actual appearance.

For four decades, the Graphic District between the main, Bayerische, and the Eilenburg train stations was the undisputed center of the German book industry. Leipzig's history as a literary mecca began in the city center, where a considerable number of booksellers had already established themselves by the early sixteenth century. While the Thirty Years

Leipzig without its Pleissenburg Castle was long unimaginable, but in 1898, only part of the tower remained

Henne Gensfleisch—with beard and as poultry

War set the local book and fair trade back a bit, Leipzig surpassed Frankfurt as the most important trade-fair city once again in the early eighteenth century, and soon thereafter as a literary metropolis, as the sale of books then was closely associated with trade fairs. One other advantage Leipzig had was the relatively harmless reach of Saxon censorship. Additionally, the presence of the university had a beneficial effect as well.

The bourgeoisie and civil service classes emerged as the primary market. Not only did they have the financial means but, more important, they could read. In the seventeenth century, fiction slowly began to emerge as a literary genre that closed the gap between (mostly theological) professional literature and simple chapbooks, and it experienced incredible growth in the second half of the eighteenth century. The number of novels published annually increased by a factor of thirty in just fifty years, and even poetry captured the market. Both genres were especially popular with women. More and more newspapers were appearing as well, beginning in the early seventeenth century. The world's first daily paper was published by Leipzig printer Timotheus Ritzsch in 1650, under the title *Einkommenden Zeitungen* (*Incoming Bulletins*), and the journal publishers in Leipzig were responsible for pioneering work in their field.

One of the main booksellers at the time was Moritz Georg Weidmann. In 1680, he founded the Weidmannsche Buchhandlung (Weidmann's Bookshop), which would remain an institution in the German book trade for centuries. Philipp Erasmus Reich took on leadership of the company in the mid-eighteenth century, after moving to Leipzig from Frankfurt, as Weidmann had. Under his direction, *Wieland* and books by authors such as Christian Fürchtegott Gellert and Christian Felix Weiße were published, along with a new edition on French grammar—an absolute bestseller in its day. Even more important, however, was Reich's role in reforming the book market, which earned him the titles "Prince of Booksellers" and "Bookseller of the Nation." He fought to suppress pirated editions, introduced cash sales to replace practice of bartering, and called for a boycott of the Frankfurt Book Fair, which diminished in importance as a result. Besides big Leipzig publishers like Johann Friedrich Gleditsch or Nikolaus Förster, who published Gottfried Wilhelm Leibniz, for example, or Georg Joachim Göschen, through whom Schiller, Goethe, and Friedrich Klopstock later released their works, Bernhard Christoph Breitkopf and his Breitkopf-Verlag (BreitKopf Publishing), founded in 1719 (becoming Breitkopf and Härtel in 1795), also deserve mention. Many musical giants released their works through Breitkopf, the oldest music publisher in the world. And Johann Gottlob Immanuel Breitkopf introduced crucial technological improvements in music publishing. The publishing house originated in the Haus zum Goldenen Bären (House of the Golden Bears) in today's Universitätstrasse, and a bear still adorns the Breitkopf crest.

It was the swan, however, that came to be the overarching symbol of all music publishing houses. The association arose, like most symbols in the book trade, from classical mythology. Apollo, Greek god of the arts, was usually portrayed with a swan and lyre, which is why that particular musical instrument is often found on the facades of buildings where musical scores used to be printed. There are a good many more owls in the Graphic District, however. In Roman antiquity, owls were faithful companions of Minerva, the goddess of wisdom, who was often depicted as well. The same was true for Mercury, god of merchants, reflecting the economic aspects of trade. He can usually be identified by his winged helmet and caduceus, and he often carries a money-bag.

Comparison of Book Cities Berlin and Leipzig

	Berlin			Leipzig		
Year	Titles	Share	Bookstores	Titles	Share	Bookstores
1850	1,107	13.5 %	171	1,495	18.2 %	128
1910	4,355	23.2 %	1,209	4,050	21.6 %	1142
2011	8,622	10.5 % (ranked 1)		929	1.1 % (ranked 11)	

In light of the book's lack of competition from other media, which did not become prevalent until the early twentieth century, the publishers' money-bags were usually well filled. In the nineteenth century, publishers were among the richest citizens in town, partly because their clientele was always increasing in numbers. This was due to the rising population and the increase in literacy, which went from 30 percent in the early nineteenth century but was close to 100 percent in 1910. All in all, the number of potential readers increased by a factor of ten during that period. New technologies developed as well, such as the high-speed printing press in 1811, without which the market would have been impossible to manage.

One of the first publishers to use the new machine was F. A. Brockhaus, who first set up shop in the Rote Kolleg (Red College) on Ritterstrasse in 1818. Crowded conditions and a ban on steam-powered machines in the city center made expansion impossible there, so facilities were built on Querstrasse, east of the city center, setting new standards for all of Germany. Not only were lexicons printed and published there but so were works by Arthur Schopenhauer, relatively unknown back then, and Casanova,

Publishing Houses in the Graphics District

Publisher	Founded	In the Graphic District	Genre	Today	Still there
Teubner	1811	1821, Poststrasse	Textbooks	Wiesbaden	
F. A. Brockhaus	1805 in Amsterdam	1818/22, Querstrasse	Lexika	Wiesbaden until 1984	
Bernhard Tauchnitz		1837, Dresdner Strasse	English classics	to Brandstetter 1934	
Giesecke and Devrient		1852, Nürnberger Strasse	Financial	Munich	x
E. A. Seemann	1858 in Essen	1861, Prager Strasse, among others	Art	Leipzig	x
Reclam	1828	1862, Inselstrasse	Classics	Ditzingen, near Stuttgart	
Oscar Brandstetter		1862, Dresdner Strasse	All	Wiesbaden	
Breitkopf and Härtel	1719	1866, Nürnberger Strasse	Musical scores	Wiesbaden	x
Baedecker	1827 in Koblenz	1872, Nürnberger Strasse	Travel guides	Kemnat, near Stuttgart	
Bibliographisches Institut	1826 in Gotha	1874, Gerichtsweg	Duden (German dictionaries)	Mannheim until 2009	
C. F. Peters	1800	1874, Talstrasse	Musical scores	New York and London	x
Georg Thieme Verlag		1886, Rossplatz	Medicine	Stuttgart	
Insel		1901, Kurze Strasse, among others		Frankfurt/Berlin	
Rowohlt		1908, Goldschmidt-strasse	Contemporary	Berlin/Stuttgart/Berlin	
Kurt Wolff Verlag		1912, Inselstrasse	Even more contemporary	Liquidated 1940	

Old Bookseller's Exchange in the St. Nicholas churchyard

which became bestsellers. In the following decades, most of the other local publishers pushed eastward, too, and many new ones came to join them.

Fifty years later, the booksellers' exchange, inaugurated in the St. Nicholas Churchyard in 1836, was too small fifty years later, it was also located in the wrong place. And so the German Publishers and Booksellers Association, founded in Leipzig in 1825, built itself a new residence on Platostrasse in 1888, which was joined a few years later by the book-trade building. With the German library created in 1912, another important institution was added to Deutscher Platz (German Square), which cemented Leipzig as the capital of the German book industry. Nearly one thousand publishers and booksellers existed in Leipzig in 1914, along with three hundred printers and 173 bookbinders. All in all, the industry employed up to six thousand workers. From May to October that same year, BuGra—the International Exhibition of Book Printing and Graphics—took place on the grounds where the Technical Fair would be held later. Attended by over 2,500 exhibitors from 23 countries and 2.3 million visitors, the show was a huge success, though the outbreak of World War I during the event completely changed things. Judging by the number of titles published since the 1860s, Berlin was the primary city of books, though its lead was slight. Not much happened after that. One out every two books was published in either of the two cities.

But Leipzig's advantage over Berlin was not just because of the concentration of associations and institutions to which the booksellers and printing academies belonged; Leipzig was also the undisputed center of the book trade on commission, where foreign and domestic wholesale and intermediate trade was organized. More than twelve thousand companies were represented by book trade on commission in Leipzig in 1914. The system, in place since the late nineteenth century, functioned so well that a book ordered on December 21 would be lying under the tree by Christmas.

Books returned because of defects were called "crabs." The crustacean was a bookseller's biggest enemy and was not usually depicted in a flattering form. It was fought, squashed, and bullied in a variety of ways—not just in illustrations but culinarily as well. So crab was always on the menu at larger gatherings of the book industry.

New Bookseller's Exchange on Hospitalstrasse (called Prager Strasse today), in the Graphic District

Public Sport Founders and Ball Heroes

On June 24, 1881, nine young men of international origin sat in the Moltke Café on Grimmaisch Street, discussing things that were hardly ever discussed. They were velocipedists—bicyclists—or simply cyclists, who founded the Leipzig Bicycle Club, one of the first of its kind in Germany. One year later, their first official race took place during the fall meeting in Leipzig, along the promenade at the zoo. Although the competition site was just a temporary one, the human and animal audiences were completely enthusiastic, and further races were planned. Beginning in 1884 the races were held on one of the first real racetracks in Gohlis's Kaiserpark, considered to be the most modern in the empire. The first German championships were held there that same year, and the German Cycling Association was founded at that event.

Steel-wheel cycling was still a young sport, not much older than the sporting equipment itself. Other forms of physical fitness had been around since the Middle Ages. Leipzig's oldest athletic association, at 570 years old, is the gun club. Today, Schützenstrasse (Gun Street) just east of the town center still marks the former location of one of the shooting ranges, though Peterssteinweg is another location, where people practiced with bows and rifles. People have also been indulging in equestrian sports for a long time, though the cost to maintain sports gear of the four-legged variety limited the

60,000 voices say, "Let the sporting begin," at the XIIth German Gymnastics Festival in 1913

number of active participants to the nobility and wealthy commoners. With the introduction of student riding in the eighteenth century, however, college students began sitting on horseback as well. At riding clubs in and near the city center, training in the art of dressage was emphasized. Horses have been known to gallop at the Rossplatz (Horse Square) now and then since 1681, and regularly at the racetrack in Scheibenholz since 1863. To date, mastery of muskets, horses, or swords has garnered a high degree of social acceptance, a mindset that has resulted in countless duels.

Yet seldom (if ever) has anyone bowled to the death, though the sport of bowling is really rather old. Friedrich Schiller and Johann Wolfgang von Goethe are said to have been enthusiastic bowlers, though there is no record of whether they were as talented at that as they were in the literary realm. Bowling did not enjoy broad appeal until the nineteenth century. Many associations with terrific names, such as Kegelmania (Bowling-mania), the Neuntöter (Nine[pin]-killers), or the Pappenheimer (Harquebusiers), were established in Leipzig. In 1891, the first German bowling alley, with nine lanes, was established on Nordstrasse. The large bowling alley opened on Elsterstrasse in 1929 was home to forty-five clubs. There were about two hundred bowling clubs in the city at that time. The most popular sport for a long time, however, was gymnastics, which has been practiced in Leipzig since 1818. Members of student leagues met at the Gasthof zur Blauen Mütze (Blue Cap Inn) and at a garden near Gohlis, where they practiced together. Because the gymnasts supported a unified Germany at a time when it was still divided up in smaller states, authorities considered the brand-new sport to be a threat to national security and went after parallel bars and pommel horses with axes and saws. Despite its illegality, people kept right on practicing, until the gymnastics ban was lifted in 1842.

Three years later, Leipzig's Allgemeine Turnverein (ATV, General Gymnastics Association) was founded. At almost the same time, gymnastics was introduced in schools, and in 1847 the first gymnasium opened on Holzgasse (named Sternwartenstrasse today). Still famous today is Friedrich Ludwig Jahn, the founding father of gymnastics, who lived in Berlin, but Ferdinand Goetz, a physician from Lindenau, is also important. Goetz was the executive director of the German Gymnastics Association for fifty-five years, during which time competitions grew to huge events of unexpected proportion. In 1863, 170,000 gymnasts participated in the third German gymnastics tournament that took place in Leipzig. By the time the twelfth tournament rolled around in 1913, the number of participants increased to 1.12 million.

While gymnastics had long been established by 1885, cycling was just getting started. That was the

Cycling fast and tall, 1885

year that Englishman George Lacy Hillier participated as a foreign cyclist in a German race for the first time. Leipzig's local elite did not stand a chance. Because power transmission via chain drive had just been invented, the high-wheeler and tricycle still ruled the track. The first cycling road races were also being held, like the 500K Leipzig–Berlin–Leipzig race won by Herbert Blank in just twenty-eight hours. The old two-wheeled steeds were still equipped with hard rubber tires then. The bicycle innertube was not invented until 1889. That same year, the first German bicycle exhibition took place in the Krystallpalast (Crystal Palace), which generated additional followers for the sport of cycling. In 1892, the new *Radsportbahn* (cycling track) was built (where the mini-fair is held today), which set new European standards as *"Lindenauer Zement"* (Lindenau Cement). The facility contained space for other sports as well, including a dozen tennis courts.

Tennis was another young sport. While its predecessor, *Jeu de paume* (palm game), had been played on indoor courts as early as the seventeenth century, the first modern tennis court came to Leipzig in 1879, just two years after the first Wimbledon Tournament. Soon people were breaking and breaking back on Waldstrasse, and later in Schleussig. Heinrich Schomburgk was particularly successful at the game. Besides numerous singles and doubles titles, he won Olympic gold in mixed doubles in 1912, with Dora Koering, and was Leipzig's first Olympic champion ever. He was talented in multiple sports along with his three brothers, who were also keen on sports. The Schomburgk brothers were the grandchildren of Karl Heine's, a pioneer of industry still famous today. Heinrich won German championships with various Leipzig teams, in ice hockey (which his brother Arthur introduced to Leipzig in 1900), hockey (which his brother Wilhelm brought to Leipzig in 1908), and soccer

Athletic wear was already hip and light by 1907

(which had already been introduced before the Schomburgk brothers).

Indeed, the Leipzig soccer players were pretty successful back then, especially those in the Verein für Bewegungsspiele (VfB, Athletics Association). In the eleven championship games played before the outbreak of World War I, the VfB played in the final five times and won in three of them. The Deutsche Fußballbund (German Soccer Federation) was established in 1900 in a Leipzig restaurant, Zum Mariengarten (Mary's Garden), in today's Büttnerstrasse. In the early years of the sport, the English *Fußlümmelei* (dribbling) was widely mocked, and struggled because of competition, especially from gymnasts. In fact, the final game of the 1903 German championship in Hamburg started forty-five minutes late because an important piece of equipment—the ball—was missing. The first German champions were the VfB, who rode home in a train after their victory, in a third-class compartment, where the players were enthusiastically received—by all three fans. Soccer was still just one of many sports, though after wins in 1906 and 1913 there was a lot more interest in it. That third championship won by the VfB, however, would also be the last won by a Leipzig soccer team.

At least as successful was the track and field association established in 1896. Theodor Schöffler, an VfB-athlete, won the first German marathon in 1897, which went from Paunsdorf to Bennewitz and back to Paunsdorf. Six additional championship titles were won in other events by 1914. Leipzigers were also successful on the water. The first rowing clubs were established in the 1860s and '70s, while swimming gained a following with the founding of the Poseidon (1900) and Otter (1902) clubs. The infrastructure was impressive. In 1913, there were

Olympic Sports in the Early 20th Century

Sport
Cricket
Croquet
Discus with right arm and left arm, added
Standing triple jump
Team handball
Weight throwing
Golf
Motorboat racing
Polo
Javelin and shot put, right and left, added
Weightlifting
Tug of war

At the pool

already thirteen outdoor and five indoor pools, and the Sophienbad (Sophia Pool) on today's Otto-Schill-Strasse, opened in 1869. Forty years later, the first four-thousand-meter Pleisse swim took place, and the German championships were held in the Auensee in 1921. In Amsterdam in 1928, fourteen-year-old Hertha Wunder was the first female Olympic athlete from Leipzig.

Not all sports were successful, however. Roller-skating was enjoyed for fun, and it was also supposedly a good remedy for anemia, heart palpitations, and nervous disorders. People could stave off such infirmities at the skating rink near the zoo, beginning in 1876. By the 1880s, though, the curative pastime was no longer in fashion. People were thinking more and more about personal fitness, and gyms started offering gymnastics, yoga, or bodybuilding, with rubber resistance bands, expanders, or fitness devices of original invention. Solar sweatboxes were also introduced, along with dietary methods that had been completely uncommon until then. In 1892, the German Vegetarian Association was founded in Leipzig. A short while later, Swedish (nude) bathing was introduced, which was especially popular around Berlin and along the north and Baltic Sea coasts. As sports were enjoyed more broadly, fashions changed, becoming lighter and more practical. But although eighteenth-century books such as *Über die Schädlichkeit der Schnürbrüste* (*On the Harmfulness of Corsets*) were already arguing against the use of corsets and stays, women were not liberated from them until the end of the nineteenth century.

At the same time—though there is probably no connection whatsoever—the Lindenau Cement was considered one of the best cycling facilities around. Leipzig's purse of three thousand gold marks was the best-known in the world. In 1901, the first world record for distance biked in an hour was set on a German track, with a ride of just over forty miles. Audience numbers might also have broken records. In 1903, 27,000 cycling fans attended the European championship, which took place in Leipzig in 1908 and 1913. The indoor world championships for professionals were also held in Leipzig in 1913, and many other cycling highlights followed, including the six-day race in the Achilleion (Soviet Pavilion) at the technology fair, where Max Schmeling also boxed in 1928. Just a few days after the last world championship in 1938, however, bulldozers rolled into Lindenau and cleared the area for the Gutenberg Book Show, which never actually took place. Besides the cycling track, twelve other sports fields and the Palm Gardens were destroyed.

The Mother of All Trade Fairs

In spring 1897, Hans Bötticher, who had just turned thirteen, fell in love with extreme intensity and frequency. The schoolboy from the King Albert Preparatory School lost his heart to twenty-three Samoan women on display between the beasts of prey and the sea lions at the nearby zoo. Unimaginable today, such so-called "ethnological exhibits" were popular then, in Europe and America alike. Unable to buy his beloveds gifts, he secretly diverted decorations from the family Christmas tree, and "soon all 23 islanders wore glass ornaments, little Santa Clauses, chocolate hearts, sugar figures, wax angels, and chains in their hair," he recalled. One day after visiting them, he arrived to class over an hour late, and his teacher was outraged. When the seventh-grader was asked where he had been, he answered proudly, "I was getting a tattoo!" It was all over then. He was expelled from school, later went to sea, and finally gained acclaim as a writer—under the name Joachim Ringelnatz.

The Samoan women, meanwhile, were shipped off to another German city, and the next colonial subjects arrived in Leipzig. These forty-seven East Africans were not put on display in the zoo's people pasture, however—they lived in an African village built just for them on April 24, in what is now known as the Clara-Zetkin-Park. Right next door was a copy of the main commercial street in Dar es Salaam, where a band marched around dressed in the sultan of Zanzibar's uniform. These were not the only attractions at the park, which contained more buildings than trees in 1897. The buildings

Sachsenbrücke (Saxon Bridge)
—always well attended. Photo 1897

were for the Saxon-Thuringian Industry and Trade Show.

The human exhibition was part of an effort to pull the Leipzig trade fair out of a severe tailspin that threatened its existence. The Samoan women were shown exactly four hundred years after the bestowal of trade-fair privileges, but that was merely a coincidence. The intent was not to glorify the past but to secure the fair's future. Despite its superior position and colossal rise, which even wars, plagues, and the elimination of privileges in 1833 could not stop, the trade fair's right to exist in a highly industrial age was suddenly being challenged. Initially, contingents of goods multiplied and the railroad facilitated accessibility, which supported the fair's development. Yet as early as 1870, it became evident that the age-old structures were no match for mass production. In addition, manufacturers and buyers no longer had to meet in a trade-fair city in order to exchange entire assortments of goods. Cheaper and simpler opportunities arose as sales could be made based on exhibited samples, and goods were no longer manually made but mass-produced. While sample stock had also been used within the old tradefair framework, the fair buildings were designed to store products, not to present them. The resulting dissatisfaction eventually led to a drastic decrease in trade-fair traffic. When the ceramic, dry goods, and toy unions announced that they were leaving Leipzig because of the condition of the buildings and would exhibit in Berlin instead, haste was in order. While Berlin's first fall fair in 1893 was not well attended, plans were already in the works for the first sample fair palace in the world.

That was not Prussia's first attempt at establishing a competing fair, of course. The Leipzigers had a considerable wealth of experience at their disposal, but the Berlin push was extremely dangerous. A fair commission and the Leipzig Tourism Office were established to tackle the problem. The Leipzig Chamber of Commerce also made exhibitors sign pledges stating that they would boycott the Berlin fair, which most of them did. Concurrently, the

The little African village was between the glass house and the large playground

decision was made to convert the municipal library on Gewandgässchen, to be used only for sample displays during the 1894 Michaelmas fair. Two years later, the building was expanded and designated a municipal store.

The Saxon-Thuringian Industry and Trade Show was supposed to inject some vigor into the fair's revival, and it truly did outshine all previous trade fairs in Leipzig's history. Neither trouble nor expense was spared. The show was not just an exhibition of Central German industry but of the trade fair itself. Preparations began with a drastic overhaul of the ninety-eight-acre grounds, and included the creation of the Sachsenbrücke (Saxon Bridge) and the two ponds that still exist today. These were followed by nine large exhibit halls; a freight depot, a power plant; administrative and logistical buildings; a post office; fire, police, and first-aid posts; and some notable smaller structures. The Wurstpavillon (Sausage Pavilion) of the Nietzschmann and Wommer Companies, designed by Paul Möbius, caused quite a sensation and was described by the Munich journal *Jugend* (*Youth*) as, "a strong departure from convention, with bold, whimsically fanciful motifs that give it a certain kick." And so the Leipzig sausage stand became an Art Nouveau pioneer.

At about the same time, the "sample fair" was established—as opposed to a trade fair, where goods are actually bought and not just sampled—and with it came a change in schedule: The fair was no longer tied to holidays movable within the calendar, such as Easter, but were held at a fixed date. First, the 1894 pre-fair for sample-stock commerce, attended by seven hundred exhibitors, was detached from the Easter feast. In 1895, when the first sample fair was established, also the Easter and Michaelis fairs were replaced with spring and fall fairs at a recurring date. The last New Year's trade fair was held in 1904.

Also, local small vendors and their pushcarts were disassociated from the trade-fair enterprise. Until then, they had been inextricably involved, but they were not able to participate in the new fair format. At first it was impossible to imagine the fair without the flair the huts gave it, but in 1906 a spatial division took place. On the Frankfurter Field (the arena area today), a separate section was established for showmen, jugglers, food vendors, and snack and beer stands. This concentration of the fair carnival, which had sufficient space available, promoted rapid growth of the small fair, which is still celebrated each spring and fall, just a few hundred yards to the west, on the Cottaweg.

The Sausage Pavillion designed by Paul Möbius became the first structure synonymous with Jugendstil (Avant Garde)

Inner-city trade-show buildings

Sample Fair Palaces

	Name	Built in	Address
1.	Municipal Market	1894	Neumarkt (New Market)
2.	Mey and Edlich	1895	Neumarkt
3.	Silberner Bär (Silver Bear)	1895	Neumarkt
4.	Reichshof (Imperial Courtyard)	1898	Reichsstrasse
5.	Grosser Reiter (Big Rider)	1900	Petersstrasse 44
6.	Moritz Mädler	1900	Petersstrasse
7.	Hansa Haus (Hanseatic House)	1906	Grimmaische Strasse
8.	Flora	1906	Petersstrasse 23
9.	Zeissighaus (Zeissig House)	1907	Neumarkt 18
10.	Riquet	1908	Reichsstrasse
11.	Handelshof (Commerce Courtyard)	1909	Grimmaische Strasse
12.	Speck's Hof (Courtyard)	1909	Reichsstrasse
13.	Lorenz	1910	Neumarkt 24
14.	Linoleum-Haus (Linoleum Courtyard)	1912	Neumarkt 7
15.	Jägerhof (Hunter's Courtyard)	1912	Hainstrasse
16.	Dresdner Hof (Dresden Courtyard)	1913	Neumarkt
17.	Gebrüder Freyberg (Freyberg Brothers)	1913	Petersstrasse 16
18.	Mädler Passage	1914	Grimmaische Strasse
19.	Zentralmessepalast (Central Trade Palace)	1914	Grimmaische Strasse
20.	Stentzlers Hof (Stentzler's Courtyard)	1916	Petersstrasse
21.	Drei Könige (Three Kings)	1916	Petersstrasse

In addition, Hôtel de Pologne, Ledig-Passage, *Königshaus* (Royal House), *Grönländer* (Greenlander), *Königliches Palais* (Royal Palace), National, *Reichskanzler* (Imperial Chancellor), historic ballroom in the Old Town Hall, Conference Center at the zoo, and the Grassi Museum

A section for bars and entertainment, where hot-air-balloon rides and other attractions were offered, was also part of the industrial exhibition. Statistics show that more than ten million glasses of beer and 786,000 wieners were consumed from April through October 1897. A total of 3,027 companies participated in the exhibition, which was attended by 2.3 million visitors, who could ride an electric tram around the area and take in the various attractions. Some of Leipzig's older buildings were replicated there life-size, including the Old City Hall and Auerbach's Courtyard. Visitors marveled at a miniature Thuringian village, complete with a mini Wartburg Castle, though no native Thuringians had to live there as part of the display. In the bicycle hall, meanwhile, people could learn to ride a bike, and of course there was also an art museum, theater, and historic exhibits. Visitors were amazed by an alpine diorama that happened to be located where the *große Warze* (big wart) looms today. About four yards high (feels like four thousand), this immensely important Leipzig sledding hill consists in part, like the *kleine Warze* (its smaller cousin), of exhibition buildings that were later torn down.

While these exhibition halls were designed to be used for just half a year, the trade-fair palaces in the city center were designed to last forever. The differences between them and their predecessors (the trade-fair compounds with courtyards) could hardly be greater. If the latter were miracles of spatial efficiency, built to house as many goods as possible, the new buildings were light, open, lavish, and usable in any kind of weather. Most important, the new structures were not meant to store mass quantities of goods but to showcase representations of products to masses of people. Modernity and comfort were in order.

Most of the buildings had electric lighting, central heating, telecommunications connections, and were designed with general security standards in mind. The fact that they had to be easy to evacuate and fireproof would be an unforeseen advantage during World War II. The large stairwells and elevator facilities were additional features. In fact, the reconstructed elevator in the municipal store is the oldest in Leipzig today. It began operating in 1901, after another expansion that involved the remaining vestiges of the block. At that time, there

Like all construction at the industrial arts show, Machine Hall was also torn down at the end of the exhibition

were another five privately funded trade-fair palaces in other locations in the city center. Most of them were added between 1908 and 1916, and were made with reinforced concrete, which allowed hanger-like floor plans. The ground floors were usually devoted to sales floors and food-service facilities, while exhibitors presented their wares above, in booths grouped around atriums. So that all the visitors could see all the products there were compulsory tours, and exhibitors in the same industry were housed together in one building whenever possible.

By 1916, more than twenty trade-fair palaces were built in the city center. World War I put an end to the construction boom and forced a transition to sample fairs in other European cities. France and Great Britain tried to establish trade shows in London (1915), Lyon, and Bordeaux (1916). Given the rush, there was no time to convert old fairgrounds, so trade fairs in other European cities moved to open fields. Because every other city followed this example (Frankfurt was the first German city, in 1916), Leipzig remained the only place where the fair center and city center were combined. In 1920, machines in the technology exhibition were moved to their own grounds, due to their large size.

Human zoos, meanwhile, continued to attract a large, wide-eyed audience all over Europe for quite some time. By 1931, there had been about forty of these exhibits at the Leipzig Zoo alone. People were put on display at larger events as well, like the World's Fair in Paris in 1889, which also served to promote colonial politics. The East Africa show in Leipzig in 1897, for example, received support from the Federal Foreign Office, which claimed that the public could gain an understanding of the people of the largest and most promising protectorate as well as the goods produced there. During the exhibitions, the native peoples among the palm and banana trees made jewelry, colorful mats, and weapons, demonstrated mock battles and ceremonial dances, or fished on a pond specifically built for the show, providing, to a certain extent, product placement. Today, the site is just a normal field, not far from the Glashaus (Glass House) and a large playground—and not a single trace of the area's past can be found in the entire park.

MÄDLER'S KAUFHAUS
REISE-AUSRÜSTUNGEN
MÄDLER'S PATENT-KOFFER
MORITZ MÄDLER
Gustav Krieg
Hoflieferant.
Gummi-Waren-Bazar.
Gustav Krieg
Hoflieferant.
C.E.KEYSER
C.E.KEYSER

Old and New

"Kalkstein forever."
—Hugo Licht

"Kalkstein forever, but English never."
—Arwed Rossbach

On October 7, 1905, at one o'clock in the afternoon, King Frederick Augustus II and his ministers arrived to celebrate the dedication of the New City Hall with Leipzig's elite and delegations from friendly cities. This jewel of a building that represented the new Leipzig like no other contained 578 rooms and many beautiful details, like metal snails on the doorknobs—reminiscent of the function of some of the municipal officials. The building was crowned with a 377-foot spire that towered over all of the other buildings in the city and every other German town hall tower—trumping Hamburg's previous record by a whole eight feet. It was not designed to be just a plain, old administrative building but to reflect the glamour and glory of the trade-fair city. Mayor Bruno Tröndlin was looking forward to moving in to his new workplace.

Tröndlin's birthplace, where he was born on May 26, 1835, was in Löhrs Square (called Tröndlinring today), and marked what was then the northwestern edge of Leipzig. Directly behind it stood various public gardens that extended to the banks of the Pleisse and Parthe rivers, dotted with fields and small groves of trees. Besides the Pfaffendorf Courtyard complex and the restorations in Rosental, such as the Schweizerhäuschen (Swiss Huts) and the Kalten Madame (Cold Madam), the next-closest buildings to come into view were over a mile away, in Gohlis. A lot of construction was taking place on the other side of the city, however. When gate tolls were abolished in 1824, there was no longer any disadvantage to living outside the city—and compared to the close quarters in the city center, there were even many advantages. And so two new city districts were added in the east, Friedrichsstadt (the area around Friedrichstrasse), and Marienvorstadt (the area around Marienstrasse), which grew steadily. By 1849, the population in the city had reached sixty-three thousand—twice as high as in 1814.

In 1849, Otto Koch became mayor in Leipzig. He and his two successors, Otto Georgi (1876–1899) and Bruno Tröndlin (1899–1908), led the city for nearly sixty years, as it transformed from a small city to a metropolis with half a million inhabitants. Yet even though Leipzig's growth was brisk, the rise in population mirrored practically every other large city in central Europe at the time. On the one hand, there were sanitation systems; water, gas, and power supplied; and a build-up of medical facilities to make life more survivable and livable, and increase life expectancy. On the other hand, there were countless new job opportunities attracting an army of immigrants.

When Tröndlin entered the mayor's office, he was in the minority as a native Leipziger. Not many had grown up in the city, which had in turn grown up with Tröndlin, as it flourished and reached unprecedented new heights of development. At the same time, however, the new era threatened to roll right over the old Leipzig. And even Tröndlin's influence and ability to protect the city's past from the dynamics of the present was limited, as the fight for the Old City Hall demonstrated. The city council was to decide the building's fate in March 1905. While one faction advocated for keeping the building for use as a museum, another faction supported demolishing the Renaissance jewel, as well as the Old Mercantile Exchange and Naschmarkt, and to put up another sample-fair palace in their place. The vote was 31 to 31. So council superintendant Dr. Junck cast the deciding vote, aligned with Tröndlin's, to keep the building. That was the second time the building was saved from demolition. The first time, twenty-five years earlier, when the New City Hall was to be built in the same location, financial issues helped save it. The new building was simply too expensive for the council.

— The Mädlerhaus (Mädler Building) opened on Petersstrasse in 1900 broke with old building traditions

Countless other buildings, however, were sacrificed, and to a much greater extent than in other cities. At the end of the Imperial Era, Leipzig was an utterly modern European metropolis, but in terms of cultural history, its building stock was relatively insignificant. Though the reasons for this were varied, they were based on a generally new orientation of city centers. After the cities' defensive role changed, the concentration of various functions seemed woefully out of date. In addition, buildings that were once indispensible, such as granaries, mills, or royal stables, lost their purpose in the modern world. And then Leipzig's city center was particularly densely populated, so the newly emerging suburbs were much better suited for living. In 1890, more than twenty thousand people lived in 4,400 apartments in the city center. Twenty years later, only 1,735 apartments remained—just about 40 percent. The central location attracted the retail industry, as well as banks, and the demand for commercial buildings in the city of Leipzig was much higher than elsewhere.

After 1895, the transition to sample fairs, which required completely new structures, fueled the process considerably. In no other city in the world would trade fairs stay in the middle of the city center. The old buildings' standards were hardly compatible with the new era's demands. Light, modern, and open structures were required, not dim relics that had sprung up in crowded spaces. Even more buildings had to give way, because the venerable transportation infrastructure originally established for a city with merely ten thousand residents would no longer suffice. Streetcars, bicycles, and automobiles were suddenly added to the mix, and the number of pedestrians grew to an unprecedented number. Narrow alleys just fourteen to sixteen feet wide would inevitably have to be widened, as Schuhmacher, Thomas, and Magazin lanes were before 1914. But many measures were achieved only because the new demands were matched with the required capital, and this claimed many senseless victims. This meant that in 1914, only one third of all buildings in the city center were more than fifty years old, and along the ring, nearly all of the old buildings had disappeared. Tröndlin's birthplace was still standing, though it, too, would fall victim to traffic twenty-five years later.

Probably the most grievous loss was the demolition of the 350-year-old Pleissenburg Castle, which was the most original and the largest structure to disappear at that time. The city had gone back and forth for a long while but eventually chose the castle grounds for the new city hall and obtained the property from the state. In 1896, an architectural contest that would at least

Pleissenburg Castle served not only the Saxon military in the 19th century, but also the Academy of Arts, the Catholic community, and as an observatory for a time

retain the tower and integrate it in the new structure was announced. Long-time municipal master builder Hugo Licht won the competition with his design, "*Arx nova surgit*—a new castle emerges." The building intended to crown the city, and it would also be a crowning achievement in Licht's life's work. The fact that its design was based on a historic use of form was anything but unusual. All over Germany, buildings were designed with historicizing features almost exclusively during the second half of the nineteenth and early twentieth centuries. Neo-baroque and Neo-renaissance dominated, but Gothic and Romantic were also revered—and commanded great respect. It seems paradoxical that during that period of creative recollection, the real Renaissance and Baroque buildings were being sacrificed by the dozen. Ironically, it is because of this redesign craze that the center of Leipzig still has relatively many old buildings today. Reinforced steel constructions were a lot hardier than half-timbered buildings, so cities that managed to retain their historic architectural legacy were much more severely damaged during World War II than Leipzig.

Yet the various architectural approaches that characterized the period before World War I are barely perceived today. Similar to the visual arts, in which Expressionism, Cubism, Surrealism, and many other styles were blazing trails, new forms of architectural expression joined the Historicism that had prevailed until then. Art Nouveau was another style, though the term is often used to describe all relatively old-looking buildings. While some old, mostly Baroque elements found their way in there as well, completely new, much snappier lines characterized the facades and roofscapes. Because many building owners considered that approach too bold, Art Nouveau remained more of an exception than a rule, even in Leipzig.

In Paul Möbius, however, it found a leading proponent in Leipzig. In contrast, adherents of reformation architecture emerging after 1900 advocated for clear structures and turned away from the floridity of Historicism. That culminated in Eclectism, which included the combination of attributes from various epochs. The best example of this is the New City Hall, which is primarily based on Renaissance forms but exhibits Classic, Gothic, and Baroque elements, particularly in its architectural decoration. Even though the building met with wide approval—the German architectural gazette, for example, described it as "one of the rare works of current German architecture"—the younger, wilder ones in the industry did not see it that way.

Tröndlin, meanwhile, who also worked valiantly to save the Old City Hall, called his move into the New City Hall as the highpoint of his life. In his celebratory speech, he said, "That sad, apoetical time in which people thought they had done enough, when a building of useful sobriety was enough, is long overcome, thank god. Art that seemed forgotten is honored once more and its exhilarating breath infuses everything, even buildings that serve practi-

"A new castle arises," announced the City Hall design by Hugo Licht

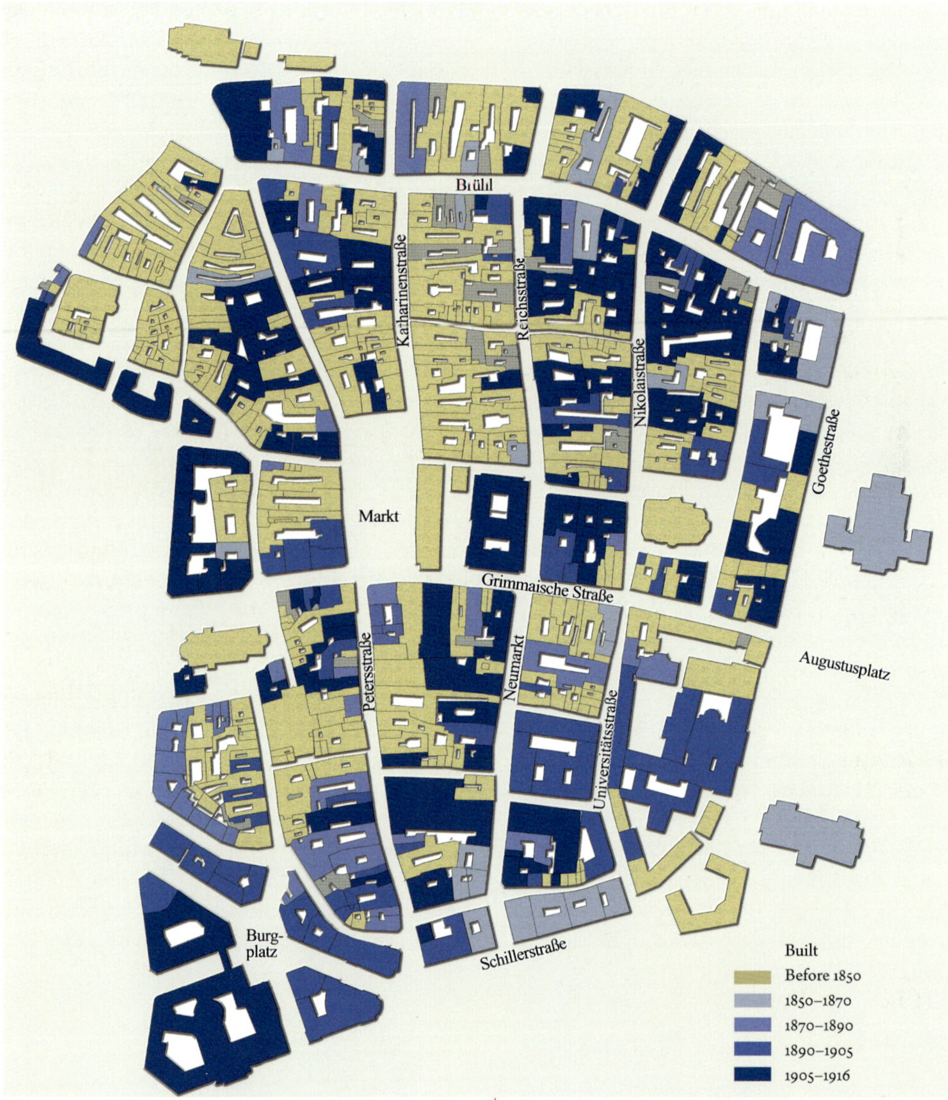

cal purposes." It was in this spirit that the decision was made two years later to start asking architects to design even public toilets. This was just one small example of the demands on the city administration, and the financial means the community had at its disposal to realize them. There was no law providing for art in construction back then because construction itself was considered an art form (today, 5 percent of the cost of public buildings is set aside for art).

Time of origin of the inner city buildings up to 1616

World-renowned University

It seems fitting that the Alma Mater Lipsiensis was in conflict again with its mother university in Prague, which had been split into two institutions, on the occasion of Leipzig University's five hundredth anniversary. This time it did not lead to another exodus of the student body, but German and Czech students did clash, culminating in street riots in 1908–09, when a state of emergency was declared. Preparations for the anniversary celebration at the daughter institution in Leipzig were hectic but much less violent. So that the day of honor would not have to be celebrated in frigid December air, it was decided to put off the festivities until the summer interim in sunny July, though it was not entirely historically accurate. The state and sponsors put up 200,000 marks (about $250 million today), but that was not nearly enough to do justice to the occasion, according to those in charge.

During the University's five-hundred-year history, 160,000 students had attended, including big names such as Leibniz, Lessing, Goethe, Wagner, and Nietzsche. Top-notch instructors included Heinrich Stromer, Christian Thomasius, Johann Christoph Gottsched, Christian Fürchtegott Gellert, and Samuel Hahnemann. Despite their vast intel-

Lobby at the university, c. 1900

lectual capacities, however, none of the luminaries mentioned took part in the celebration, due to, one can say, insufficient liveliness. Instead, the current generation of geniuses was on hand. It was by no means a matter of course, though, that Leipzig University offered them a home. Back in the nineteenth century, the institution experienced a difficult structural crisis. Building deficiencies, debt, and outdated curricula set the tone, and very few nationally known experts were teaching in Leipzig at the time. The main reason for the situation was the institution's nearly feudal statutes, which had hardly changed since the university was founded.

Long disputes raged over how to reinvigorate the educational fossil. Finally, in 1830, university reforms were introduced that launched the Alma Mater Lipsiensis into the modern age. Not only was the principle of nations abolished then, to which Leipzig was the last European university still clinging, expenditures for scientific endeavors increased tenfold within a short period of time. Besides transforming into an applied university, the institution was now under the direct supervision of the Saxon state, which also massively increased its financial support. In addition, the prominence of the philosophical college increased, and it now oversaw nearly all of the new scientific subfields. These changes quickly paid off, although other (German) states were giving more attention to the sciences as well.

A Selection of Leipzig Nobel Laureates

Year	Name	Nobel Prize
1902	Theodor Mommsen (antiquity scholar)	Nobel Prize for Literature (first German)
1909	Wilhelm Ostwald	Nobel Prize for Chemistry
1925	Gustav Hertz (with James Franck)	Nobel Prize for Physics
1930	Nathan Söderblom (religious historian)	Nobel Peace Prize
1932	Werner Heisenberg	Nobel Prize for Physics
1936	Peter Debye	Nobel Prize for Chemistry
1970	Sir Bernard Katz (1911–2003)	Nobel Prize for Medicine (with Ulf von Euler-Chelpin and Julius Axelrod)

In 1909, there were only 66,000 university students in all of Germany (0.1 percent of the total population, whereas today it is 3 percent). One quarter of those were enrolled at one of eleven technical colleges or at a mining or forestry college, and the rest were at the twenty-one classical universities. The institutions in Berlin (c. 8,700 students), Munich (c. 5,500), and Leipzig (c. 4,600), were considered to be the top dogs, where there were especially a lot of foreign students as well. At times, foreign students constituted 15 percent of the student body in Leipzig, with Russians, Rumanians, Bulgarians, and Americans particularly drawn to the university on the Pleisse. The number of women was only 2 percent, though they had not been able to enroll as students until a few years prior. While women had been allowed to study at universities in Sweden and France as early as the 1860s, and ten years later in Great Britain, they were not allowed to do so in Germany until the twentieth century, and not until 1906 in Saxony—which was still two years earlier than in Prussia. The battle over that subject had been long and intense. Leipzig psychiatrist Paul Julius Möbius held an opinion on the subject that was extreme even then. He wrote in *Über den physiologischen Schwachsinn des Weibes* (*On the Psychological Weakness of Women*), published in 1900, "As animals have always done the same thing throughout all time, the human race would also have remained in the same primitive state if there had been only women. All progress is man's doing." Eight editions of the book were released within quick succession.

During the anniversary celebration, female students played no role at all, despite hard-won rights. Saxon King Frederick Augustus III played a much larger role. Yet he was not the only guest of honor on July 30, 1909. Twenty German and eighty-seven foreign universities sent representatives to Leipzig, along with twenty-seven academies, scientific societies, and technical colleges—a grand array with which a host of additional guests of honor and former students mixed. Representatives of the archenemy SPD (Socialist Party of Germany), however, were not invited. One highlight of the festivities was a 2,500-man parade, which the masses cheered on from the sidewalks. The current student body presented fourteen different themes from the university's history and dedicated one to Goethe, of course, though his attitude toward his studies was notoriously not the least bit exemplary. Prior to that, Wil-

helm Wundt gave an hour-long celebratory speech in the lobby of the Augusteum.

Wundt was called to Leipzig in 1875, and retired after teaching for forty years. He was particularly renowned for establishing a chair in psychology in 1879, the first of its kind in the world. Scholars in psychiatry were similarly outspoken, with the subject first taught in Leipzig in 1822, another first in the world. Of particular note were Paul Flechsig, Wilhelm His, Wilhelm Erb, Julius Cohnheim, and Adolf von Strümpell. The men liked to debate at social gatherings in the Baarmann on the market square, at *Nervenkränzchen* (neural parties), which did not diminish Leipzig's reputation as a center of neurology and brain research in the least. The city was also renowned in the field of chemistry at the time, particularly because of Wilhelm Ostwald's huge contributions, for which he'd just won the Nobel Prize in 1909. The Physiological Institute, established in 1869 by Carl Friedrich Ludwig, also served as an international role model. It should be mentioned that the first chair of medical history in the world was created in Leipzig in 1905 as well. Additionally, the city was the first German home to a weather station, built in 1878, and an observatory and a seismological station in the Medical-Science District.

Because the university's space needs could no longer be met in the city center, the institution branched out into southeastern Leipzig in the mid-nineteenth century, where many other new institutions were established. In the late-nineteenth century, the central region also underwent a general overhaul. That would not have been possible without adequate funding, so the university budget increased from 720,000 marks in 1872 to 3.05 million marks in 1906 (about $39.9 million today; the university budget was $127 million in 2012, but with six times as many students). The thriving economy required skilled labor, and the state needed officials, so the future elite was drawn more heavily from the existing aspiring academic elite than it had been in the past. In 1909, only six out of the eleven hundred freshmen came from working-class families. Instead, children of the petit-bourgeoisie (white-collar employees, officials, or teachers) were predominant on campus.

In conformance with the existing elite, the students were far less liberal than in the first half of

The Augusteum in Augustus Square, c. 1900

the nineteenth century. College student sentiment was characterized by Nationalism, which had an effect on the sixty-three student fraternities in the city. Because Leipzig University functioned as an applied university, the number of students who were members of such organizations—about one third at that time—was smaller than it was in other places. The fraternities included singing and gymnastics associations and orders that emerged during the Enlightenment, similar to the Freemasons.

The fraternities were dominated by those that had emerged in the wake of the battles for independence against Napoleon, however. They represented national and Christian positions, which they clearly expressed. They also were defendants of German Imperialism, which considered Social Democracy and Judaism to be enemies of the fatherland. These fraternities, meanwhile, had merged with the much older territorial associations or corps, which had more regional connections. This was evident in their names: Saxons, Thuringians, Franconians. Leipzig's largest fraternities were the North Albingians, Arminians, and Germanians.

The leitmotifs of instruction, meanwhile, were further influenced by Ancient Greece. It was no coincidence that Max Klinger's mural on the theme of *"Die Blüte Griechenlands"* ("Greece at Its Prime"), was unveiled in the Augusteum just in time for the anniversary celebration in 1909. Ancient ideals such as improving the intellect and mind and promoting history characterized not only science but other social realms—architecture, for example, which promoted new humanistic concepts in Historicism. The fact that things were not all that humane in reality was evidenced by the twenty-seven hundred detainees in student prisons between 1870 and 1909, sent there primarily for dueling, brawling, and drinking sprees.

At the anniversary celebration, however, the positive aspects of university history were the main focus. The festivities took place in a temporary party venue on the trade fairgrounds, which could hold ten thousand guests. The New Theater and Church of St. Paul, which hosted a worship service attended by two thousand people, were also involved. And there were gifts, of course. Thirty-six patrons donated 405,000 marks for endowments or scholarships. Fritz Baedecker, recent recipient of an honorary degree, gave 50,000 marks alone. The university also became an international university largely because of physics professor Emil Warburg, who taught in Berlin. His university would also celebrate a significant anniversary the following year, though Berlin's was only the one hundredth.

Higher, Faster, Farther

"I believe in horses; the automobile is just a temporary phenomenon."
—Kaiser Wilhelm II

When the year 1909 began, winter had a lock on Leipzig, and nearly a foot of snow covered the municipal area. Adventuresome tobogganists besieged Wart Hill and the Gohlis Scherbelberg, and ice-skaters lived it up on the pond in Johannapark and the Rödel River. But the eight hundred workers responsible for keeping the roads clear were swearing under their breath. In early February, a sudden change in the weather came to their aid, bringing mild temperatures and plenty of rain. The glorious white stuff melted in record time, and the river levels rose quickly. Yet, unlike in the past, when primitive engineering methods were insufficient in combating the seasonal forces, nature was largely stripped of its potential to wreak havoc.

For the last fifteen years or so, there was a good deal of tinkering around going on by the Parthe, Pleisse, Elster, and their countless tributaries. There was still flooding, as in 1899, but the annual misery of flooding that had plagued the interior delta was a thing of the past. The water, meanwhile, flowed between numerous dams through Leipzig's western region. The elevation there had been increased by about five feet, which is still visible on the small slopes leading into the parks. River branches were straightened or capped, swamps drained, and ponds filled in to prevent flooding and reduce the mosquito population, which was the source of malaria, cholera, and other ills. Other means were employed to battle the insects, including Saprol and petroleum, for example. But when it was discovered that these methods had a fatal effect on fish as well, biological weapons in the form of mallards and frogs were applied instead. City administrators soon discovered, however, that the frogs were often subject to theft.

100-year flood in 1909. The Frankfurt Fields served as a flood area, where the Sport Forum is located today

An even healthier effect resulted from the expansion of a stronger medical infrastructure. In 1872, the new St. John's Hospital, with 380 beds, was dedicated, and a year earlier, the first buildings of the university clinic were opened on Liebigstrasse (still known as St. Jacob Hospital then). This was a completely new kind of facility in Europe, with 340 beds at the outset and a nearly threefold expansion capacity. The new St. George Hospital was still under construction but would eventually have space for one thousand patients. Starvation and malnutrition, meanwhile, were also mostly a thing of the past. According to the *Statistical Yearbook* for 1910, the average person consumed about 150 pounds of meat per year, which is higher than today, and milk consumption was almost 23 gallons. Lasagna, sushi, and pizza were eaten much less frequently than today. New scientific discoveries led to a measurable increase in life expectancy, which had risen by thirteen years since 1871. The life expectancy for men was forty-seven years, and fifty-two years for women. While that might seem relatively low, infant mortality was higher then, about 20 percent. Those who survived early childhood usually reached an age of about sixty years. Because the official retirement age was seventy, the number of retirees was pretty low, especially compared with the under-eighteen group, which amounted to nearly one third of Leipzig's total population.

Leipzig's ancient rivers were not affected by any of that. In February 1909, the water level had a mind of its own and set a few records. First the Parthe and Rietzsche rose to unprecedented heights, though damage was minimal. But when the Pleisse and Elster brought the spring thaw down from the Ore Mountains during the night of February 6, where the snow had been up to five feet deep, the water surged into the northern area of the city, which was soon noticed downstream. The Frankfurt Fields were completely underwater. Not long after, the dams broke on the Rödel and Elster rivers, flooding Schleussig like a bathtub, which lay between them. The water in the streets was over three feet high in some places.

In light of the advances of that time, it hardly seemed possible to be surprised by something as banal as a flood. The world—which meant Europe and America back then—had entered the modern age. While there were still one thousand horses registered in the Leipzig area in 1909 (71 in the city center), bicycles had surpassed them in number during the previous fifteen years, and motor vehicles had started joining them. There were 41 trucks and 701 personal vehicles in Leipzig in 1909, including 34 hackneys, or taxis. Because the tires and chassis could not handle full car bodies yet, only convertibles were made. Dust from the untarred streets spoiled the fun of driving, however, so drivers always wore protective glasses and special clothing, and stored their vehicles in coach houses in winter. Seat belts, turn signals, and actual driving exams were as uncommon as traffic lights or street signs. As a result, the

A driver and his wife in traffic

number of traffic fatalities in relation to the number of vehicles existing at the time was more than fifty times higher than it is today. And that was with a speed limit of under ten miles per hour in town.

Trams, meanwhile, went a little faster. Begun as horse-drawn trams in 1872, all lines of the Great Leipzig Streetcar-System (the Blue system), converted to electric operation in 1896—within eighteen months. At the same time, the Leipzig Electric Streetcar-System (the Red system) also began operating, followed by a third, the Outer Web (the Green system). Because the different operators only rarely used the same sections of track, the tracks passed through even the narrowest streets, and by 1909 the total network had grown to over 123 miles of track. The billing increment for heavily traveled lines was three to five minutes, and fares ran ten pennies (about $1.50) per day. The myriad new modes of locomotion would expand to include air traffic, with the dedication of the Lindenthal airship station in 1911 and the Mockau Airport in 1913.

Like locomotion, lodging gained fresh impetus. Nearly one quarter of all apartments had bathrooms and toilets by then. In the buildings that still had cesspools, the toilets were usually outside the apartments and halfway down the stairs, due to the odor. Only one out of every twelve Leipzigers still used an outhouse. After the first two power plants were built on Magazingässchen and Eutritzscher Street in 1895, soon followed by others, electrification progressed. Though only 1,700 primarily public buildings were connected to the power grid in 1909, the number grew to 7,500 by 1914. Because the cost of a kilowatt-hour of electricity initially exceeded a craftsman's hourly wage, it was used primarily for light at first, but electric irons and sewing machines were also in use by then.

Of much greater significance was the introduction of the elevator, which also turned the building world upside-down. Until then, the financial elite lived predominantly on the first floor, or the *belle étage*, and left stair-climbing to the poorer folk, despite the better views. The elevator made that unnecessary, and so the areas where servants or simple workers had been living began to be marketed as penthouse apartments. The *belle étage* lost its appeal. In bourgeois districts, those penthouse apartments usually took up the entire first floor and consisted of eight rooms or more, and at least 3,200 square feet. In better neighborhoods, the floors above were divided into two apartments; or into three in working-class areas. In the Music District, often called "Protzendorf," there were four-story residential buildings with just one apartment on every floor. These could be 4,800 square feet and have ceilings over 13 feet high. And those

The new era was also expressed in poetic form, as it was here by Robert Zimmermann (not Bob Dylan)

Ausgunfd

Uffn Fußsteig loofd ä Frauchen ganz verängsdidgd hin un her
mechde niewer iewern Fahrdamm,
doch zu doll is dr Vergehr.
Ganz besonders die Geleise von der schdädt'schen
Schdraßenbahn
blinzeld se mid scheien Oochen
aus dr Ferne ängsdlich an.
Schließlich faßd se sich ä Herze
un gehd uff ä Schudzmann los:
»Sie entschuld'chen, liewer Härre, eene eenzche Frahche bloß:
Wenn ich nu hier niewer mache un ich drede aus Versähn
mid'm Beene uff die Gleise,
gann mir da nich was geschehn?«
»I bewahre!« sahchd dr Schudzmann,
»da kann Ihnen nischd bassiern,
wenn Se mid'n andern Beene de Oberleidung nich beriehrn!«

Inquiry

A frightened woman on a sidewalk paces,
Afraid to cross, too much traffic races.
Especially the tracks of the local streetcars
She eyes warily from afar,
Mustering courage, she hails the police,
"Excuse me, sir, a question please,
If while crossing I accidentally
step on a track, will something happen
to me?"
"Why, no!" his reply, "No harm will
come to you,
unless your other foot touches the
overhead wire!"

dimensions were easily exceeded in villas in Gohlis, Leutzsch, and the four outlying districts. The western and northern districts were the most expensive areas in Leipzig, where a room cost an average of 190 marks per month. In Kleinzschocher, prices were in the double digits, though the trend moved upward quickly. Rents had risen 50 percent during the previous twenty years. Leipzig's real estate market offered an above-average number of upscale apartment buildings, as evidenced by the large number of large apartments. The 138,200 apartments available in 1910 were divided into:

1-Room	1,680	1.22 %
2-Room	2451	1.78 %
3-Room	22,367	16.21 %
4-Room	55,224	40.02 %
5-Room	28,376	20.56 %
6-Room	13,071	9.47 %
7-Room	6,277	4.55 %
8-Room	3515	2.55 %
9-Room	1,915	1.39 %
10+-Room	3,317	2.40 %

Source: *Statistical Yearbook of the City of Leipzig*, 1910

An average apartment had 4.67 rooms, of which only half were heated. In 1910, 4.26 people lived in every household; in 2012, while the average was only 1.7. The number of children per family was higher back then, and there were also fifteen thousand household servants living with their employers, and another five thousand lived outside the homes they served. Working-class families often took in strangers. Besides thirty-five thousand boarders, there were twenty two thousand bed lodgers who rented beds by the hour. Such arrangements emerged in response to a shortage of residential space. While about three thousand new apartments were built each year, five hundred old ones were torn down, which was only enough to keep the vacancy rate at 1 to 3 percent.

Analogous to the growing population, the economy also grew vigorously. It was not until 1908 that it experienced an unusually intense downturn. The unemployment rate ranged from 1 to 2 percent for decades, and it did not increase because workers had their hours reduced instead of losing their jobs. Except for Sundays, people usually worked 9.5 hours per day. Because of the economic crisis, however, working hours decreased to six, and the labor force struggled with lost wages. National unemployment benefits did not exist yet, though unions supported those affected.

Meanwhile, the city administration tried to help the flood victims. On February 6, the day of the flood, gangways were placed in Schleussig. The civil engineering department sent boats manned by fishermen and lock operators to Oeser- and Schnorrstrasse to rescue people and large valuables. Rödelstrasse was hit especially hard, and two buildings in danger of collapsing were reinforced, though later they would have to be torn down anyway. Installation of a real flood-control system would be very expensive, but planning for it progressed briskly. The Elster Basin, however, would not be completed until 1925.

Development of the Infrastructure

1837	City center equipped with gaslights
1839	First long-distance train line, Leipzig–Dresden
1850	Underground telegraph line completed, Leipzig–Dresden
1856	Connewitzer Waterworks launched, first drinking water supplied to taps
1860	Construction begun on sanitation system still in use today
1871	St. George Municipal hospital opened
1894	Saxony's first wastewater treatment plant opened in Rosental
1895	Electric streetlights introduced
1896	First electrified streetcar in Leipzig
1911	Second oldest German airport opened in Lindenthal

The *Scherbelberg* (hill made of trash) in Rosental was opened in 1896. Probably the city's most brilliant attempt to reach new heights

Amusements

"You dance—you dance—until the last moment!"
—"Die oberen Zehntausend" (High Society), an 1909 operetta by Gustave Adolph Kerker and Julius Freund

The festivities surrounding the dedication of the Monument to the Battle of Nations were over, and the circus had left town. Even a real circus, Barum's Circus, packed everything up after the evening show on October 19, 1913. They were to leave that night, so the beasts of prey were tucked away in two wagons to be taken to the Berlin freight yard. On the way there, the driver grew extremely thirsty, and fortunately the Graupeter (Gray Peter) on Berlin Street still had its lights on, and alcohol when behind the wheel or a horse was not yet detectable. So they moved their after-work beer up a little and went inside. Bears and lions were not permitted.

In 1913, the Graupeter was a Leipzig tavern, which had been registered in 1398. There were an additional 206 pubs for non-alcoholic beverages. Auerbachs Keller (Auerbach's Cellar) was not one of them but it was closed for renovation. Initially the new owner, trunk manufacturer Anton Mädler, wanted to tear down Goethe's apartment and Auerbachs Hof (Auerbach's Courtyard), but protests at home and abroad convinced him to preserve the cellar. It would reopen in 1914, larger and even more traditional, of course. The Thüringer Hof (Thuringian Courtyard) was also famous and

Albert Hall, one of many attractions in the Crystal Palace

would be expanded in 1932. It contained seventeen dining halls, with two thousand seats that were always full during the trade fairs.

Besides the many other traditionally furnished venues, the modern era also found its way into the food service industry, in the form of vending machines, for example. "Stick a sausage in up there, and a mark comes out below," was a running joke about the devices that served up creature comforts, music, and entertainment. Other places, like the Nordpol (North Pole) or the Dschungel (Jungle), had an exotic allure or were popular sites for political gatherings. Alfred Brehm and August Bebel, among others, some of whom had criminal records, debated new social ideas at the criminal table in the Guten Quelle (Good Fountain) on the Brühl. The Taubenschlag (Dovecote) on Goldhahngässchen, however, was where the rightwing conservatives congregated. It was even more intense in 1916 at the Schützengraben (Trench) on the Brühl, where true patriots could take a stand surrounded by murals depicting various battle fronts.

This correlation was by no means new. The Panorama on Rossplatz was adorned with a diorama depicting the 1870 cavalry battle of Mars la Tour, entitled, *"Eine der größten Waffentaten unseres Heeres"* ("One of Our Army's Greatest Feats of Arms"). Now and then a soft whinny could be heard from the nearby Café Bauer, which had a 278-foot addition that housed a riding arena and horse stalls. Similarly noble yet even more famous was the Café Francais (French Café), renamed Café Felsche (Felsche's Café, after the name of the owner) after World War I broke out. Because that name also sounded too French, the establishment was soon renamed yet again—Kaffeehaus Felsche—definitely no French fries there. Other institutions settled in the red-light district on Preusser and Sporergässchen and especially south of the city center, which used the term "Café" in their names as well. The area around Seeburgstrasse was long called the Wild District. At one time, there were up to fourteen houses of ill repute—still called women's homes at the time—near Pleissengasse.

The Graupeter, however, was a little-known ale house, which was about to change with the carriage driver's arrival. The beasts of prey were sitting in the open, in view of the cart horses parked outside the pub, which were growing increasingly nervous and soon tried to flee. They did not get far, however, because they were attached to a rig, but they did manage to move the wagon with the lions onto the streetcar tracks. Because it was dark and foggy, the tram that soon came along was not able to stop in time and crashed into the lions, liberating the eight big cats from their cage. And there they stood on an October night in Leipzig. They did not remain alone for long. A policeman on patrol in the area soon arrived at the accident site and, confronted by the unusual situation, called for backup. Countless policemen and the circus director rushed to the scene, and the zoo was also notified.

They were well acquainted with lions at the zoo. A pair of lions had been part of the inventory since the zoo was established. A livestock yard was originally located on the zoo grounds, the last place for animals waiting to be slaughtered. A popular restaurant destination had also been located there, known as the Pfaffendorfer Hof (Pfaffendorf Courtyard), operated by Ernst Pinkert since 1873. He attracted customers with jugglers, tightrope walkers, balloon rides, and a "magnificent-giant-monster-fireworks show," in addition to a gardening exhibition.

Beginning in 1876, guests were amazed by exotic animals, which Carl Hagenbeck also offered for sale. In 1878, his marketing trick eventually became an institution on its own, although the zoo grounds were hardly bigger than the market square. A roller-skating rink, music pavilion, curiosities of all kinds, and sporting contests were also on the program, including many human exhibitions, where people were on display. Many old Leipzig institutions disappeared during that time, as most of the public gardens and outlying estates that had long served to distract people with beer, coffee and cake, music, and theater, gave way to the expanding city. The same was true of the Schimmelsche Ponds and their island of entertainment, Buen Retiro, once the top site for ice cream and ice skating. The Music District sprang up there. The Gose-beer houses had to contend not only with the triumph of pilsner but with establishments that served up a whole lot more than beer.

The halls, restaurants, salons, cafés, and beer gardens at the Crystal Palace on Wintergartenstrasse could seat up to fifteen thousand guests. The facility—the largest entertainment venue in Germany—included a mountain, a hang-gliding cliff with a viewing platform, trick fountains, a hall of

fame, and bowling alleys, among other things. The program was just as varied and included open-air and pre-lunch cocktail concerts, automobile exhibitions, conventions, theater productions, and massive parties attended by the emperor and the Saxon king. Since 1887, circus, variety, and sports shows had been thrilling up to thirty-five hundred spectators at a time in Albert Hall. Musical greats were also guests there, from the Don Cossacks to Josephine Baker, to the Gewandhaus Orchestra, which would establish its annual New Year's concerts in the hall in 1918. Its polar opposite in the west was the Palm Garden, opened in 1899, which, according to its advertisements, was "Leipzig's finest recreation area! Concerts by first-rate local and visiting music ensembles, first-class hospitality."

Its star, however, was botany. The Palm House alone encompassed nearly fourteen thousand square feet. The park required an admission fee and offered gondola rides, illuminated fountains, pony-carriage rides, and a rose garden. In 1939, all of the Palm Garden buildings would be demolished to make way for the Gutenberg Show that would not take place. Four years later, wartime bombing turned the entire Crystal Palace into ash and rubble. Many establishments fell on hard economic times in the 1920s or during the global economic crisis. That is why the Charlottenhof—the Palm Garden's small, Asian-inspired brother—Meusdorf Park, with its fruit wine bar and children's giant playground, and the Lunapark on the Auensee, complete with a mountain rollercoaster, hippodrome, and public beach, all closed.

The biggest sensation of 1913, however, were the lions on the loose in Leipzig's northern region. They did not run for long, though. After one of the big cats pounced on a passing horse pulling a carriage, the policemen opened fire. They killed five animals in quick succession, and caught another one a short while later. Meanwhile, Polly the Lion jumped through a window at the Blücher Hotel and bounded through the lobby and up the stairs to find the men's restroom. The French guest using it at the time gladly yielded the room to the lion, and Polly was locked inside. Only Abdul the Lion was left on the run, followed by hundreds of curious onlookers.

That was the kind of thing normally seen only in the cinema, in black and white and without sound. Film was a completely new genre but it had already earned a spot in the entertainment industry. At the turn of the century, the "biggest sensation of the modern age"—the "presentation of living giant photographs"—could be seen only at carnivals and annual fairs. As the quality improved, however, the first permanent movie houses were established in 1905, though most were simply darkened shops. So Leipzig's first cinema was actually a pub—the Eldorado, at 4 Pfaffendorfer Street, where a world cinematograph was permanently installed in 1906. That same year, the American Theater opened at the Königshaus, along with the Weiße Wand (White Wall) on Wintergartenstrasse, establishments that were much more like cinemas. Because movies were often just a few minutes long, early shows were

Charlottenhof (Charlotte Courtyard), once a site of swinging oars, now an athletic field

composed of many different productions shown one right after the other. Some of the movie hits of 1906 were, *Sich selbst besiegende Ringkämpfer* (*The Self-defeating Wrestlers*), *der Apachentanz* (*Dance of the Apaches*), and *Die Flucht und Verfolgung des Raubmörders Rudolf Hennig über die Dächer von Berlin*, (*The Flight and Pursuit of Robber and Murderer Rudolf Hennig Over the Rooftops of Berlin*), which was also the very first film banned by the government.

Because there were no subtitles yet, movie interpreters were used. A short while later, silent films started playing to musical accompaniment. Today's movie lengths were introduced by the industry in 1910. The new medium's quality and popularity increased, in part through films like *Atlantis*, the most expensive production of its time, and *Quo Vadis*. By 1913, there were sixty-seven cinemas in Leipzig, although a few closed soon thereafter. The largest movie theater was the Astoria Lichtspiele (Moving Pictures) on Windmühlenstrasse, with sixteen hundred seats and equipped with air-conditioning and various other extras, including a thirty-member orchestra. Around that same time, the first cabarets were opening in Leipzig, such as the Nachtfalter (Moth) on Hainstrasse, as well as other vaudevilles, dance halls, and dance cafés. Large new halls, like the Neuen Felsenkeller (New Cliff Cellar) or the convention center at the zoo, also served the booming entertainment industry.

The growing population was not the only thing driving increased demand. People now had more time and money for going out, as hours were declining and wages were rising. New trends fostered additional stimulus. While the emperor himself preferred marches to waltzes, polka, and Rhinelanders, which he thought were too modern, the young population was hungry for more. So wiggling and shuffling made their way onto the dance floor with unprecedented momentum—despite all legal measures to stop them. In 1913, the tango, in particular, caused near manic situations all across Europe. It was clearly a shuffle, or as playwright George Bernard Shaw called it, a "vertical expression of a horizontal desire." Dances like the maxixe (Brazilian tango) and the cakewalk, or even ragtime, a predecessor to jazz, also contained auspiciously fresh configurations.

Hits emerged from operettas and were met with enthusiasm, so a tenor superstar such as Enrico Caruso performed in Leipzig many times. Music was presented more and more on shellac, however. These new musical influences were deemed fashionable. Tango dresses and flat shufflers' caps defined fashion, as did the permanent, patented in 1906. Yet as intense and eclectic as the time was,

King of the jungle after the slaughter

it was soon abruptly interrupted. In that regard, the title song of a Berlin Revue sounds prophetic: "We're dancing on a powder-keg, and that's what, that's what, that's what's so much fun! You dance and when the fuse ignites, you dance, you dance until the last moment!" That moment came when war broke out and the general ban on dancing that came with it, without a doubt.

Abdul, the last lion running free on the northern outskirts of town, did not live to see that moment. Zoo and circus workers had almost managed to lure him into a trap, when an onlooker threw a rock toward the lion. As the startled Abdul leaped to the side, the constables on the scene opened fire. An autopsy later revealed that the animal was hit by over a hundred shots.

The Great War and What It Prevented

> *"Wars, one might say, are getting more and more benign."*
> —Umschau, *October 1914*

Caspar René Gregory, born in America, had lived in Leipzig for forty-one years and had long held Saxon citizenship. Holding multiple doctoral degrees, the professor of theology enjoyed a great deal of esteem, far beyond the German border. He had explored the vast Orient and mastered fifteen languages, some of them long forgotten, which were imperative standards for his research on the *codex sinaiticus*—the oldest known version of the New Testament. He was also described as a philanthropist, always helpful and kind, to scholars as well as simple laborers. No one expected the 68-year-old to volunteer to serve as a soldier in the First World War. Yet that is exactly what he did. The Army command was not exactly enthusiastic, however, especially because Gregory insisted on fighting on the front line. The generals were worried that the French might think the German Army was done in, if it was resorting to old men to do the fighting.

In fall 1914, victory was certain—all over Europe, but especially in the German Empire. Millions euphorically heeded the call to arms, and in the national frenzy an entire generation charged off to the slaughter. No one dreamed that the war would not end until four years later, and even fewer suspected that the glorious fatherland would be on the losing side. Development during the preceding decades seemed practically to preclude such a

Caspar René Gregory on his way to the front at age 68. Photo 1914

scenario. After the playful campaign against France in 1870–71, and the subsequent proclamation of a finally united empire in the Hall of Mirrors at Versailles, a dream that had been decades in the making was finally fulfilled. Forty-three years had passed since then, during which time the population of Germany increased from 41 to nearly 68 million, and the number of major cities rose from eight to over fifty.

The economy ascended just as quickly. Though the boom of the industrial *Gründerjahren* ended in 1873 with the founders' crash, when the stock

Population Rates by Comparison

Rank	City	Population, in 1000s	
		1910	2013
From 1 to 3	London	7,256	8,416
From 2 to 9	Paris	2,888	2,273 urban area 12 million
From 3 to 5	Berlin	2,071	3421
From 4 to 12	Vienna	2,031	1781
From 5 to 4	St. Petersburg	1,962	5,132
From 6 to 1	Moscow	1,533	11,971
From 7 to 68	Glasgow	1,000	596
From 8 to 13	Hamburg	931	1,746
From 9 to 2	Constantinople	910	8,872
From 10 to 14	Budapest	880	1,744
From 11 to 15	Warsaw	872	1,724
From 12 to 28	Birmingham	840	1,092
From 13 no longer in the Top 100 today	Liverpool	753	436
From 14 to 35	Naples	722	989
From 15 to 25	Brussels	720	1,138
From 16 to 92	Manchester	714	514
17 (remained)	Barcelona	710	1,611
From 18 to 6	Madrid	600	3,207
19 (remained)	Munich	596	1,407
From 20 to 81	Leipzig	590	531
From 21 to 20	Milan	579	1,339
From 22 to 41	Amsterdam	574	810
From 23 to 72	Copenhagen	559	572
From 24 to 39	Marseilles	551	850
From 25 to 83	Dresden	548	530
From 26 to 8	Rome	542	2,868
From 27 to 29	Cologne	517	1,034
From 28 to 60	Breslau	512	632
From 29 to 32	Odessa	506	1,017
From 30 to 7	Kiev	505	2,868

exchanges plummeted and sent the economy into years of stagnation, economic boom and rapid industrialization were the name of the game beginning in the 1880s. Around 1910, German industrial production surpassed even that of Great Britain and put Germany just behind the United States, which was surging ahead. Science represented a particularly effective bastion. Until 1914, one out of every three Nobel prizes was awarded to a German researcher. Saxony especially profited from all of these developments. This was manifested in population growth and the high level of industrialization, which no German state had achieved yet.

Leipzig took on a leading role in Saxony during this development, and in 1910, the year when Stötteritz, Möckern, and other communities were incorporated into Leipzig, the city surpassed even Dresden as the largest urban metropolis in Saxony for the first time in nearly three hundred years. Right before the war began, 625,000 people lived in Leipzig—exactly one hundred years earlier, there had been about 31,000 plus another 50,000 in the incorporated villages. Hardly any other city in Europe grew so quickly, placing Leipzig in the top twenty largest cities on the continent. Within Germany, only Berlin, Hamburg, and Munich were larger. Economically, Leipzig was at the zenith, thanks to the booming trade-fair business, the fur and book trades, and a variety of industries. Leipzig had 17 percent of all major German corporations headquartered there.

The city's urban building capacity was also enormous. In 1913 alone, 756 new buildings were completed. The projects under construction concurrently included the main railway station; the Monument to the Battle of Nations; the Mockau Airport; a municipal pool; the Russian Memorial Church; the Royal-Saxon Building School (HTWK); the Palm Garden dam; the new Saint George; five trade-show palaces, including the Mädlerpassage and the Central Fair Palace; half of Nikolaistrasse; the Runde Ecke (Round Corner); the Althoff (Karstadt), Ury, and new Held department stores; and the buildings for the International

Canons at the Victory Monument

Building Exhibition (Alte Messe, [Old Trade Fair]), including the model city section of Marienbrunn. That level of development was maintained during the early years of the war, as evidenced by the Haus der Handlungsgehilfen (House of Commercial Clerks, dedicated in 1917, now the LVB at the Karli) and the German Library (dedicated in 1916). But the pace decreased significantly as war raged on. An even more serious effect of the war was the shortages that soon set in, leading to the turnip famine in winter 1917, the likes of which the majority of the German population had never seen before. Tuberculosis and other illnesses also took more victims than usual. The main reason was the conversion of the economy to support more and more of the war effort, combined with the food embargo on the Atlantic. Women worked in the factories then, all over Europe, manufacturing the munitions eventually fired by their husbands.

Caspar René Gregory saw a lot of dead people. After fighting on the front line, he was given his own command in 1915, charged with rescuing and burying fallen soldiers. This was more in line with Gregory's motive for joining the war. Besides his sense of duty, his willingness to help played a role, as strange as this may have sounded. He said he could not sit in his professor's apartment while the simple laborers fought for the country in which he lived.

The terrible toll the First World War had on Leipzig is best demonstrated by the city's population. If the population had continued to grow at its pre-war rate—the city had been gaining about nine thousand people each year—it would have reached nearly 700,000 after the incorporation of Mockau and Schönefeld at the end of 1918, instead of 538,000. The economic decline and subsequent loss in tax income were similarly devastating and resulted in the delay or cancelation of many planned projects. One of those was the construc-

Population Growth in Leipzig Between 1800 and 1914

Year	Population	Year	Population
1800	32,146	1880	149,081
1815	33,773	1885	170,340
1830	40,946	1890	295,025
1840	51,712	1895	399,995
1852	66,724	1900	456,156
1861	78,495	1905	503,672
1871	106,925	1910	589,850
1875	127,387	1914	624,845

Catching a cab to the *"Völki"* (Völkerschlachtdenkmal) in 1913

tion of a tunnel connecting the main and Bayerische train stations, on which work stopped at the beginning of the war, after reaching a length of 2,300 feet. Work was to continue when funds were available again, which city administrators thought would be by Christmas 1914, at the latest. In reality, though, Leipzig would not have a financially strong national structure until Christmas 1990, and the project now called Citytunnel would not be dedicated until 2013—exactly one hundred years after construction began. Work on the Elster Basin was also interrupted, after beginning late anyway, in 1913.

At first there were endless discussions about whether the facility should be like Hamburg's, with an inner and outer Elster, or a flood basin wide enough to exceed that of the Elbe in Dresden by nine or ten feet, coincidentally or not. The latter option was the one eventually chosen, along with the idea of crowning the new banks with a magnificent new city center, with stores, fair buildings, and event venues. Construction should have begun in 1918, after comprehensive ground work was completed. But the war and economic crises saw to it that the basin was not finished until 1925. The city planners in the new era decided it made more sense to use the area for sports and recreation, however, but new crises postponed those plans for another thirty years.

Leipzig's connection to the oceans remains an eternal dream. The Leipzig and Merseburg Canal Company, founded in 1908, raised funds for the fifteen-mile Elster-Saale-Canal. Even the Prussians were on board, ready to provide half of the twelve million marks needed for construction. Yet despite great efforts, that project would remain only a dream in subsequent years.

Other major projects that were never completed included relocating the university on the edge of town, though a construction site in Probstheida had already been obtained, and the already planned expansion of the Graphic District. Developing the area south of town, especially the Street of October 18, was simply postponed—by about sixty years. Various squares, including Deutsche Platz (German Square), were supposed to open on the already existing street. The German library that was located there, along with three other residential buildings closer to the city center, remained the only buildings from that time, and partially

How the Elster Basin might have looked if World War I had started just a few years later indicate the intended exclusivity of that prestigious area. Because no plans made by either the Weimar Republic or the National Socialists were ever realized (thank goodness), the area was not architecturally formed until the 1970s. The brand-new buildings made from prefabricated slabs did convey exclusivity, but only in the context of that era.

Caspar René Gregory's time was up on April 9, 1917. The oldest volunteer in the German Empire was seventy years old by that time, but he was still in good physical condition. That did not stop the grenade that killed him, however. His last words were, "I'm slightly injured, having sustained a terrible blow to the abdomen." He was one of sixteen thousand Leipzigers who lost their lives at the front.

Albert Riemann
Porzellanfabrik
COBURG
Weisslackmöbel
Oswald Tannert
Wehrsdorf Sa.
Photohaus „Bezee"
Mädler-Passage
früher Auerbachs Hof
Mädler-Passage
früher Auerbachs Hof
DUX AG
FRANZ MERTL
GLADENBECK
Cigarren
Bezee

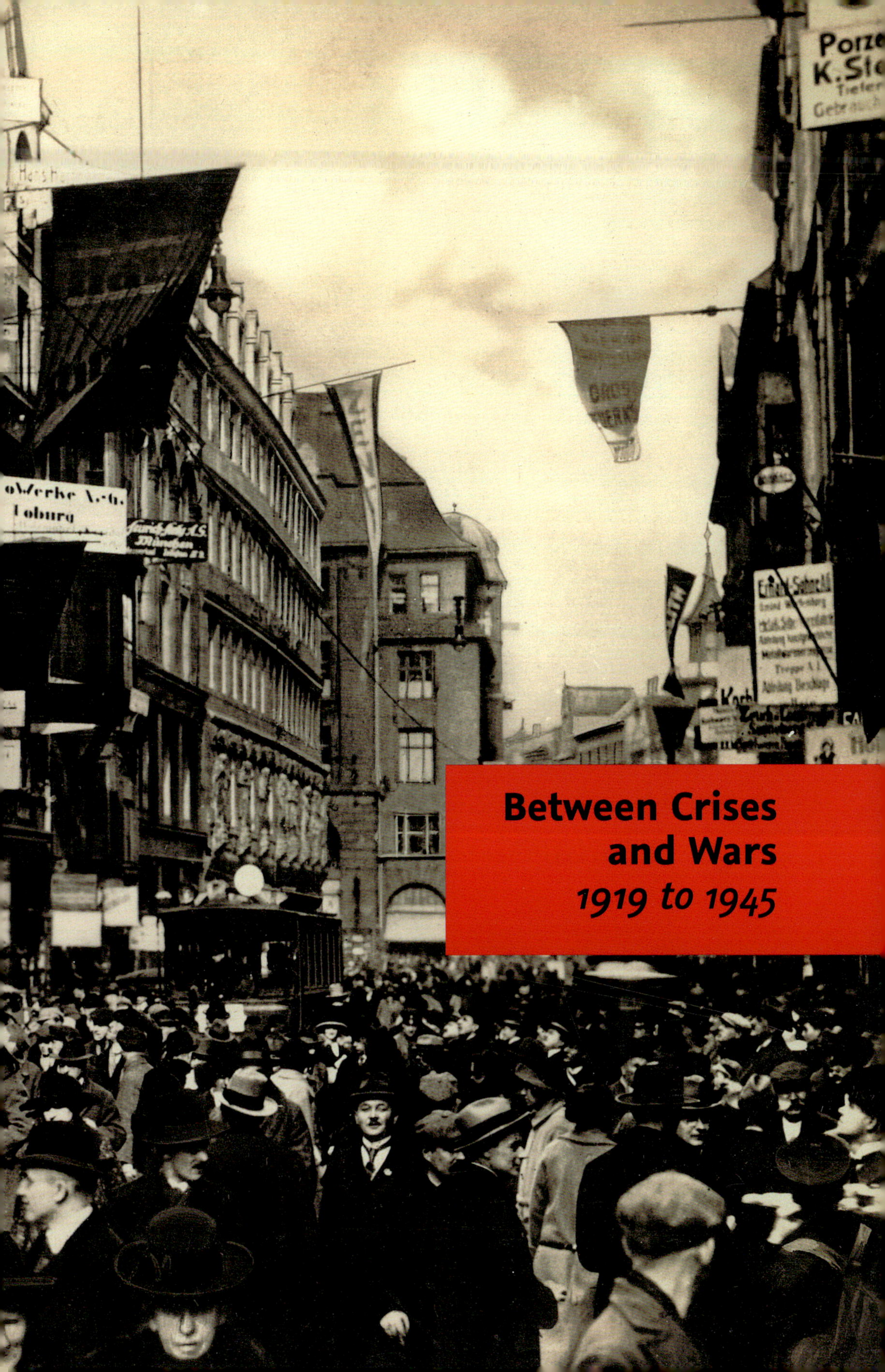

Between Crises and Wars
1919 to 1945

Crisis Years

"The bullet intended for me has already been cast."
—Matthias Erzberger

It just wasn't getting any better, Ludwig Ebermayer thought on November 10, 1923, as he sat with his afternoon coffee and a couple of newspapers at Café Felsche in Augustusplatz. That morning, an Austrian by the name of Adolf Hitler had attempted a putsch, or coup, in Munich, his Bavarian homeland, though the Mussolini-wannabe's march had ended a few hundred yards later. And just two weeks earlier, there had been an uprising in Hamburg led by Communist leader Ernst Thälmann, which Ebermayer was currently investigating. Since September 1918, Ebermayer had been president of the Second Criminal Division of the Reich's Supreme Court in Leipzig and frequently made appearances as the Weimar Republic's chief prosecutor. His first major appearance had been at the proceedings against WWI war criminals, the Leipzig Trials. Those had made him uncomfortable. "We should never have to submit to the dishonorable obligation of prosecuting our fellow countrymen for these alleged war crimes," he remarked later.

The Great War had ended five years earlier. Within four years, the war had claimed 17 million lives worldwide, and 2.2 to 2.8 million in Germany alone. An unfathomable, somber record. The Spanish Flu

In the 1920s, the trade show grew larger than the city could handle

Destroyed community center after the Kapp-Putsch in 1920

raged even more dramatically, spread primarily by soldiers marching all over the world. At least 25 and up to 50 million fell victim to that epidemic, with especially high numbers during the final weeks of war. The fact that it carried off inordinate numbers of young adults in good physical condition lent the illness an even more sinister character. Germany got off relatively mildly, losing about 250,000 citizens to the flu, including about 2,000 Leipzigers.

In that deadly age, the epidemic hardly seemed remarkable after it abated. Other topics dominated the scene, such as politics, especially. On November 9, 1918, Social Democrat Philipp Scheidemann proclaimed the Weimar Republic. For the first time, everyone over twenty-one years of age had the right to vote, including women. But the transition to democracy was anything but smooth. Communists, Socialists, bourgeoisie, monarchists, nationalists, militarists, and racists tried everything they could to dominate, support, or blow apart this new form of government. Violence escalated in the young republic during the Spartacist uprising in January 1919, after which army veterans murdered Marxist spokespersons Rosa Luxemburg and Karl Liebknecht, a Leipzig native. Soviet republics created in Bavaria, Saxony, and other places ended in bloodshed.

When the Treaty of Versailles was finally signed in June 1920, it deeply wounded the pride of many Germans. The treaty called for substantial cessions of territory (including Elsace and Lorraine, West Prussia, Posen, and Upper Silesia) and huge reparation payments, and declared Germany solely responsible for the war. German sentiment against the victorious countries rose sharply, but also against their own government for ratifying the treaty in the first place.

The treaty also called for a reduction of the *Reichswehr* (imperial army), which affected many soldiers, some of whom refused to disband their units. And so the Ehrhardt marine brigade and the *Freikorps,* led by Walter von Lüttwitz and Wolfgang Kapp, marched into Berlin on March 13, 1920, and took over the government. Because the putsch had no public backing, it led to a general strike with 12 million participants, the largest in German history. Everything ground to a halt in Leipzig as well—factories, public authorities, and streetcars. Massive rallies were held, with one in Augustusplatz (Augustus Square), where a temporary volunteer regiment composed mainly of students faced off with a *Reichswehr* unit. Without warning, the soldiers fired into the crowd, killing forty demonstrators, on what came to be called Leipzig's Bloody Sunday. It was followed by barricade battles all over the city. One of the central locations of the resistance, the *Volkshaus* (public house), was completely destroyed during the putsch (it would later be rebuilt, only to be destroyed again by a bomb in November 1922). Five days later, the putschists gave up. Berlin (and Leipzig) was free once more. Then putsch opponents, however, led by the Communist Party of Germany (KPD) and the Independent Social Democratic Party of Germany (USPD), tried to establish a Dictatorship of the Proletariat in various parts of the country. In late March, the Red Ruhr army controlled wide areas of the Ruhr. Twelve hundred people died when the movement was defeated, which involved armed units that had also taken part in the Kapp putsch. And still there was no peace.

Supreme Court President Ludwig Ebermayer felt this on a professional level. Over four hundred political murders had been committed in the last five years. Most by the right, but the judges, as members of the old elite, were much more sympathetic to them than they were to the left. The victims included high-ranking ministers, like center party politician Matthias Erzberger and Bavarian Prime Minister Kurt Eisner. What caused the biggest firestorm, however, was the murder of Jewish German Foreign Minister Walter Rathenau, a liberal who had also been the object of Jew baiting by conservative politicians in parliament. The Organization Consul, an association of former *Reichswehr* members with links to Leipzig students, was revealed as the instigator of the attack, which had not been a solitary occurrence. "At night, Leipzig is full of Rathenau-murderers and those who would like to be," Viennese journalist Joseph Roth reported after

Germany on November 9

Year	Event
November 9, 1848	Robert Blum hanged
November 9, 1918	Weimar Republic declared by Philipp Scheidemann
November 9, 1923	Hitler's Putsch
November 9, 1938	Pogrom Night
November 9, 1989	Fall of the Wall

visiting Leipzig in fall 1922. "I heard student troops marching through the streets three nights in a row. They came from Goldhahngässchen, where the Taubenschlag (Dovecoat Tavern) was located."

Just how weak the country was at that point was also evident in the fact that Gustav Stresemann was already the seventh imperial chancellor to take office. And Saxony was already on its fourth prime minister after Social Democrat Erich Zeigner was removed from office in October 1923. The replacement in quick succession of national leaders was accompanied by the inflation of the national currency, which was devalued at an unprecedented rate. The reason for this was due to armament credits from World War I, which had driven Germany's total debt to 100 percent of economic output. Germany now had to repay not only the cost of the war but also—according to the Treaty of Versailles—"its consequences." Because Germany had lost the war, it had to finance the peace that was negotiated. The price of a dollar rose from 4.20 marks at the end of 1918 to 7,260 marks in January 1923. Yet total collapse would not happen until Belgian-French troops occupied the Ruhr, reparation payments came to a halt, and another general strike was called. That one was supported by the government. The currency required was simply printed in larger and larger quantities by 124 printing houses, where a total of thirty thousand people were employed. By early July, a dollar cost 160,000 marks, rising to 321 billion marks by early November. The already dismal economic status of broad sectors of the population became downright catastrophic. Those left behind by Germany's two million fallen soldiers were hit particularly hard, along with five hundred thousand disabled veterans depending on retirement benefits, whose payments did not keep pace with inflation. Destitution took over the entire city. Beggars and starving people were everywhere, even on the steps of the proud theater. The economic drama was accompanied by a quick rise in criminal activity, which often occurred out in the open. As it happened on July 4, when hungry people stormed the Café Felsche. Among those affected, however, were large numbers of the bourgeoisie, who had remained relatively unscathed until 1922, when they lost their fortunes to inflation. Any faith the old elite had in the new republic was completely destroyed. Some made money from the destitution, especially speculators who acquired entire factories for mere pennies. Robert Steidl's *Wir versaufen unsrer Oma ihr klein Häuschen* (We're Drinking Away Granny's Cottage) was the hit of the year.

While Ludwig Ebermayer was not directly a victim of the misery, it shaped everything around him. By November, inflation was galloping at incredible speed. People everywhere were frantically pushing money—much too much money—back and forth, sometimes in laundry baskets or wheelbarrows. Even Ebermayer pulled out a bundle of brand-new fifty-billion-mark notes, which were blank on the back. When the waiter politely handed him the check, there were two coffees listed on it—one for 600 billion marks, and the other for 800 billion. Begging his pardon, the waiter explained that the price had increased between the two orders. Five days later, on November 15, 1923, the horrific episode was finally over. The Rentenmark replaced the paper mark, at an exchange rate of one to one trillion. At least the Reichsmark bonds issued during the war could be repaid in one stroke—suddenly worth only sixteen pennies.

Time Flies

In fall 1927, Erich Kästner packed his bags after eight years at 51 Hohen Strasse in Leipzig and moved to Berlin, the cultural capital of Europe, where his big literary break would soon come. Other luminaries were already living in the cosmopolitan city, like quintessential Berliner Kurt Tucholsky, Bertold Brecht from Augsburg, and Egon Erwin Kisch from Prague. Kisch, known as the "raving reporter," had traveled throughout the entire republic in one year, during which time he had also reported from Leipzig—with prolonged repercussions. After his article on the *Mendebrunnen* (Mende fountain), in which Kisch erroneously (or not) described the fountain benefactor's widow, Marianne Pauline Mende, post mortem as a brothel operator, the Neo-baroque decoration in Augustus Square came to be known as the *"Nuttenbrunnen"* (whores' fountain), and still is by some old Leipzigers today.

On the west side of the square, work had begun on Leipzig's first skyscraper, the Kroch building, which was also a popular topic of conversation and debate. The building was so controversial that the four upper levels of the twelve-story building were just a wooden mock-up for a time, and then a film simulation. Finally, a building permit was received for the entire height of 137 feet, though the architectural vision for the structure of the early 1920s had included many more. Many high-rise building projects by private investors had landed on the officials' tables at the building administration, including the Frankfurt Fields and the Rossplatz (Ross Square). In 1920, a construction site was even reserved in Schulplatz (School Square, along Goerdelerring today, near the natural history museum), for a 354-foot trade-fair tower. It was to have thirty exhibition floors, each 196 feet wide. Even huger plans were presented the following year. Between the main

The international trade-show city was to be furnished with appropriate architecture in the 1920s, but the trade-show tower would remain just an idea

train station and Augustusplatz (Augustus Square), the 314′ × 918′ Welthandelspalast (Palace of International Trade) was to be built, with sixteen floors and 2.1 million square feet of exhibition space. Unlike most other industries, the trade fair was booming, indeed, and prewar records were being easily broken. The long-pioneering effort was now really paying off. Édouard Herriot, mayor of Lyon, expressed his awe of Leipzig by calling it the "mother of all trade fairs." What developing the new trade-show format would mean for the city was also expressed in 1917, when the double-M logo was chosen for the Leipzig trade show.

Because the existing spatial capacity could not keep pace with growing demands, gaps were filled by renting schools, gymnasiums, music halls, and other temporary spaces. Wooden auxiliary halls adorned municipal squares, like Königsplatz and Augustusplatz, and even the market was home to the so-called *Reklameburg* (publicity mountain) for a few years, until the underground trade-show hall was built in 1924, providing an unusual, longer-term solution. By the time the global economic crisis broke out, ten new trade-show palaces had been built. All in all, thirty buildings were created for the new fair format in and around the city center, some of which occupied entire city blocks. These were joined by an assortment of repurposed buildings, like the Hôtel de Pologne (Pologne Hotel), the Königliche Palais (Royal Palace), and the Haus zum Grönländer (Greenlander Building), so the trade show had over forty buildings near the city center at its disposal, with some 1.6 million square feet for exhibition space. The area added in 1920 for the Technical Trade Show had grown to over 1.4 million square feet of exhibition space. One of the seventeen halls built before 1928 was the Achilleion (later known as the Soviet Pavillion), which also served as a sports arena, hosting events like the six-day race. Eight thousand people watched Max Schmeling become European middleweight boxing champion there in 1927. It was now the largest sports arena in the city and the largest trade-show building in Europe. The trade-show office did not limit its activity to its home turf, however, but staffed offices in eighty-six different countries to hold competition from London, Lyon, and Milan in check. Within Germany, Leipzig's position was so dominant, however, that only border shows in Königsberg, Breslau, and Cologne could gain anything beyond regional significance, and Frankfurt's, meanwhile, had almost completely dissolved.

Spring Trade Show Exhibitors

Year	Exhibitors
1905	2,930
1910	3,682
1914	4,213
1916	2,438
1918	3,681
1920	12,345
1925	13,996
1928	10,106

The world trade palace, planned to be located between Augustus Square and the main train station, was not built either

Leipzig's fur industry developed along with the trade show, though business dropped off sharply during the First World War, particularly because Russia and the United States, the primary suppliers, had become wartime enemies. But prewar levels were soon reached again, and surpassed a short while later. One reason was because fur traders profited from Germany's good relationship with the Soviet Union during the Weimar Republic, while the competition in London and New York struggled with trade restrictions. In 1928 one third of all international fur trade was transacted through Leipzig.

Even Erich Kästner worked at the trade show now and then, during his early years in Leipzig. In 1919 he enrolled at the university to study history, literature, theatrical arts, and German. His hometown of Dresden paid his stipend, but it was barely worth anything in light of the runaway inflation. He managed to keep his head above water as a working student with various part-time jobs. He sold perfume, recorded stock prices, and, after winning a short-story competition sponsored by the *Leipziger Tageblatt* (*Leipzig Daily News*) in February 1923, was able to earn some money with his writing. Fittingly, he lived in the Graphic District at the time, then on Senefeld Street, and later in Czermak's Garden, as a boarder. In 1925 he received a doctoral degree in philosophy with a 1 (the highest score). But how does the saying go? "Lucky with the dissertation, unlucky in love." After a long-term relationship with Ilse Julius, which lasted nearly seven years, it all went to pieces in 1926. Because both were native Saxons, it happened while they were drinking coffee. At least according to Kästner's account in the poem, *"Sachliche Romanze"* ("Non-nonsense Romance"):

... Sie gingen ins kleinste Café am Ort
They went to the smallest café in town,
und rührten in ihren Tassen.
where in their cups they stirred.
Am Abend sassen sie immer noch dort.
They were still there as the sun went down,
Sie sassen allein, und sie sprachen kein Wort
sitting alone, not speaking a word,
und konnten es einfach nicht fassen.
in utter disbelief, all around.

Kästner, after all, was a passionate patron of coffeehouses. The Felsche in Augustus Square and the Café Merkur (Mercury) on Dittrichring were among his favorites. He called the latter the literary café on the Pleisse, though other creative folk also gathered there, including painters, musicians, and actors. Presumably a few passionate news-

At trade-show time, according to this postcard, suitable lodgings were not always available

paper readers as well—as many as three hundred papers were published in Leipzig in the mid-1920s. The press was still the most important medium by far, though radio was just making it onto the scene. With "Hello, hello—Leipzig here, fair-office transmitter of the Reichs-Telegraph Administration for Central Germany, broadcasting on wavelength four-fifty," the MIRAG station, predecessor of today's MDR, greeted its audience on March 1, 1923. The second German broadcasting company transmitted initially from the Alten Waage (Old Scale), the trade-show building on Market Square.

As the modern age was finding its way in technology, social roles were changing. The New Woman, emancipated, professionally ambitious, and self-confident, was characteristic of the new republic. While subtle gender-equity trends were already developing during the late imperial era, nothing really changed until the First World War, when women became an indispensible part of the workforce. Because one out of every four young men returned from the Great War with a permanent disability, or did not return at all, working women became a permanent change to the social framework. Just as important was the democratization of the country, because when the republic was proclaimed, women were also allowed to vote. Their new self-confidence quickly took new forms of expression. Skirts shortened, cigarette holders lengthened, and bobbed hair became a sign of the times. At least in big cities. Such displays in villages, however, were still reason to call an exorcist.

The different pace at which urban and rural areas developed was particularly evident in the nightlife. Electricity and advertising turned large cities into veritable paradises of light. New, shiny, glittery bars, dance cafés, and music salons emerged in the mid-1920s, especially in Berlin. In Leipzig, life was a riot in the city center then, but also in the south and southeast, particularly around Windmühlenstrasse. The fact that Gundorfer Strasse (part of Georg-Schwarz-Strasse today) was commonly referred to as the *"Reeperbahn"* (after a particularly lively street in Hamburg) because of the many bars and cinemas there, demonstrates that Leipzig's western region was not exactly a snooze either. Musically, jazz won over many ears, hearts, and dancing feet, followed later by swing, the shimmy, and the Charleston. The movie-orchestra era was drawing to a close. In 1927 the first full-length talking film debuted, and musicians' protests and campaigns did nothing to deter the cinematic triumph. In January 1929 the city's first theater for talking films opened, known today as the Passagekino (Passage Cinema) in Hainstrasse. Half a year later, the Capitol opened on Petersstrasse, whose 1,700-seat capacity set a new Leipzig standard. By comparison, Leipzig's largest cinema in 2014, the Lichtburg Essen, seats only 1,250. In 1929 two million people went to the cinema in Germany—daily—nearly six times as many as today.

That same year the first Oscars were awarded in Hollywood. *Wings* won Best Picture—a film about two WWI pilots who fall in love with the same woman. In Leipzig, nude dancer Josephine Baker's appearance at the Crystal Palace in January 1929 caused an uproar. "A ruckus in Berlin, after scandal

Writers in Leipzig

Writer	Time spent in Leipzig
Paul Fleming (1609–1640)	10 years
Johann Christoph Gottsched (1700–1766)	42 years
Christian Fürchtegott Gellert (1715–1769)	32 years
Christian Felix Weiße (1726–1804)	43 years
Gotthold Ephraim Lessing (1729–1781)	3 years
Johann Wolfgang von Goethe (1749–1832)	3 years
Friedrich Schiller (1759–1805)	4 months
Jean Paul (1763–1825)	3 years
Johann Gottfried Seume (1763–1810)	20 years
Novalis (1772–1801)	3 years
Theodor Fontane (1819–1898)	2 years
Friedrich Nietzsche (1844–1900)	4 years
Clara Schott (1858–1942)	61 years
Joachim Ringelnatz (1883–1934)	15 years
Lene Voigt (1891–1962)	70 years
Hans Fallada (1893–1947)	2 years
Erich Kästner (1899–1974)	7 years
Hans Mayer (1907–2001)	15 years
Erich Loest (1926–2013)	27 years
Uwe Johnson (1934–1984)	6 years

in Vienna, and outrage bubbling up even in Scandinavia, and now Leipzig, the first city in the German province, has the pleasure of seeing Josephine Baker. And lo and behold, we Saxons are the better ones after all! It doesn't even occur to us to be outraged. On the contrary, Baker is showered here with kindness . . ." the *Neue Leipziger Zeitung* (*New Leipzig Newspaper*) crowed.

It was that same *Neue Leipziger Zeitung*, however, that had reacted much less impassively in 1927 to Kästner's poem "*Nachtgesang des Kammervirtuosen*" ("Night Song of the Chamber Virtuoso"), illustrated by Erich Ohser. "Too indecent," was the verdict, and soon Ohser and Kästner, who had written numerous commentaries and theater reviews for the paper, were shown the door. Kästner would later describe the occurrence as *"Fußtritt Fortunas"* (Lady Fortune's boot), because it prompted his move to Berlin. Half a year later, his first book was released, *Herz auf Taille* (*Tailored Heart*), a collection of poems from his Leipzig years, which had already been published individually in many journals, such as *Simplicimus* (*Simplicism*), *Weltbühne* (*World Stage*), and *Jugend* (*Youth*). The book was a big hit.

The Big Crash

"Stock prices have reached what looks like a permanently high plateau."
—Irving Fisher, October 16, 1929

Wall Street's Dow Jones Industrial Average had been climbing since October 1924. That was a 370-percent gains in just five years. Amazing. European stock exchanges posted similarly steep price increases, including the German Statistics Office's stock index, which had been utterly eroded by crises just a few years earlier. Unlike past price increases, this kind of inflation made people happy, so now everyone wanted to be an investor. Even common workers borrowed money to get in on the boom. A lot of fun—until October 24, 1929.

The real economy actually did improve all over the world during the Roaring Twenties, though not by 370 percent—more like 37 percent, at most. And the growth was largely based on private borrowing. Germany's boom was particularly strong, although real earnings reached prewar levels for the first (and last) time only in 1928. The greatest dynamic, as usual, was in larger cities. Within ten years, Leipzig's population grew by 175,000, of which 35,000 came through the incorporation of Grosszschocher, Leutzsch, Wahren, and Paunsdorf. In 1930 statisticians recorded a population of 718,000, the highest in the city's history. It did not occur to anyone that Leipzig might shrink instead of grow in subsequent decades. Not even to Hubert Ritter, who was municipal master builder at the time and presented the city's first general development plan in 1928. The plan's prognosis for the future extended to the year 2000, when the population was predicted to be 1.75 million. In 1928 that was a completely realistic hypothesis. So Ritter's initial measures were characterized by growth. He had city hall's vacant attic renovated to accommodate the ever-growing city-

The Supermarket Halls under construction, soon nicknamed the Kohlrabi Circus

planning staff. He adopted a similar approach for the space needs of the entire city center. To protect the center's already decimated stock of old buildings, new buildings around the Ring would be built two stories taller. Additional space would be added with the construction of individual high-rise buildings, which would form dominant pillars in the city's crown.

With the onset of the global economic crisis, the demand for new office space took such a nosedive that the Kroch high-rise and Europahaus remained Leipzig's only skyscrapers. Ritter's ring-city concept influenced future Leipzig city planners, as demonstrated by the Ring Café and Wintergarten high-rise. The Ring itself, both in Ritter's concept and in reality, plays a huge role in dispersing traffic. In 1928, there were about twelve thousand motor vehicles in the city, five times as many as in 1914, but only 5 percent of today's number. Though there was less traffic back then, it needed regulating nonetheless. On Augustus Square it was managed by a traffic policeman at a dizzying height—the *Eiserner Schupomann* (iron policeman). A short while later, the first traffic lights followed on the Ring. Parking was already a big problem, as well. Large parking garages would soon help with that. In addition, complaints increased about buildings shaking because of passing trucks. Meanwhile, Leipzig's two large streetcar companies merged to form a joint municipal entity. On the one hand, that meant that redundant tracks from the once double routes disappeared, but also that new connections to distant city districts were added. Annual tram use amounted to 170 million passengers back then. For air traffic, new landing sites were created in 1927. The central-German Zentralflughafen (Central Airport) joined the Mockau International Airport, angering Leipzigers because it was built in the Schkeuditz corridor, which meant that it was in Prussia (not Saxony). Planners assumed that planes in the future would need much less room for takeoff and landing, so space for an inner-city airstrip was reserved at the horse track, and Augustus Square and the roof of the main train station were also considered as runways. For non-motorized traffic, Ritter envisioned a series of linked paths in the form of long stretches of green space connecting urban spaces.

On October 24, 1929, however, all plans went out the window. Known as Black Thursday in the United States, the crash hit in Germany on a Friday, due to the time difference. There was no strategy for what to do if stock prices fell. In the days leading up to the crash, the Dow Jones average had already lost

"Schupomann" (policeman) in Augustus Square, 1927

15 percent, so investors were uneasy. When prices began to fall at eleven o'clock that Thursday, too, investors panicked. Everyone wanted to sell, and trade collapsed multiple times. When the market stabilized somewhat in mid-November, the index had already lost 200 points, from a starting point of over 350. It hit rock bottom in the summer of 1932, with 41 points, after nearly 90 percent of asset values were lost. Some stocks simply did not exist anymore. These were numbers games with very real outcomes.

Almost every economy struggled with crises. It shook the United States particularly hard, where industrial production took a 47-percent hit, and Germany, where losses were nearly just as big. In Leipzig, the trade-show and fur industries collaborated. Because the boom of the Roaring Twenties was mostly financed by short-term credit, which foreign financial backers would no longer extend, banks were in trouble. Their equity ratios, meanwhile, no longer reached 25 or 30 percent, as before the First World War, but were down around 10 percent, causing widespread bankruptcy and collapse. Leipzig was less affected in that regard, because the largest bank in the city, the Leipzig Bank, had already failed spectacularly in 1901. Unlike 1923, the new crisis did not cause inflation but deflation, instead. Yet the results were just as dramatic. Unemployment figures in Leipzig, which were around 4,500 in 1910, and 15,000 in 1926, rose to 103,000 by 1932. Broad levels of the population faced hunger and poverty again, and because tax income also took a massive nosedive, subsidies were drastically reduced. The same was true for residential construction, still plagued by the aftereffects of the previous crises, the responsibility for which moved increasingly to local communities. Fewer than eighty-four hundred new apartments were built between 1916 and 1925. Many families were refused subleases, and in 1925 more than twenty-five thousand families did not live in their own homes. The gap in supply decreased slightly during the Roaring Twenties, when 175,000 apartments were built but there was still a housing shortage, and it would remain a problem in Leipzig in subsequent years. Unlike the houses in imperial times, the new ones were far more convenient. Bathrooms with toilets had become standard, and ceilings were no longer ten to thirteen feet high, but often under eight feet. Architectural adornment was also used much less often, and in the intense debate about roofs, advocates of flat roofs prevailed, with Ritter's support.

Aerial view of the city center, 1930

Another change was that instead of individual buildings with different forms, most new residential constructions were designed with uniform exteriors. The Kroch neighborhood, the construction fair residential area on Zwickauer Strasse, and the new buildings on Thaerstrasse were some of the most innovative examples of the time. The most famous residential project, however, was the *Rundling* (circular settlement) designed by Hubert Ritter. The architect was also famous for his large covered markets, which people soon came to call Kohlrabi Circuses. Each one spanning 246 feet, the two free-standing domes were the largest of their kind in the world—a last record for Ritter. Plans to build a third dome failed when the municipal budget collapsed. Much more serious, however, was the fact that the recently pacified political situation was drifting toward a state of emergency.

Incorporations

Year	Community
1889	Anger-Crottendorf, Reudnitz
1890	Eutritzsch, Gohlis, Neureudnitz, Neuschönefeld, Neustadt, Sellerhausen, Thonberg, Volkmarsdorf
1891	Connewitz, Kleinzschocher, Lindenau, Lössnig, Plagwitz, Schleussig
1892	Neusellerhausen
1904	Lössnig manor estate
1909	Kleinzschocher manor estate
1910	Dölitz, Meusdorf, Dösen, Möckern, Probstheida, Stötteritz, Stünz
1915	Mockau, Schönefeld
1922	Grosszschocher-Windorf, Leutzsch, Paunsdorf, Wahren
1925	Dölitz manor estate, Grosszschocher manor estate with outlying Windorf, Leutzsch manor estate with Barneck, Möckern manor estate with barracks, Paunsdorf manor estate, Schönefeld manor estate, Stötteritz manor estate with outlying Meusdorf, woodland estate, castle pastures
1930	Abtnaundorf with Heiterblick, Knautkleeberg, Schönau, Thekla
1935	Portitz
1936	Knauthain
1979	Lausen parish parcels and Grossmiltitz
1993	Hartmannsdorf
1994	Flickert, Göhrenz parish parcels
1995	Lausen, Plaussig
1997	Seehausen
1999	Böhlitz-Ehrenberg, Engelsdorf, Holzhausen, Knautnaundorf, Liebertwolkwitz, Lindenthal, Lützschena-Stahmeln, Miltitz, Mölkau, Wiederitzsch, Rehbach parish and Bösdorf, sections of Eythra parish
2000	Burghausen parish, Rückmarsdorf parish

Election results for the radical parties, especially the National Socialist German Workers' Party (NSDAP, or Nazi Party) exceeded one record after another, mostly because they knew how to use the disastrous financial situation to their political advantage. So the Leipzig Nazis focused particularly on the Leipziger Stadtbank (Leipzig Municipal Bank), established several years earlier by the municipality. In 1932 loan defaults of thirty million Reichsmarks had to be made up, because larger enterprises had to file bankruptcy as debtors in the wake of the global economic collapse. This was yet another scandal that generated votes. From then on, those who'd had the foresight to buy stock in the weapons industry especially profited on the stock market.

Nazis

Rudolf Haake was a Leipzig Nazi right from the start. The nineteen-year-old business apprentice was one of the thirty people in attendance when the local NSDAP (Nazi party) was established in November 1922. While members of the equally nationalist and anti-Semitic Deutschvölkischen Schutz- und Trutzbundes (German Nationalist Protection and Defiance Federation), which boasted 180,000 members throughout Germany, tried to interrupt the event, they did not succeed. In 1923 both organizations were banned, but the ban on the NSDAP was lifted again by December 1924. Haake was on hand again for the group's reestablishment, ready to devote his life to the hostile ideology. First he took on the responsibility of organizing Leipzig's Hitler Youth (HJ), and after completing party training in oration, he became a spokesman and author. Neither he nor his party would have any social impact until the Crash of 1929, though.

Until then, the NSDAP, founded in Munich's Hofbräuhaus in 1920, was a rather loud but politically insignificant fringe group. In order to conceal its insignificance, member ID numbers started at 500. During the postwar turmoil, Hitler did manage to win a few votes in the Reichstag elections in 1922. After Hitler's Munich putsch in 1923 and the subsequent party ban, interest in the party waned, and the more the Twenties roared, the less the Germans warmed up to his abstruse slogans. Unfortunately, it also worked the other way round: when times got worse, the Nazis gained more votes. While the

While the Nazis planned to demolish Naundorf, the Allies made it happen in 1943

NSDAP did not get even 3 percent of the vote in the Reichstag elections in 1928, votes increased five-fold just two years later. Winning 37.4 percent in the first election in 1932, the Nazis became the strongest political power in the Weimar Republic. In Saxony, they won with 41.4 percent. Due to strong labor representation in Leipzig, however, they rated far below the national average. Even in the 1932 city council election, the NSDAP gained only one fourth of the seats. The Social Democratic Party (SPD) still held the most power in Leipzig, where their roots were unusually deep. 3.3 percent of all Leipzigers—twice the national average—were members of the SPD, whose own ranks opposed the right-wing terror that grew ever more pervasive after 1930.

There was also opposition from the Leipzig media, like the *Leipzig People's Newspaper*, and public authorities, including Leipzig's chief of police. The university, on the other hand, proved to be a right-wing bastion; the Nazi German Student Association dominated the scene, beginning in 1930. Shortly after the seizure of power, over one hundred professors welcomed Hitler's national government in an open proclamation. At the same time, Communist and Socialist student associations were banned, more than thirty university instructors dismissed, and syllabi adapted to promote the new attitudes. The new policies had an even graver effect on minorities—the Jews and the Romany, but also on the homeless or those supposedly adverse to work. In addition to imprisonment and forced labor, more than three hundred thousand forced sterilizations were performed throughout Germany. In September 1939, Hitler's mania eventually led to the eugenic murder of over one hundred thousand physically, mentally, or intellectually disabled persons, including the blind and deaf. Five thousand of those were children. Leipzig physician Werner Catel played an especially inglorious role, as one of only three file reviewers in all of Germany who decided whether people lived or died. As a result of his work, an estimated five hundred children were killed at the pediatric clinic on Oststrasse and later at the Dösen Sanitarium.

Haake, meanwhile, had secured an important role within the NSDAP. In 1930 he was promoted to executive director of Leipzig's local chapter and he joined the city council, where his verbal abuse attracted attention. He was issued multiple fines for libeling officials. Beginning in 1935, he led the housing, trade-show, Gutenberg Exhibition, and harbor departments in the mayor's office, and he was also deputy to Carl Goerdeler, who opposed the Nazis. Upon Goerdeler's resignation, Haake ascended to the top position in 1937, even if only as acting mayor. It was then that he wrote the blatantly National Socialist memorandum, *Leipzig, Stadt ohne Raum* (*Leipzig, City Without Space*), in which he demanded the incorporation of forty surrounding communities. Unsuccessfully, though. Still, he did manage to expand his domestic realm by fathering seven children.

The economy as well was overexerted. Using job-creation programs, most of which had been designed during the Weimar Republic, large projects were kick-started all over Germany, creating new jobs. The largest stimulus began in 1934, however, was spurred by the armament industry. Leipzig became the center of aerial weaponry, first around the Mockau International Airport, and a short while later across the entire municipal area. The Erla-Werken plants were of particular importance, as the second-largest German manufacturer of fighter planes—the General Material Handling System Corporation and the Junker Shipyard. The Hugo Schneider Corporation, Saxony's largest arms factory, was also based in Leipzig. By 1943, there were 221 weapons-related companies in the greater Leipzig area, in which more than 150,000

Führer Cities

City	Role
Munich	Capital of the movement
Berlin	Imperial capital
Linz	Hitler's adopted city
Hamburg	Gateway to the world
Nürnberg	Rally site

Additional Cities with a Nazi Perspective

City	Role
Stuttgart	City of expatriates
Weimar	City of Goethe and Schiller
Bremen	City of colonies
Essen	City of labor
Frankfurt am Main	City of German craftsmen

people worked up to sixteen hours a day, one third of which were forced laborers.

The construction of new industrial facilities was also promoted, but aside from that there was relatively little built in Leipzig during the Nazi era. One reason was the prioritization of other cities, particularly the five so-called *"Führerstädte"*: Berlin, Munich, Hamburg, Nürnberg, and later, Linz. Leipzig was not among the twenty-seven cities in the Reich that Hitler wanted to redesign. Only its appointment as the Reich's trade-show city in December 1937 increased Leipzig's prestige. The trade-show office reported directly to Joseph Goebbels's Ministry of Propaganda during that time. Because the number of trade-show visitors after the global economic crisis climbed sharply again, at least for those interested in domestic manufacturing, three new show buildings and the Bugra-Exhibition building were built in 1938. Creating an international fairgrounds that would extend from the technical trade show to the Bayerischer train station was postponed until after the war was over.

Hardly anything happened within the city, except for the construction of bunker systems. The Mercury exhibition building completed in 1936 remained the sole new inner-city structure of the Nazi era. Construction activity by private builders languished almost completely, so despite the rallying economy throughout the entire municipal area, very few residential and commercial buildings were created, while construction of small and public apartments was accelerated. Much more was torn down, some of it to make way for large projects that were never realized. The most prominent example of this was the demolition of the cycling track, Cow Tower, and Palm Garden building to make way for the Gutenberg Show planned for 1940. Demolition was also planned in the historic district, in the Tanners' District and Naundörfchen. An additional thirty properties between St. Matthew's Churchyard and Richard-Wagner-Hain were to make way for a new municipal administration building.

Some of those projects were realized, at least in Johannisplatz and the Seeburg District, about which the *Neue Leipziger Zeitung* (*New Leipzig Newspaper*) reported, "It is generally known that this district contains not only the most miserable living quarters but also harbors Marxism and criminal activity in its poorly constructed buildings." Haake's first blow was widely celebrated. The press, forced by the Nazi government to toe the line, reacted with similar enthusiasm, although only flood control on the Luppe and Parthe rivers, the Elster Basin, and the stretch of autobahn linking Leipzig and Halle were ever completed. There were plans for a Richard Wagner National Monument along the Elster Basin, and Hitler was on hand to officially kick off

Richard Wagner Square in 1935. Ten years later, there was only rubble here

the work in 1934. While the monument was largely finished—including a fourteen-foot-tall base created by Emil Hipp—the city refused to accept it after the war.

Lindenau Harbor, considered to be Germany's most technologically modern inland harbor in 1942, was also completed. But because the Elster–Saale Canal that was supposed to connect to it was not finished, Lindenau Harbor had no access to any bodies of water. Many other large projects, however, like the tunnel connecting the Bayerisch and the main train stations or the development of the Frankfort Fields, never even made it to the groundbreaking ceremony. Instead, the reshaping of German cities was taken over a short while later by Allied bombers.

Rudolf Haake's political career ended then, too. After Alfred Freyberg, mayor since 1939, accused Haake of corruption, he was removed from office in Leipzig in 1943 and he went on to be party spokesman in distant Lithuania. When the Red Army occupied the Baltic region in summer 1944, the 41-year-old, who was nearly blind by then, moved back to Kelbra. On April 12, 1945, American soldiers seized that area. With the final victory in his blurry sight, Haake opened fire from the town hall and wounded a commander before turning his weapon on himself.

RES·SEVERA·VERUM·GAUDIUM.

Resistance

"To base enduring peace on a deal with the devil is a bizarre illusion."
—Carl Friedrich Goerdeler

The election in 1930 of the relative unknown Carl Friedrich Goerdeler's as mayor of Leipzig came as a huge surprise. Not only did the bourgeoisie vote for him, but individual city councilors from the KPD and NSDAP did, too. His task would not be easy. The republic was heading toward political and economic chaos. Yet within a short time, the East Prussian earned an excellent reputation as a financial expert and was appointed to the cabinet of the Weimar Republic in 1931. The fact that he was so popular in Leipzig was one of the reasons he was able to stay in office even after 1933—only four mayors who were not NSDAP members were able to keep their positions after the Nazi accession to power in Germany. While Goerdeler was skeptical of these new, noisy rulers, some of their political convictions did match his own.

Others shared his ambivalence. The bourgeoisie especially longed for political stability and continued to advocate fervently for repeal of the dictates from Versailles. Plans that Hitler recklessly but successfully advanced. Hitler could also point to economic successes, even though surmounting the fading global economic crisis was promoted by covert loans and excessive armament. On a superficial level, things were looking up, and many accepted restrictions of their democratic rights in exchange. Furthermore, the Nazis had already imprisoned or forced the emigration of a considerable portion of their active rivals. Authorized by the Reichstag Fire Decree and the Enabling Act, nearly all social realms were soon brought into line.

In March and April 1933, political police made more than a thousand arrests in Leipzig alone. Political parties and unwelcome media, like the *Leipziger Volkszeitung* (*Leipzig People's Daily*) were banned, Jews and nonconforming officials were expelled from city and state administrations, the *Volkshaus* (public hall) was laid to waste, and the unions became political tools. Judicial cooptation was not yet completely in effect in 1933, as demonstrated by the December 23 verdict of the Reichstag fire trial that was intended to be a propaganda campaign. The Nazis wanted a group of Communists led by Georgi Dimitrov to be sentenced for the fire. Dimitrov was a Communist official from Bulgaria who had just been arrested in Berlin. Only one perpetrator was found guilty: Dutch Communist Marinus van der Lubbe (and even that verdict was hotly contested). One year later, though, judicial cooptation was complete when the party-conforming People's Court was created. By 1945 the People's Court handed down eighteen thousand death sentences. Covert resistance continued, however, with an ever-increasing base.

Goerdeler began to disagree more and more with the new system, although he worked with the Nazis at the national level. He found much of it disconcerting. So he refused to hoist the swastika flag on city hall, and made a point of going to Jewish businesses on April 2, the day after the Nazis invoked a boycott of Jews. He also tried to stop the expulsion of Jewish artists, though not successfully. When the monument for composer Felix Mendelssohn Bartholdy was torn from its base in his absence in November 1936—after he had fought long to preserve it—and was not returned despite his ultimatum, he resigned, disillusioned. He remained politically active. Just not in an official capacity.

In light of the severity with which the Nazis persecuted their opponents and their strong hold on society, resistance was meager for quite some time. Members of unions and the banned KPD and SPD parties were especially spied on. Nevertheless, small underground circles managed to operate covertly. When war broke out in September 1939, and particularly after the attack on the Soviet Union in June 1941, their numbers and spheres of influence increased. Resistance fighters printed underground leaflets and newspapers, sabotaged production at arms factories, and urged the population to rise up. Tiny pinpricks that were very dangerous. Many of

— Leipzig's second Gewandhaus, with a Mendelssohn memorial

the activists were arrested or even executed. The resistance movement in Leipzig known as the National Committee for a Free Germany, was one of the largest groups nationwide. Its leaders, Georg Schumann, Otto Engert, and Kurt Kresse, along with fifty-six others, mostly Communist members, were arrested in November 1944, and most were sentenced to death shortly thereafter.

There were others in Leipzig who put up a fight, not just Communists and Social Democrats. Cologne had the Edelweiss Pirates, and similar groups of youth known as gangs rebelled in Leipzig. Their archenemy was the Hitler Youth (HJ), which until the mid-1930s had relatively little influence in Leipzig. Half of all ten- to eighteen-year-olds in the nation were Hitler Youth members, but in Leipzig, it was just one third. But in 1936 the Nazis increased the pressure considerably. "Gang" members, most of whom came from working-class families, resisted HJ membership and for a long time represented the antithesis of the Hitler Youth's drilling and military nature. Modeled after the naturalist youth movement *Bündische Jugend,* which was banned in 1933, and other leftist youth organizations, they often wore *lederhosen* with suspenders and plaid shirts. A third of them were girls, who wore dark skirts, blouses, and hiking shoes.

There were over twenty groups like that in Leipzig, and they usually functioned independently of one another. They distributed leaflets condemning Nazi Germany or destroyed NSDAP showcases, and they vandalized Hitler Youth homes and attacked and beat up members, causing the Leipzig HJ branch to complain to Hitler Youth leadership in Berlin that they were afraid to wear their uniforms on some city streets. About fifteen hundred youth in Leipzig belonged to one or more gangs. The largest, with about one hundred members, was the Reeperbahn Gang, named after the group's meeting place on Schlageterstrasse (named Georg-Schwarz-Strasse today), which was known locally as Reeperbahn, after Hamburg's famous nightlife district. Other well-known Leipzig gangs were the Hundestart (in Kleinzschocher), Arndtstrasse, Lille (in Reudnitz), and Eisenbahnstrasse. In 1939 nearly all of them were broken up by the Gestapo and the members placed in juvenile detention.

By that time, Goerdeler had already distanced himself so much from the Nazi regime that he was using his contacts to warn top politicians abroad about Hitler. Above all, he feared that the Nazis would ruin Germany, An opinion that other conservative elites had come to share. Thus a cir-

Resistance Fighters

Name	Life span
1. Communist and Social-Democratic Resistance	
Richard Lipinski	1867–1936
Alfred Kästner	1882–1945
Alfred Frank	1884–1945
William Zipperer	1884–1945
Rudolf Hartmann	1885–1945
Georg Schumann	1886–1945
Otto Engert	1895–1945
Georg Schwarz	1896–1945
Alfred Schellenberger	1898–1963
Arthur Hoffmann	1900–1945
Richard Lehmann	1900–1945
Karl Jungbluth	1903–1945
Kurt Kresse	1904–1945
Karl Plesse	1906–1978
Kurt Roßberg	1906–1991

Name	Life span
2. Bourgeois Resistance	
Carl Friedrich Goerdeler	1884–1945
Walter Cramer	1886–1944
Hans von Dohnanyi	1902–1945
3. Religious Resistance	
Arkenau-Group – Father Aurelius Arkenau OP	1900–1991
4. Others	
Margarete Blank	1901–1945
Wolfgang Heinze	1911–1945

cle of subversives formed around him and Ludwig Beck, a general close to Hitler-assassin Claus Graf Schenck von Stauffenberg. Their plans failed, however, along with those of the leftist opposition. Goerdeler was one of the central figures in the bourgeois resistance. If their overthrow worked, he was intended to take the office of Reich's chancellor. But that did not happen. One week prior to Stauffenberg's assassination, a warrant was issued for Goerdeler's arrest. At first he was able to avoid capture, but he was soon caught and then executed on February 2, 1945.

Jewish Life

In 1891, Henri Hinrichsen was twenty-three years old and had just moved to Leipzig after completing his apprenticeship, to work as a music distributor in the publishing company owned by his uncle, Max Abraham. After Abraham's suicide in 1900, Hinrichsen became the director at C. F. Peters, one of the most important music publishers in that era. It was not just in his capacity as a publisher that he was convincing, but in his involvement in other fields, too. He donated the Henriette Goldschmidt School to the city in 1911, and acquired the Heyer Collection of 2,600 musical instruments in 1926, which became the core of the Grassi Museum exhibit. Already recognized by the Kaiser for his services, he also received an honorary degree from Leipzig University in 1929.

The Ez Chaim Synagogue was located west of Leipzig until 1938

In the late 1920s, nearly 13,000 Leipzigers belonged to the Jewish religious community, and there is evidence that Jews lived in Leipzig as early as the thirteenth century. In that historically deeply religious time, when 99 percent of all residents were Christians, people of other faiths met with suspicion and were often thought to be the cause of otherwise inexplicable misfortune. Superstition and myths played a huge role. As late as the nineteenth century, some people still believed that Jews killed Christian children and offered up their blood for ritualistic purposes. The resulting fear, and the fear of losing privileges, led to violence and to laws almost all over Europe prohibiting Jews from practicing certain professions. During the sixteenth century, Jews were exiled to rural areas almost everywhere in the empire. Even in Leipzig, for a long time Jews were around only during the trade fairs, where they had to pay higher taxes than Christians.

It was not until the Enlightenment that some began advocating for equality. Gotthold Ephraim Lessing's play *Nathan der Weise* (*Nathan the Wise*), is the most prominent example, but it was more of an exception than the rule. Following the French Revolution, when French Jews became the first in Europe granted full citizenship in 1791, legal principles eventually changed in the German states as well. Saxony did not react until much later. It was not until the mid-1830s that commercial restrictions on Jews were lifted. Beginning in 1838, Jews were allowed to settle in Leipzig and Dresden, and in 1868, Jews could finally become Saxon citizens. At that time, there was an impressive Jewish community, which had built a synagogue on Zentralstrasse in 1855. In 1925, it was the sixth largest Jewish community in the Weimar Republic—at 1.8 percent of the population, the number of Jewish citizens in Leipzig was twice as high as the national average.

That was not unusual. Large cities offered much better prospects, especially Berlin, where 3.8 percent were Jewish. In Leipzig, 35 percent of working Jews were officials, 10 percent had professions, and 41 percent were merchants. Besides the textile industry, retail was a Jewish domain, especially the establishment of department stores. The majority were in the fur industry, however. More than half of the 794 fur companies registered in Leipzig in 1928 were run by Jewish merchants, whose ancestors emigrated mostly from Eastern Europe and especially Brody and Krakow. With the political situation improved, they moved their headquarters closer to the center of Leipzig. Because many Jews traditionally moved to the Brühl District during

Synagogues

1925: 13 Synagogues and four houses of prayer

Name	Former address	Notes (built/destroyed)
Large Congregational Synagogue ("The Temple")	Formerly at 3 Gottschedstrasse, corner of Zentralstrasse	Built 1854/1855, destroyed November 9–10, 1938; first and primary synagogue in Leipzig
Brodyer Synagogue	4 Keilstrasse	Built 1897/1898
Ez Chaim Synagogue	Formerly at 4 Apels Garten (orig. 6–8 Otto-Schill-Straße)	Built and dedicated 1922, destroyed November 9–10, 1938; largest orthodox synagogue in Saxony
Beth Jehuda Synagogue	11 Färberstrasse (courtyard building)	Synagogue incorporated in 1921, closed 1939
Ballroom at the New Israelite Cemetery	Formerly at 224 Delitzscher Strasse	Built between 1926 and 1928, bombed Februar 24, 1939
Merkin Synagogue	7 Ritterstrasse	Established in 1830, building remains
Hindenburg Synagogue (24th Synagogue)	Formerly at 24 Humboldtstrasse	Established 1916/1917, destroyed during war
Schaare Zedek Synagogue	31 Schillerweg (in courtyard building "Schillerlaube" tavern)	Established 1922, building remains

Others included: Tiktin Synagogue, Bochnia Synagogue, Jassy Synagogue, Kolomea Synagogue, Krakau Synagogue, Ohel Jacob Synagogue, Mischnajos Assoc. Synagogue, Ahwat Thora Synagogue, Lemberg Synagogue, Bikur Cholim Synagogue, Tifereth Synagogue.

trade fairs anyway, many began establishing their permanent residences there. A short time later, the sections of town developed in the northern municipal area became popular residential neighborhoods. A lot of Jewish families moved into the Waldstrassen District and the northern outskirts of town. Jewish schools, cemeteries, and seventeen synagogues and prayer rooms were also established there. While that period was by no means free from hostility, coexistence generally worked well.

After Hitler took power, that would change. In 1933, Henri Hinrichsen was forced to step down from the committees of all of his foundations. The social climate was changing drastically. For many Jews, including the Hinrichsens, who felt just as German as they did Jewish, suddenly being considered archenemies was as unbearable as it was inexplicable. While four of Hinrichsen's seven children were able to leave home by 1938, the other three and parents Henri and Martha stuck it out in Leipzig. During *Reichskristallnacht* (Night of Broken Glass) on November 9, 1938, they fell victim to a new level of hostility. When Nazis roamed the streets setting fires, the publishing business on Talstrasse was destroyed. A professional ban and the "Aryanization" of Jewish business followed. Henri Hinrichsen was given just a few minutes to leave forever the company in which he had worked for nearly fifty years. From then on, an SS-colonial would serve as trustee over Hinrichsen's life's work. In January 1940, he and Martha immigrated to Brussels.

Initially, the German Jews still felt relatively safe. During World War I many Jewish soldiers had fought in the German Army, and their national pride was no less evident than that of other Germans. One indication of that is revealed in the inscription on the bell in the Kroch high-rise: "Developed and strengthened with the flourishing young Reich, the Kroch Jr. Company Ltd. built this tower in 1927–1928, the fiftieth year of this bank's existence, as a symbol of undaunted German might." While the Nazis blotted out the Kroch name in 1933 because of its Jewish connotation, the rest of the inscription was left intact.

Many streets and buildings were renamed after the Nazi takeover. Jews were prohibited from public bidding and forced out of official positions. Gustav Brecher, conductor of the Leipzig Opera, and Bruno Walter, director of the Gewandhaus, lost their positions along with numerous other city and state officials. In July 1935, city administrators banned Jewish citizens from using public pools, and the Jewish cemetery in Johannistal was leveled one year later. *Reichskristallnacht* brought things to a whole new level. The reason given for the severe backlash was a Polish Jew's attack on a German envoy in Paris. National leaders ordered a spontaneous public reaction, an order also sent to the NSDAP district office at 10 Gottschedstrasse. SA-members in civilian clothing rode through the city in cars and trucks, setting fire to Jewish establishments. Besides the Grand Synagogue, the Höhere israelitische Schule (Higher Israelite School) on Gustav-Adolph-Strasse was also burned down, along with the Bamberg & Hertz and Ury department stores, the Ez Chaim Synagogue, and the hall of mourning at the Israelite Community Cemetery. Because most Jewish homes were in apartment buildings, they were *only* vandalized and boarded up. More than five hundred people were arrested; violence was now an officially approved tool.

Six thousand Jews still lived in Leipzig, but they struggled with arbitrary measures that grew harsher and harsher. In 1939, rent control was lifted for all Jewish families, and they were forced to move to forty-seven "Jewish homes." Not only did their terrible living conditions add to their ever-more intolerable situation, but they were subjected to curfews, exclusion orders in parking garages, forced labor, confiscation of property, and constant surveillance by the authorities. In 1941, Leipzig Jews were also forced to wear the Star of David. October that same year saw the first transports to concentration camps, and Jewish citizens were prohibited from leaving the country. In January 1942, the last 2,000 Leipzig Jews were hauled away, and in January 1945 the person in charge of the Jewish office declared with pride that the city was *"Judenrein"* (free of Jews), as the Nazis called it.

Henri and Martha Hinrichsen did not escape the Nazis either. They fled to Brussels and were waiting for a visa to England when the *Wehrmacht* (armed forces) marched into Belgium in May 1940, and into France one month later. As a result, Martha, who was diabetic, could not get any insulin anymore. She died in 1941, when her sons Hans-Joachim and Paul were also killed in the Perpignan concentration camp. One year later, 74-year-old Henri Hinrichsen, alone and financially destitute, was arrested in Brussels and sent to Auschwitz. He died on September 17, 1942.

Bombed Out

Robert Saundby was an ardent fly fisherman, and his passion influenced his career as well. As deputy commander in chief of the Royal Air Force Bomber Command, he devised the Fish Code in 1941, a list of ninety-four German cities given fishy code names. "Haddock" was the order given on the afternoon of December 3, 1943, for the assault the following night—when over five hundred fighter jets took off for Leipzig. They reached their destination shortly before four o'clock in the morning. Contrary to the weather forecast, the city lay under a light cloud cover. Nevertheless, the assault was executed with precision.

In 1943 the Allies responded to Hitler's crazy declaration of war on the entire world by targeting Germany itself more and more. A circumstance for which the Führer had obviously not planned. In any case, the Reich's situation no longer seemed sensible or advantageous. While millions of German soldiers were supposed to help provide the self-proclaimed *"Volk ohne Raum"* (people without space) with more of the same in the Russian tundra or Caucasus, increasingly unsuccessfully, the home front remained completely unprotected, and the only spatial prospects began opening up in German city centers—with new ones every night.

The Nazis initially set about destroying their own cultural assets without any help from others. During WWI, acute shortages of raw materials were addressed by recycling, among other means. As the war continued, the March 1940 call for metal donations from the public meant that not only were all coins containing copper and nickel melted down, but practically everything else that might be relevant to the cause: grave markers, musical instruments, bridge railings, architectural decorations, fountains.

Nine thousand church bells alone were sacrificed to the war, along with countless monuments—excluding busts of the Führer, of course. Among the objects spared in Leipzig was the Vic-

Bombardment Timeline

Date	
August 16, 1940	First air-raid alert
October 10, 1940	First light damage from individual aircraft
March 27, 1943	Single drops cause large fire in Gohlis
August 31, 1943	Drops over Eutritzsch and Schönefeld initially claim the first lives (four)
October 20, 1943	First major attack, primarily on Stötteritz and Paunsdorf, 40 dead
December 4, 1943	Massive attack causes large-scale fires, about 1,800 killed; large sections of the inner city and surrounding areas destroyed
February 19–20, 1944	Double attack on the southern and southwestern areas of the city, including the Mockau Airport, 920 killed; during the Big Week (second Gewandhaus hit)
February 27, 1945	Large-scale attack
April 6, 1945	Major attack (central train station hit)
April 10, 1945	Last major attack
April 15, 1945	Official end of wartime bombing
April 18, 1945	American ground forces liberate Leipzig

38 attacks were recorded, of which most were carried out over industrial complexes by the US Air Force, and in which over 5,000 people were killed.

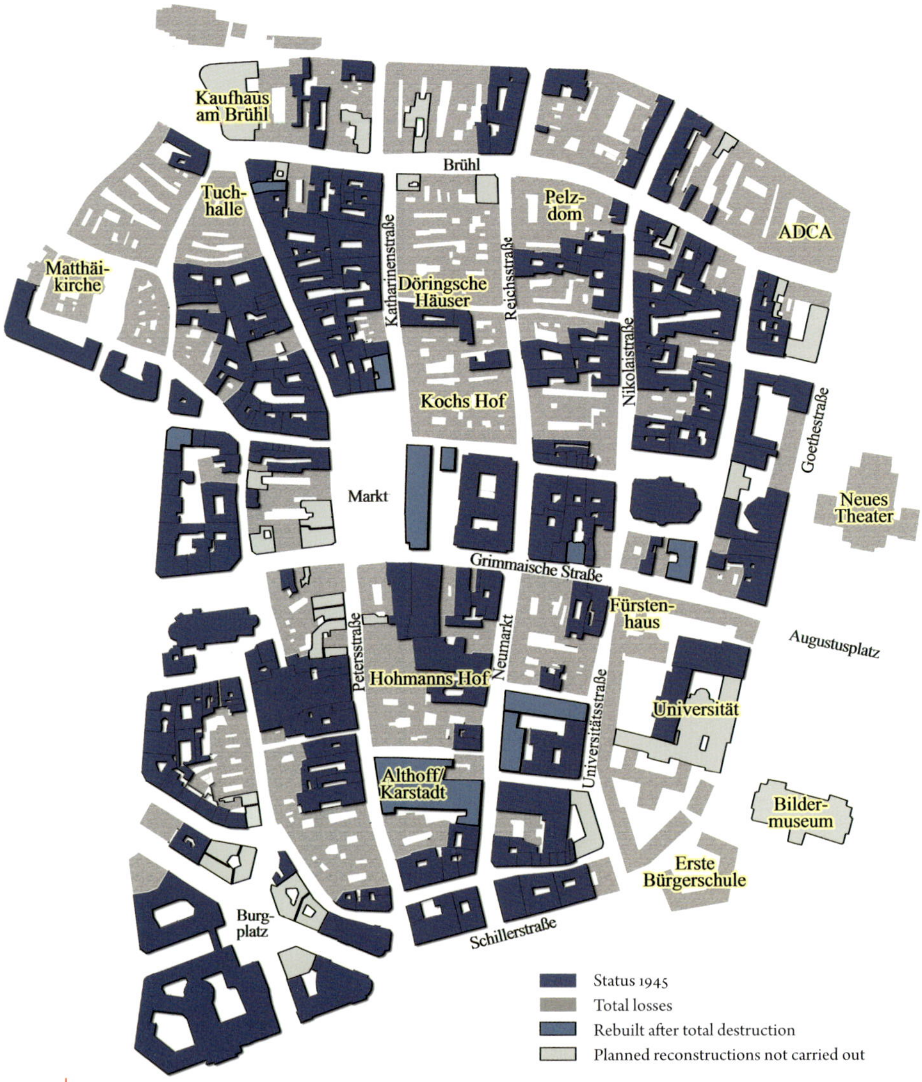

Map of damage to Leipzig's city center in 1945

tory Monument, of all things, which escaped unscathed and towered pathetically over a landscape of ruins at the end of the war. The Soviets tore it down shortly thereafter. The Karl Heine Monument (restored later), Luther Melanchthon Memorial, Fechner Memorial, and other monuments were destroyed as early as 1942, when bomb impacts came closer and closer. Cologne, Dortmund, Hamburg, and Berlin reported massive devastation, and British bomb squadrons showed up occasionally over Leipzig as well. The first local damage was to Gohlis in March 1943. Greater destruction and the first deaths occurred in Eutritzsch and Schönefeld in September, and Stötteritz in October, although the perfectly sound NS-propaganda continued to declare Saxony to be the bomb shelter of the German Reich. But there's a big difference between castles in the air and air defense.

On December 3, 1943, at 3:58 a.m., a cascade of light and so-called Christmas trees—lights hung on parachutes to mark bomb targets—lit up the city. A spectacle ceremoniously announcing the beginning of the destruction. In the next moment, the first flight squadrons crossed a sky that was lit up as bright as day, from north to south, dropping bombs to break up the roofs. The entire city center shook with the resulting concussions. The force of countless detonations tore windows and doors off their hinges and crumbled the mortar in basement walls, where men, women, and children clung to each other in the dark, seized by mortal fear. When the hellish noise waned twenty minutes later, silence descended. There was no all-clear signal since the sirens had been destroyed. Despite the explosive power, only a few buildings collapsed. The actual destruction was yet to come. In a corridor three miles long and almost a mile wide, from Uferstrasse in the north down to Connewitz, about five thousand fires were blazing.

Aerial assaults had been a military tactic in the war since 1939. While the Allies first concentrated on individual strategic targets, the German air force's attacks employed carpet bombing right from the start. Warsaw, Rotterdam, Coventry, and London were the most severely damaged. Pressured by their own destruction and in the wake of advances in air force armament, the British eventually also shifted their targets to densely developed civilian areas in early 1942, unlike the Americans. The change came about not least because of new Bomber Command Chief Arthur Harris, who went on record after the war, saying, "Besides Essen, we never actually considered any particular industrial sites as targets. The destruction of industrial sites was always some sort of bonus for us. Our real targets always were the inner cities." Mortal bombing was intended

Buildings Destroyed

Building	Designation
Cultural buildings	Old and New Theaters, second Gewandhaus, Central Theater, Playhouse (Shakespearestrasse), Art Museum
Churches	St. Matthew's Church, St. John's Church, Anglican Church (western outlying area), St. Andrea's Church (southern outlying area), Old Redeemer's Church (Thonberg)
Public buildings	New Exchange, main post office, planetarium, observatory, market hall, old and new booksellers' exchange, Eilenburg train station, Bavarian train station (left section and hall)
University	Of the university's 103 buildings, only 16 were not significantly damaged, more than 15 were total losses, whereby the city's central region was hit hardest, where only the Church of St. Paul was slightly damaged. Additionally, about 70 percent of library holdings were destroyed.
Destroyed or heavily damaged but rebuilt	Old Exchange, Old Weigh Station, main train station (entire concourse), Old City Hall (attic level), book industry building, Reformed Church, convention center, Grassi Museum, Ringmessehaus, Grosser Blumberg, among others

During the December 1943 attack alone, 3,350 buildings were destroyed, including 1,067 commercial buildings, 221 significant to the arms industry, 56 schools, and 29 trade-show buildings. The Crystal Palace, Café Felsche, Bauer, Panorama, Thüringian Courtyard, Royal House, Greek House, Large Fireball (Goethe), New St. John's Hospital, New St. Nicholas and New St. Thomas Schools, artists' house, and the Horseshoe were left in ruins.

not just to disrupt the public and economic orders but, above all, to provoke the civilian population to revolt.

But this consequence did not occur, not even in spring 1943, when air supremacy shifted to the Allies and the bombing grew more and more intense. The Nazi reaction was soon reduced to deploying a few antiaircraft units, evacuating children to the countryside, and various propaganda initiatives. Of the one hundred largest German cities, only Görlitz and Heidelberg were spared.

It was only 25 degrees Fahrenheit on the morning of December 4, 1943. The sun had not yet risen, but the flames lapping up the city made the sky bright as day. Every attempt to contain the fires failed. The water system in the city center had collapsed, and rubble blocked the fire engines' way. In addition, the majority of Leipzig's fire department had been called to Berlin, which had been targeted several nights before. The external forces responding were faced with the problem that Leipzig's fire hydrants were not equipped with standard connectors, so they could not connect their hoses. Two hours after the attack, Allied pilots were just arriv-

Degree of Destruction of German Cities in WWII

City	Percent
Düren	99
Paderborn	96
Cologne	70
Dresden	60
Hamburg	54
Berlin	37
Munich	33
Stuttgart	30
Leipzig	**25**
Potsdam	20

The heavily damaged north side of the Market Square. Rubble from the Old Weigh Station was already removed in 1944

ing back at home, when individual fires merged into larger ones, unleashing a firestorm on Leipzig's inner city. The unquenchable hunger of the flames generated so much suction that trees snapped and people and even cars were whipped around. Days later, individual fires continued to flare up. Amazingly, only about two thousand people lost their lives that night.

The Socialist City
1945 to 1989

Reconstruction Resistance

"It has to look democratic, but we'll have to keep everything in hand."
—Walter Ulbricht, 1945

June 17, 1953, began as a pretty normal Wednesday morning. People ate breakfast, went to work, the streetcars squealed along the tracks, and there was discussion at Free German Youth (FDJ) Headquarters on Ritterstrasse about Walter Ulbricht's sixtieth birthday, which he wanted to celebrate with his fellow Leipzigers two weeks later. During the morning hours, though, ten thousand people suddenly took to the streets in demonstration, and the most unusual thing about it was that no national organization had called on them to do so. Protests began because of a strike initiated on the previous day by construction workers at Berlin's Stalinallee. A spark that soon lit up the entire republic, as discontent was huge over supply bottlenecks and continually rising work quotas.

Eight years earlier, the Nazi horror and Second World War had finally ended. Hitler's mania had claimed fifty million lives in Europe. Vast swaths

Tomato plants on Ernst-Thälmann-Strasse, 1981

National Front Pavillion on fire in the market

of the thousand-year empire lay in ruin, a thousand years behind the twentieth century. Leipzig, which got off relatively easy, was liberated by the Americans on April 18, 1945, and handed over to the Soviets in July, who installed SPD-politician Erich Zeigner as mayor. "The city was bleeding from countless wounds," he said of the situation. Only half of all buildings in the municipal area were unharmed, and nearly 20 percent were declared total losses and listed as debris, which amounted to 162 million cubic feet, enough to cover 100 hundred soccer fields with a nineteen-foot layer. The majority was hauled away in railway cars and dumped onto a 130-foot-tall pile on Fockestrasse, once a scenic vantage point.

In addition, twelve hundred bomb craters disrupted streets and squares, electricity and gas supply were not functioning in various districts, and the health care system was severely impaired. Typhus, dysentery, diphtheria, and increased infant mortality took their toll. The city center was hit particularly hard, including Leipzig's central institutions: the trade-show complex, university, and book industry. The loss of nearly all major cultural sites was perhaps the most emotionally difficult one to handle. Only the convention center at the zoo survived, which was "just" heavily damaged, while the art museum, Gewandhaus, and initially even the New Theater would have to be rebuilt. Of the 225,000 apartments, only 78 percent were habitable, a number that could be increased by maintenance work. Though Leipzig's population in 1945 was just eighty percent of its prewar total of 585,000, two out of every five Germans were no longer in their hometowns, because they had fled, been evacuated, or deported, leaving countless people wandering around, looking for their homes. Another eleven million were German soldiers held as prisoners of war, and about half that many had been killed at the front. So for every (potentially disabled) man between the ages of eighteen and thirty in the Soviet Occupation Zone in 1946, there were nearly three women of the same age. That meant that rebuilding the city was largely women's work.

By 1950, Leipzig was relatively clear, though rubble removal continued until 1956. The Old City Hall, the Old Exchange, and other destroyed buildings were rebuilt. Meanwhile, 617,000 people were living in the city, the biggest population from post-1945 until today. After that, though, population development and reconstruction came more and more to a standstill, and not just in Leipzig. Throughout the entire newly established German Democratic Republic, reality lagged far behind political intentions and behind West German development

Rubble removers on Petersstrasse

as well. This was one reason why work quotas were continually rising.

Construction workers felt particularly under pressure, and some protested in Leipzig as well. Industrial laborers also quickly joined the protests, and about eighty factories went on strike. Their workforces filed into Karl-Marx-Square from every direction on June 17. According to the German Socialist Unity Party's (SED) internal estimate, about forty thousand people took part in the demonstrations, and observers say it might have been closer to one hundred thousand. Because management wanted to ride it out, the situation was peaceful until noon. But when various national and party institutions were seized and occupied, the political leadership changed strategy. Initial warning shots were fired, and shortly after 3:00 p. m. several demonstrators were wounded by bullets when they tried to storm the detention center on Beethovenstrasse. Nineteen-year-old foundry worker Dieter Teich was killed. His corpse was carried along the Ring in a protest and funeral march. Later, the police reported to Berlin, "On the way to the main train station, people shouted at the People's Police and threw flowers on the deceased." At 4:00 p. m. a state of emergency was declared, and Soviet tanks rolled into position.

The Soviet Union was controlling in every regard, and its presence extended beyond tanks. After the war ended, the country went straight from one Führer to a new, socialist one, in Steely Stalin—as if the Nazi Führer had not been enough. Three months before the uprising, "the greatest man of our time," as super-Stalinist Walter Ulbricht described him, died and was replaced by Nikita Khrushchev. Leipzig native and furniture-maker Ulbricht remained general secretary of the Communists, and the extension of Moscow, though he did falter briefly in the face of de-Stalinization.

Ulbricht was born in 1893 in an attic apartment at 25 Gottschedstrasse. Seven years earlier, composer Gustav Mahler had lived in the same building for a while, and in 1899, economics student Gustav Stresemann moved in and was Ulbricht's neighbor for half a year. About thirty years later they met again at the Reichstag. Ulbricht was a German Commu-

"Post-war acrobatics" under "Iron Stalin's" gaze, in the market

nist Party (KPD) delegate, and Stresemann was the foreign secretary and a Nobel Peace Prize winner. A career to which Ulbricht definitely did not aspire. As a powerful man in the Soviet Occupation Zone, he presented a manifesto for developing Socialism at the Second Party Congress in July 1952. The plan did away with the states, whose functions were assumed by fifteen districts. Officially, Saxony no longer existed, but people kept on speaking Saxon, including Ulbricht. Additional factories were expropriated, and heavy industry was prioritized at the expense of other branches of the economy. The resulting shortages of consumer goods were one reason for the national uprising, which was directed primarily at the institutions of the new government. The Pavilion of the National Front on Market Square went up in flames, the Free German Youth (FDJ) building was raided, but the storming of the Runde Ecke (Round Corner) was especially fierce. As one of the few buildings in the inner city that was still usable after the war, the building, with its characteristic semicircular façade, first served the American Army and later the Soviet Ministry of the Interior, until the *Stasi* (East German State Security Force) eventually moved there in 1950 and built its first extension in 1958—the school museum today—followed by a second one in 1983.

On June 17 a demonstrator was killed at the Round Corner, too. One of twelve people who lost their lives in Leipzig that day, including a policeman accidentally shot by a Soviet soldier. Throughout the entire GDR, at least thirty-four demonstrators and five members of the security forces were killed during the fighting, and another twenty-six death sentences were enforced. The SED denounced the riots as the work of provocateurs and Fascist agents from other countries. Despite the casualties, strikes continued throughout the next several days, but the uprising had already failed. The city did not return to normal until July 11, however, when the state of emergency prohibiting gatherings of more than three people was finally lifted. Meanwhile, Walter Ulbricht had not celebrated his sixtieth birthday with his fellow Leipzigers, nor was the Ring named after him as originally planned.

Names Changed

Name Today	Former Name
Markt (Market)	Platz des Friedens (Peace Square, 1950–54)
Augustusplatz (Augustus Square)	Karl-Marx-Platz (Karl Marx Square, 1945–1990)
Eisenbahnstrasse (Railway Street)	Ernst-Thälmann-Strasse (Ernst Thälmann Street, 1945–1991)
Goerdelerring (Goerdel Ring)	Friedrich-Engels-Platz (Friedrich Engels Square, 1945–1991)
Willy-Brandt-Platz (Willy Brandt Square)	Karl-Legien-Platz (Karl Legien Square, 1945–1953), Platz der Republik (Republic Square, 1953–1993)
Prager Strasse (Prague Street)	Leninstrasse (Lenin Street, 1950–1991)
Karl-Liebknecht-Strasse (Karl Liebknecht Street)	Zeitzer Strasse (Zeitz Street, 1839–1933)/Südstrasse (South Street, 1874–1933), Adolf-Hitler-Strasse (Adolf Hitler Street, 1933–1945)
Ranstädter Steinweg (Ranstadt Stone Lane)	Stalinallee (Stalin Avenue, 1950–1956), Strasse der III Weltfestspiele (Street of the 3rd International Festival, 1951–1956), Friedrich-Ludwig-Jahn-Allee (Friedrich Ludwig Jahn Avenue, 1956–1991)
Dresdner Strasse (Dresden Street)	Strasse der Befreiung (Liberation Street, 1951–1991)
Delitzscher Strasse (Delitz Street)	Strasse der Deutsch-Sowjetischen Freundschaft (Street of German–Soviet Friendship, 1950–1991)
Rittergutsstrasse (Manor Street)	Strasse der Jungen Pioniere (Young Pioneers Street, 1966–1991)
Dieskaustrasse (Dieskau Street)	Strasse des Komsomol (Komsomol Street, 1950–1991)

Long Live Sports!

The year 1964 was downright eventful in the realm of sports. The summer Olympic Games were held in Tokyo, the last time a unified German team participated, and the newly established Bundesliga (West German national soccer league) held its first championship in Cologne. In Steinheidel-Erlabrunn, meanwhile, Jens Weißflog was born, Täve Schur ended his cycling career, and the television program *Mach mit, mach's nach, mach's besser* (an exercise show encouraging the audience to follow along) debuted on East German TV-station DDR1. Unusual things were happening in Leipzig, too. Before the beginning of the fourth-division soccer season in 1963–64, GDR athletic officials initiated further structural changes intended to result in a "concentration of achievement potential," in GDR official-speak. The best players from both of Leipzig's fourth-division teams, SC Rotation and SC Lokomotive, were delegated to the newly established SC Leipzig (which became the first FC Lokomotive Leipzig after 1966). The SC's home field was the old VfB arena in Probstheida, the Bruno Plache Stadium. The "rest of Leipzig" played under the name BSG Chemie (Chemical Factory Athletic Association) and coach Alfred Kunze in the Georg Schwarz Sportpark in Leutzsch. Innercity rivalry games were played in the Central Stadium, dedicated in 1956.

Swimming arena—the first structure in the Sport Forum

Planners in the Weimar Republic had already envisioned athletic and recreation fields along the shores of the Elster Basin. The design made public in 1926 included a covered stadium seating sixty thousand to seventy thousand, bleachers for aquatic sports, an institute for small-team sports, a civic center, and a swimming pool, among other things. While execution of the plans was interrupted by the global economic crisis, the German Reich's Association of Physical Education, directed by Werner March, architect for Berlin's Olympic Stadium, took up the plans in 1935. March envisioned a large athletic complex with a stadium for ninety thousand spectators, but it never made it beyond the planning stage. Converting Ranstadt pastures into the Adolf Hitler Field was the only part that actually happened, so where several hundred head of cattle once stood, now several hundred thousand Nazis could stand.

Athletic complexes would not be built in the athletic complex until after the war. First came the 9,200-spectator swimming stadium in 1952. Many international competitions took place there, such as the 1962 European Championships and the international competition between the GDR and the US in 1971, and world records were set there, by Mark Spitz, among others. The Elster Basin itself had served as an aquatic sports venue in the 1920s, and regattas returned there after the Luppe River dam was damaged in 1960. Business was brisk at Central Stadium, whose rampart was built by 180,000 volunteers working for 360 days to pile up rubble from the Second World War. Because of its capacity, it came to be known as "100,000 Stadium," though the official record was 110,000 spectators—set in 1956 for the legendary 5:3 match between FC Kaiserslautern and Wismut Aue. Because 400,000 tickets were ordered in advance and the barriers were relatively low, the unofficial spectator count was closer to 150,000. Before the stadium's renovation in t 2000, it was the second largest stadium in Europe, after the 250,000-seat Strahov Stadium in Prague. Soccer games were not the only events that sold out. Gymnastics tournaments, sports festivals, and track-and-field championships also drew sell-out crowds. Even a handball match between East and West Germany in 1959 drew about 93,000 spectators.

At that time, Bruno Plache Stadium could seat fifty-five thousand, but in the 1963–64 season, only ten thousand spectators came on average, while twice that many went to watch the Chemical team at Georg Schwarz Sportpark. Even more surprising was the first inner-city match on the sixth day of play, in which the alleged elite (the Leipzig Locomotives) fell 3:0 to the team from Leutzsch, catapulting the "rest of Leipzig" to the top of the standings. The same was true of the Dresden Dynamos, who played one level lower. Unlike the Elbflorenzer, who were known as an elevator team at the time (continually rising and falling), teams like

Athletics and Socialism—closely connected

BSG Motor Steinach and BSG Lokomotive Stendal made it to the top flight.

New teams were established after World War II in other sports as well. The old league structures were dissolved completely in 1945 and were now subject to the new Socialist state. The government's new emphasis on sports was visible in its efforts to build up the athletic infrastructure, and not just in Leipzig. Selection and training methods were also of considerable importance. One of the most central components was the Deutsche Hochschule für Körperkultur (DHfK, German Academy of Physical Culture), for which buildings were erected in the athletic complex in the mid-1950s. An offshoot of the Institut für Leibesübungen (Institute for Physical Education) founded in 1925, the facility served as an educational institution for a total of sixteen thousnad certified sports educators and coaches, who later worked in competitive and recreational sports. One out of every four students came from abroad, where DHfK research and training enjoyed a great reputation. Graduates came from over one hundred countries. With 93 Olympic victors and 136 world champions, the affiliated DHfK Sport Club is still considered to be the most successful club in the history of international athletics.

International athletic success would win the little Socialist country some respect both at home and abroad. The results were impressive indeed. After ranking second in Montreal and Moscow, the GDR placed second one last time in total medals at the 1988 Olympic Games in Seoul, the last Olympics in which the country participated—behind the Soviet Union and ahead of the United States. But how much of that success may have been due to doping is hard to say.

The 1964–65 soccer season, meanwhile, defied all classification, for the expected top performer did not come out on top, but the "rest of Leipzig" topped the chart on the last day of competition, followed by the eternal runners-up SC Empor Rostock and the vastly superior local rival Leipzig Sports Club. For the city, it was the most successful season in all of division history, which was no consolation to SC fans. The championship title had gone to Leipzig once before, in 1951. The Chemical team had won then, too. The decommissioned team's victory was all the more important, because it was the last national championship any Leipzig soccer team has managed to win.

Olympic Medal Winners

Athlete	Sport	Medal	Most Successful Event(s)
Margitta Gummel	Track and field	1 (1 × G)	Gold, shot put, 1968
Bärbel Eckert	Track and field	4 (4 × G)	Gold, 200 m dash, 1976 and 1980, Gold, 4 × 100 m relay, 1976 and 1980
Thomas Munkelt	Track and field	1 (1 × G)	Gold 110 m hurdles, 1980
Kristin Otto	Swimming	6 (6 × G)	Gold, 50 u. 100 m freestyle, 100 m butterfly, 100 m backstroke, 4 × 100 m free relay, 4 × 100 m medley relay (all in 1988)
Klaus Köste	Gymnastics	4 (1 × G, 3 × B)	Gold, vault, 1972
Angelika Bahmann	Kayaking	1 (1 × G)	Gold, indiv. kayak, 1972
Anett Schuck	Kayaking	2 (2 × G)	Gold 4-man kayak, 1996 and 2000
Christian Gille	Kayaking	3 (je 1)	Gold, double-Canadian 1000 m, 2004
Siegfried Brietzke	Rowing	3 (3 × G)	Gold, double w/o coxswain, 1972; Gold, 4-man w/o coxswain, 1976 and 1980
Gustav-Adolf Schur	Cycling	2 (1 × S, 1 × B)	Silver, team sprint, 1960
Uwe Ampler	Cycling	1 (1 × G)	Gold, team sprint, 100 km, 1988

Gateway to the East

On March 11, 1984, Franz Josef Strauss looked out the window again in the suite set up for him in the GDR Council of Ministers' guesthouse. Outside, People's Policemen and State Security forces patrolled in front of the building. The temperature was well below freezing that morning, and the air was thick with the reek of two-stroke engines and a whole lot of burning brown coal. The ultramodern building usually housed GDR elites visiting the trade shows and was one of the few in the area with central heating. It loomed like a gleaming modern fortress over the grey-brown residential buildings nearby. But Strauss, prime minister of Bavaria, had not come to survey facades. In just a few minutes, he would head to Leipzig's trade-show grounds, where East and West German journalists were already waiting impatiently for the traditional opening tour of the spring trade show. Oskar Lafontaine from the SPD and Otto Graf Lambsdorff from the FDP would also be there, and American President Ronald Reagan had sent his regards.

As in in past centuries, the Leipzig trade show was an almost unavoidable institution for trade between Eastern and Western Europe, even during the decades after World War II. Although now the points of view had changed completely. It was no longer the city's advantageous geographic location or the exemplary development of the trade show's infrastructure that attracted people to Leipzig, but its position within both of the European power blocs at the time. The trade show was the point of contact between capital and Socialism, between market and planned economies. Because that function could be experienced only behind the Iron Curtain, Leipzig remained a factor, far more than

cities like Poznan, Brno, and Budapest. West German trade shows had long since phased out trade within Western Europe. Leipzig's position was occupied by Frankfurt, Cologne, and especially Hannover, where an elaborate counter-fair had been established in 1946.

At that same time, Leipzig had worked hard to rebuild the trade-show infrastructure so heavily damaged during the war. Speck's Courtyard, the Trade Palace, and the Union and Ring trade-show buildings were repaired at great expense, and the first and for a long time the only new building in the inner city was the Trade-show Courtyard, dedicated in 1950. The trade show had not only served trade for a long time but had functioned as an advertising tool. Twice a year, real Socialism was presented to visitors from capitalist countries. And as a result of this big production, Leipzig citizens enjoyed products twice each year that were not usually available in their local stores.

The face of the city was also spruced up, at least in areas expecting fairgoers from the West. Even more important, Leipzig maintained a level of internationality through the trade show unlike anywhere else in the Socialist republic. The world declared off-limits since the Wall was built was always dropping by the city on the Pleisse. Direct contact with the class enemy holding hard currency was pretty much unavoidable. Due to a shortage of beds, some guests stayed in private quarters—with trade-show moms. Cab drivers and employees in the hotel and trade-show industry were also pleased, and entrepreneurs were available for private amusement on Nordstrasse, which was prohibited but also tolerated. The end justified the means. One reason that even the Socialist government claimed, which had borrowed billions from the capitalist class enemy.

Franz Josef Strauss had negotiated the loan of those billions during his first visit to Leipzig one year earlier. The fact that the Communist-hater, of all people, would orchestrate such a deal with the anti-capitalists was pretty incredible, but Strauss wanted to show the leaders in Bonn that Bavaria could make international policy, too. Financial imbalance in the GDR budget created good opportunities for that. Boldly confident SED slogans were evident all over Leipzig, especially on the trade-show grounds, such as, "Victory in Socialism, always forward, never back," and, "The German Democratic Republic saves peace; as we work today, we shall live tomorrow," and, "Learn-

The trade-show's double-M logo and the Soviet Pavillion

ing from the Soviet Union means learning how to win" (which in the Saxon dialect sounded more like "how to be sick"). Real circumstances, however, did not stand up to these slogans, especially not when compared to conditions in West Germany.

The East German economy had grown considerably in decades past, though on a much more limited basis than its West German counterpart. Productivity per capita there in the early 1950s was more than twice as high, partly due to the isolation of East German industry in the southern part of the country, but also because of reparations paid to the Soviet Union, resulting in 3,000 East German factories, 7,332 miles of railroad tracks, 2,367 cranes, 155,100 tons of instruments and spare parts, and much more being sent east, where the German invasion in WWII had caused heavy damage. Capital funds, know-how, and people immigrated to the West, because economic policies in the Soviet Occupation Zone severely limited entrepreneurial freedom.

Nationalization was part of that, right from the start. At first it affected large corporations, but by 1972 most of the trades and smaller companies were also expropriated, and private companies comprised less than 5 percent of all economic enterprise in East Germany. Instead, production took place in publicly owned companies (VEBs), which were linked to technical combines. The most significant industrial area in the GDR was the region of Halle-Leipzig, which generated about one quarter of total GDR production. Many of those industrial sectors were located in Leipzig.

Most production occurred in factories that predated the war. While some new industrial buildings were added, such as Robotron (an electronics company), Chemieanlagenbau (a chemical plant), or Brühlpelz (Brühl Fur Company), those were more exceptions than the rule. Production was further concentrated in traditional industrial cores—in Plagwitz alone, there were eighteen thousand industrial jobs. The book industry was largely still located in the Graphic District. In 1971, of seventy-eight total publishing companies in the GDR, thirty-two were located in Leipzig. Most of the original publishers had left in summer 1945, in an American convoy headed for southern Germany. Some publisher that remained initially, like Reclam, left the Soviet Occupation Zone a short time later. The old publishers' names were still employed but were now preceded by VEB, meaning publicly owned (e.g. VEB Reclam, VEB Bibliographisches Institut, VEB Brockhaus). To keep book prices low, the state subsidized the industry, along with culture in general, but also basic foodstuffs and rent. Electronics, vehicles, or upscale products (like coffee), were more expensive.

GDR citizens spent twice as much on coffee in the 1970s than they did for shoes. When international coffee prices increased sharply in 1976, which could be bought only with hard (Western) currency, GDR leaders were compelled to curb imports, which led to shortages and unusually strong protests. Attempts to relieve the situation with Kaffee-Mix (a coffee beverage enriched with ground peas and grains) failed dismally, and the product was lampooned as *"Erichs Krönung"* (Erich's best), after Erich Honecker, the last general secretary of the SED and chairman of the GDR state council.

Residents at the guesthouse on Schwägrichenstrasse lived far removed from such problems. There, along with the best goods from the GDR, western imports were available, from toilet paper to DAB beer in cans. The latter was reportedly preferred by Erich Honecker, the biggest of all Party comrades—further indication of his proletarian origins. Whether Franz Josef Strauss ever had a beer with him (a Radeberger, perhaps) was never recorded, unfortunately. The guesthouse is still there, despite numerous threats to tear it down, still in contrast with its surroundings, though now it's the other way around. While Protzendorf has been properly refurbished since then and its bourgeois luster restored, the former Socialist fancy flophouse has stood empty for twenty years and has deteriorated considerably.

Beautify Our Cities and Towns

> *"The old University building will be rebuilt."*
> *—Walter Ulbricht at the first building conference in 1955*

Six Leipzig churches were destroyed during World War II, including the Catholic Church, St. Matthew's Church, and St. John's Church. The latter also contained the gravesite of Johann Sebastian Bach and brothers Christian Fürchtegott and Christlieb Ehregott Gellert, whose remains were first salvaged in 1949, after the nave had collapsed. While Bach was immediately moved to St. Thomas Church, the Gellerts found a new final resting place in the Church of St. Paul. Debris from the nave was hauled away, and only the 187-foot tower remained of St. John's Church, though it was badly damaged. It was refurbished in 1956, and the brand-new Baroque tower stood tall and a little lonely over war-damaged Johannis Square, for seven whole years.

"Redevelopment of the square at St. John's Church is not one of the city's most urgent missions. But the tower must not be left to deteriorate," Leipzig's head architect Walter Lucas said in March 1956. Preserving architectural heritage was one of the priorities of redevelopment, which corresponded to the style employed for new construction. As in the Soviet Union, where Socialist Classicism had been the only architectural style permitted since 1934, traditional elements crept into architecture in the Socialist sister states—commonly referred to as Stalin-Baroque or gingerbread style. The first ensemble was built in Leipzig in 1951–52, on Windmüh-

The Brühl after renovation, 1969

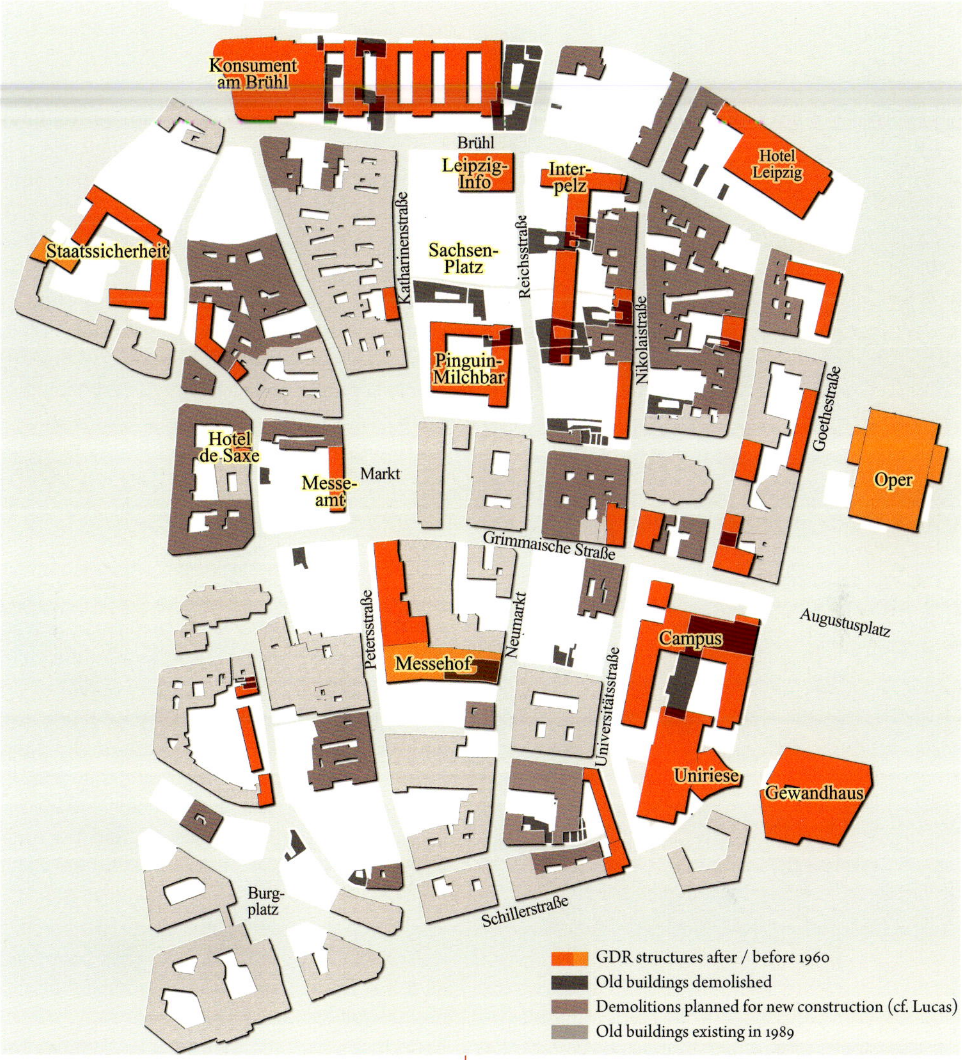

Buildings from the GDR Era

Building	Erected	Remark
Trade-show Courtyard	1950	
Apartment blocks Windmühlenstrasse	1952	
Ring Café	1955	
Opera	1960	
Trade-fair Building at Market	1963	
Main Post Office / Hotel Deutschland	1964/65	
Milk bar Penguin	1964	
Trade Fair Office Building	1965	demolished
Interhotel Leipzig	1965	demolished

Building	Erected	Remark
Interfur Brühl	1966	
Brühl Buildings/"Tin Can"	1968	demolished
Saxonia Square	1970	demolished
University and "Uni Giant"	1972	
Highrise "Winter Garden"	1974	
Hotel Merkur (Westin)	1981	
Gewandhaus / Concert Hall	1981	
Bowling Hall	1987	
Dorotheen Place	1989	

Construction in downtown Leipzig during the GDR era

lenstrasse and the Strasse der III. Weltfestspiele (Ranstädter Steinweg). The most terse examples of Leipzig architecture from that era, however, are the Ring development with the Ring-Café (1953–1955), and the Opera House (1956–1960), which was originally supposed to sport a much more ostentatious facade. Since 1957, however, leading GDR architects suddenly switched to completely different concepts than before. "What's new is definitive, and the old must defer to it or get out of the way," Walter Lucas said.

He had already demonstrated his capacity to change. After he joined the NSDAP in 1928, which awarded him numerous contracts and the Golden Party Insignia, he was sentenced to five years in prison in Bautzen, only to swear his loyalty to Socialism and be promoted to the highest position in Leipzig's city planning office. Like his predecessor, he first promoted rebuilding the Augusteum, Gewandhaus, and the art museum. In 1957 he began advocating just as vehemently for their demolition and reworked a design for Leipzig's city center. More than half of all inner-city buildings was to make way for a modern Socialist city center, including Barfussgässchen, Nikolaistrasse, and the Reformed Church.

The plan was initiated by a veritable construction boom, at least relative to prior years. Since the end of the war, only three new buildings had emerged inside the Ring—the Trade-show Courtyard, the expansion of the Round Corner, and the Opera House—which was the subject of much criticism.

That was about to change, partially because the city's eight hundredth anniversary was to be celebrated in a presentable city center. Historic characteristics, however—except in the rebuilt Alte Waage (Old Weigh Station), the historic trade-fair building—were not present in the new buildings, as they were frowned upon after de-Stalinization. At the same time, many old buildings were stripped of their culturally historic significance. Even Paul Fröhlich, first SED secretary of Leipzig's district administration, said in 1967, "The complex completion of the ensembles chosen for the development of the city center requires the removal of old buildings and partial ruins." Gerberstrasse, the western and eastern outlying areas especially, and the center, were subject to clear-cutting until 1968, a process in which even buildings repaired after the war were torn down. That is also what happened to St. John's Church tower—it fell victim to the absurd building policy in May 1963.

Five years later, the level of restraint sank so low that the demolition expert was even sent to Karl Marx Square. The central post office and Hotel Deutschland on its eastern side had already been given a Socialist facelift. The western side was still marked by the Augusteum, spared by the war, and the 700-year-old St. Paul's Church. Rededicated by Martin Luther as the University Church, it had been the spiritual core of the intellectual center for many generations. But the thing was to be removed, despite all of its history, its status as a protected monument since 1962, and its sound architectural condition. And so it was detonated on May 30, 1968, at 9:58 a.m., followed several days later by the Augusteum. Christian Fürchtegott Gellert, whose casket had been preserved in the choir since 1949, had to

Newly renovated and then demolished, St. John's Church spire, c. 1960

be moved again. He was more fortunate than any of the other people buried in the three-story crypt under the church. The whereabouts of only three of the eight hundred laid to rest there are known.

Old buildings were not losing prestige only in the GDR, however. The substance of West German cities greatly diminished in that era as well, though sound churches hundreds of years old were not the usual architectural victims there. War was declared on Historicism in particular, which in light of financial opportunities in the West could be waged more efficiently. De-ornamentation, demolition, and the expansion of car-friendly roads were common.

While the GDR was extremely open to that approach, a lack of financial means limited dealing with the architectural legacy to an almost nonexistent degree, and that included ignoring overdue renovations. One reason was low fixed rents, about one East mark per square meter, which made repairing properties impossible. Loans for private landlords would not pay themselves off, and in cases of inheritance, the buildings were often rejected, which meant that they became the property of the VEB Gebäudewirtschaft Leipzig (GWL, Leipzig Public Building Industry). In 1989 barely 10 percent of all Leipzig apartments were privately leased, 25 percent through government-owned cooperatives, and 65 percent through the GWL.

Their financial means for rehabilitation were all similarly limited, however, because almost all the available funds went to new apartment construction. For the average citizen living in old buildings, the neglect was evident in the ashen cityscape, the communal bathroom down the stairs, the stove heating, and the construction defects, all this on top of the massive industrial pollution. Because construction of new buildings lagged behind demand, thirty thousand Leipzig families still had no home of their own in the mid-1970s, and had to share with other renters. A problem the SED Central Committee tried to fix with a new apartment construction program in 1973. Three million apartments were to be built, most on the edge of

One of the most tragic events in Leipzig's post-war history—demolition of St. Paul's Church, 1968

the city, where it seemed like it would be the most economical.

Thus Socialist Modernism was headed for greener pastures—in Berlin's Marzahn district; Halle's Neustadt; and in Leipzig's Paunsdorf, Mockau, Schönefeld, and especially Grünau districts. For the Lieipzig's largest large-scale housing complex, about 38,500 new apartments were built beginning in 1976, all with central heating, modern plumbing facilities, water-tight roofs, schools, daycare centers, grocery stores, and all kinds of large-scale housing flair. All in all, ninety thousand prefabricated apartments were built in Leipzig, in which more than two hundred thousand Leipzigers lived in 1989, with eighty-five thousand of them in Grünau alone.

St. Paul and St. Martin's churches served those, along with two newly created houses of worship, and the Trinity Congregation (Waldstrasse District) and the Mormons (Schleussig) dedicated new churches in the 1980s, made possible in part by a development program cofinanced by West Germany. St. Mark's Church in Reudnitz, meanwhile, was condemned due to dilapidation and demolished in 1978, after decades of neglect. A fate that threatened countless other old buildings as time went by. While all kinds of work was done on the edge of town, Leipzig's core was rotting away. Meanwhile East German city planners had distanced themselves from the brutish methods of the 1960s and devoted themselves to preserving and developing old city neighborhoods in the post-modern style in the early 1980s. Some neighborhoods were on the verge of collapse, however, with some of them even lived in until they were torn down.

Industrialized Apartment Blocks in Leipzig

District	Beginning of Construction	Number of Apartments
Grünau	1976	36,000
Paunsdorf	1987	6,300
Schönefeld	1974	4,500
Möckern	1961	4,500
Mockau Ost/West	1976	4,500
Lößnig	1971	3,000
Street of October 18	1968	2,400
Großzschocher	1964	1,800
Thekla	1976	1,700
Inner Western Suburb	1971	2,600

Augustus Square with new university structure and the Gewandhaus, after 1981

"Ruinen schaffen ohne Waffen" (make ruins without weapons), Leipzig residents joked bitterly.

At the time, because most buildings erected around 1900 did not need renovation before the global economic crisis and later were not renovated due to insufficient funds, Leipzig consisted of tens of thousands of buildings that had not been refurbished in a whole century. The number of demolitions increased sharply in the mid-1980s, many executed by military vehicles from the National People's Army. At the same time, city planners tried to close the housing-shortage gap that had resulted, but because of insufficient funding, that often meant they used prefabricated buildings to do so. The WBS 70, the most heavily used prefabricated building model in the GDR, became a universal weapon of choice in the country's architectural arsenal. Nearly 650,000 apartments of that type were built. Through design kits, they could be equipped with recessed balconies, bays, and other extras, with a total of thirty-nine different options available—not bad. The Colonnade District was probably the most expensive redesign effort in Leipzig at the time, but Seeburgstrasse, Reclamstrasse, and other districts—most in the eastern part of the city—were similarly transformed, after a great deal of demolition.

The year 1989 also saw the beginning of the first large-scale demolition in the municipal area, which affected primarily Connewitz's Biedermannstrasse. In Plagwitz, too, the old "oppressive architecture," as it was called in the GDR. would make way for new apartment buildings of the prefabricated variety, as later GDR travel guidebooks boasted. The plans would run into resistance, however, at a time when general resistance was growing. Both went hand in hand, because the political elite's ineffectiveness was reflected in the cities' appearance. Many Leipzig residents took to the streets in protest, some prompted by their fear of losing the city's cultural heritage.

Lunar Landscape

It was another magnificent day on the coast of Saxony. Crystal-clear water beyond pristine beaches devoid of people, flanked by subtropical plants. In the pleasantly warm Tertiary period, Leipzig's lowland bay actually had direct access to the sea, along with truly Caribbean qualities. Fifty million years ago, flora and fauna flourished so splendidly that the massive accumulation of their dead biomass is still in the ground today, although it has been used as an energy source known as brown or bituminous coal.

Coal has been mined and used there since the preindustrial era. Problematic effects did not emerge until the early twentieth century, however, when the demand for the raw material increased sharply as it began to be used for generating electricity, and new technologies enabled mining on a massive scale. Until 1907, coal was still mined by hand, but first excavating machines and later conveyor bridges were developed. Instead of underground mining, as was still practiced in the Dölitz shaft that opened in 1895, extraction shifted to surface or strip mining. After the first mines of the kind were developed at Borna and Bitterfeld in the central German mining district, the Böhlen surface mine south of Leipzig was added in 1921, and another in Espenhain just a few miles away in 1937. The mines secured supply for the Böhlen industrial power plant and the Espenhain power plant built in 1942, but they also supplied numerous briquetting plants and coal refineries and fuel extraction facilities. Because untreated industrial sewage flowed directly into the Pleisse River, the river soon no longer resembled a river, and after a huge fish die-off in 1939, it was entirely devoid of life.

That the means of industrial production came at an increasing cost to nature was nothing new. The eastern Rietzschke River had already been turned into a sewage canal fifty years earlier and was eventually encased in tile. With continually increasing production, the quantity and quality of pollution increased in scale and affected local natural areas as well as distant regions across. World War II did not change that trend, and the division of Germany only increased its momentum. There were hardly

The brown coal refinery Espenhain in the Borna area. The nearby town of Mölbis had the sad distinction of being "the dirtiest town in Europe." Photo from 1990

any black coal deposits in GDR territory, where oil and gas were too expensive, especially after the oil crisis (the price for crude oil from the Soviet Union increased fivefold between 1970 and 1980), and hydro and nuclear power remained marginal technologies. In the mid-1980s, over 70 percent of power generated was from brown coal, which came primarily from Lusatia and the Halle-Leipzig area. Which might have been a good thing, if mining and processing it had not had huge consequences for the land, water, air, and people.

The fact that Leipzig's water was ruined by industrial carbon-chemical sites upstream could not be overlooked, however, so the political leadership finally felt compelled to do something about it. The idea of treating industrial sewage in advance did not occur to the cadres, but they did direct first the Pleisse millrace in 1951, and then a nearly three-mile stretch of the Elster millrace underground ten years later. These sections of waterway were not tiled, however, and they created a jet-black substance topped with frothy foam, the odor of which evoked a wide variety of unpleasant associations. Casting a line into the water may have been considered an act of subversion, or an indication of an unsound state of mind, but definitely an attempt to catch *any* fish.

The Pleisse's fate was not an isolated example but served as the most drastic of that era. Rivers all over Europe were degraded to components of the process of production. No longer seen as life veins, they came to be considered a cheap means of removing industrial sewage as it accumulated. The industrial centers' treatment of air in the 1960s was also appalling, all over Europe. The GDR's investment in environmental protection was just 0.5 percent, whereas West Germany's was 1.6 percent. The Leipzig area was hit especially hard in that regard. Many industrial cooperatives were concentrated in the city, whose emissions combined with those of the many brown coal power plants. Fine-particulate and sulfur-dioxide pollution reached levels that would give today's Chinese metropolitan areas a run for their money. In addition, there were two large chemical sites in the immediate vicinity—one twenty-five miles north, near Bitterfeld, and the other in the Böhlen area, to which the town of Mölbis belonged, in the south, just six miles from the edge of Leipzig. Mölbis has the sad distinction of being the most polluted place in Europe.

The landscape in the region, though, could hardly be characterized as European anymore. Giant mining fields, including the conveyor bridge at the Espenhain surface mine, which was one of the largest in Europe, have gobbled up one mile of land after another, leaving craters 160 feet deep and several miles wide. Groundwater levels in the entire region sank sharply, and the course of rivers in the area were rerouted. The Pleisse was diverted four times, until it eventually flowed straight north, penned in by highways and railway lines. The river and the two roadways are on a sliver of land nearly four miles long and barely 300 feet wide, between the Espenhain and Böhlen surface mines. The towns of Gaschwitz and Grossdeuben were boxed in there within a few years, as the excavators came within a dozen feet of the villages, first from the west and then from the east.

Other towns were less fortunate. Eythra, Bösdorf, and Magdeborn disappeared entirely. In Leipzig's southern region alone, twenty-three thousand people in more than six towns and districts had to relocate because of coal mining. And that was just the tip of the planned iceberg. The oil crisis in 1973 increased the country's dependence on its own sources of raw materials, and the SED's response was to call for a policy of radical coal extraction. The plan was to mine the brown coal deposits in Leipzig's southern area nearly completely by 2060. A plan that would have meant doing away with the cities of Zwenkau, Pegau, and Groitzsch.

The mining facilities had already nibbled away at some of Leipzig's municipal territory. The Cospuden surface mine was opened in 1981, which in addition to the towns of Prödel, Cospuden, and the Lauer estate wiped out considerable portions of the riparian forest, along with the 250-year-old Napoleon Oak. Excavation was to continue as far as Brückenstrasse, but vast protests in 1990 stopped it. Several years later, the same happened at the Espenhain surface mine, and at the Böhlen/Zwenkau mine in 1999. Excavation has not yet stopped completely. In 2000, the third brown coal power plant was opened in Lippendorf, with plans to operate for forty years. Surface mines at Profen and incorporated Schleenhain will operate at least as long, which claimed the town of Heuersdorf in 2006. In general, though, mining of this prehistoric fuel source has decreased significantly, and the mutilated landscape is slowly taking (a new) shape again. Like the good old days in the Tertiary period, there are real coasts in Saxony once more, though without the palm trees.

From Free German Youth to Punk Rock

"Whatever tact the youth chooses is up to them. Just as long as it's tactful."
—Walter Ulbricht, 1963

In January 1978, 26-year-old Michelle Bachelet, who fled to the GDR from her home in Chile four years earlier, began a one-year course in German at the Herder Institute on Leipzig's Lumumbastrasse. Angela Merkel, just three years younger and also newly married, was in the final stretch of her physics degree. No one suspected then that both women would begin long careers as female heads of state twenty-eight years later—Merkel in a united Federal Republic of Germany, and Bachelet as the president of Chile. Back then they were just normal students. Angela Merkel was also active as a latent *Trümmerfrau* (woman who removed rubble, especially after WWII). Beginning in 1973, a total of thirty thousand volunteers worked to excavate the Moritzbastei (Moritz Bastion) and convert the centuries-old treasure into a central club for the Free German Youth (FDJ), as it was officially called then. The first concerts were held at the construction site in 1974. At construction site concert number five in November 1974, Leipzig's Klaus Renft Combo played, just a year before the group was forced to disband. Again.

The band was banned for the first time in 1962. Before that they had devoted themselves to rock 'n' roll for five years, which along with Bebop was considered by Socialist leaders to be a spearhead of American imperialism. *Junge Welt* (*Young World*), the FDJ's central news agency, published the rarely objective assessment of Elvis Presley, "His 'singing' was just like his face: stupid, mindless, and brutish." The 1958 ordinance on dance and popular music programming attempted to ban the specter. According to the rule, GDR-DJs—which were referred to as *Schallplattenunterhalter* (SPU, record entertainers) to avoid using an English term—could play only 40 percent capitalist songs, and the rest had to come from Socialist producers. At the Bitterfelder Conference in 1959, Walter Ulbricht advocated for a pop-music build-up. "It is not enough to judge Capitalist decadence with mere words, to campaign against trashy literature and bourgeois customs, or to argue against the hot music and ecstatic vocals of someone like Presley. We must come up with something better to offer." As a result, the Lipsi (Leipzigers) were created to stand up to rock 'n' roll as Socialist adversaries. The 6/4-beat group was named after creator René Dubianski's hometown. Critics from the newspaper *Neues Deutschland* (*New Germany*) were completely enthusiastic. "The progression is full of harmony, and with solos detaching from and finding their partners again, the sound is thoroughly modern." Except this Socialist dance music fell flat with the Socialist youth and was ignored, at best.

More liberal GDR youth policies in the early 1960s were more open to Beat music, partly because the Beatles came from working-class families. On the occasion of the 1964 Deutschlandtreffen (Youth Festival), a new radio station, DT64, was established to supply Socialist youth with plenty of the latest rhythms. The Butlers, Klaus Renft's new band, was even recognized for its musical appeal. But political opposition in fall 1965 was suddenly harsher again, not least because of the legendary outdoor concert by the Rolling Stones and the change in leadership in the Soviet Union. Beat music had already conquered Leipzig, however. Officials reported only six groups of Beat fans in the municipal area in early 1965, but by October, the number had swelled to eighty-three. The phenomenon had gotten out of hand and soon became subject to sanctions. The *Leipziger Volkszeitung* (*Leipzig People's Newspaper*) warned, "The long, shaggy hair they adopt as an outward symbol of their attitude constrains their horizon to the point that they no longer see how abnormal, unhealthy, and inhumane their behavior is."

Beat bands became subject to permits, which was essentially the same as a ban. Even the Butlers were affected. Just how serious the GDR leadership was about enforcement was evident on October 31 in Leuschner-Platz. More than two thousand Beat fans gathered for a demonstration, which government forces brutally dispersed with canine units, billy clubs, and water cannons. They arrested 267 young people, 100 of which were sentenced to several weeks of forced labor at a brown coal–mining operation. Among the generally restrictive measures was the forced enrollment in juvenile work centers. There was no way to stop the phenomenon, though. Fans began meeting in secret. The risk was just part of the appeal. Years later, the political leadership tried a new approach—using musical passion to their advantage instead of prohibiting it.

These new freedoms benefited the Moritzbastei project as well, which was supported by the city and FDJ district management. Though only three students showed up for the first volunteer effort, that would soon change. All in all, volunteers spent 150,000 hours through May 1976, when rubble removal and repair work were complete, for the most part. After provisional approval was finally granted in February 1982, the entire complex was dedicated as the largest student club in Europe—at least that was the claim. Those who had volunteered over fifty hours to the project received builder's cards entitling them to special visitor privileges. While the program was under supervision, it was colorful and controversial right from the start. Besides concerts, the Academixer student cabaret performed there, along with the readers' theater company Der durstige Pegasus (Thirsty Pegasus), established in 1974.

The FDJ did much more than rehabilitate underground medieval chambers. About twenty thousand members of the government-owned youth organization worked nationwide to cut down antennas in 1961, for example. Under the slogan, "The sun rises in the East and sets in the West; we're establishing peace, so down with antennas in the West!" FDJ members carried out sabotage against reception of capitalist propaganda, which did not accomplish much. Western radio remained an uncontrollable influence and developed a completely different kind of attraction than FDJ programming. Though no one was forced to join the FDJ, refusing to do so could result in considerable personal disadvantages, such as not being allowed to enroll in university. As a result, more than 80 percent of all 14- to 25-year-olds were FDJ members.

For most GDR youth, the FDJ's blue shirt or blouse never became more than the inevitable work clothing and was seldom as cool as scarce commodities such as leather jackets and jeans. The things that truly motivated the youth have always been outside the reach of politics. It became harder and harder for party comrades fifty years their seniors to maintain an overview, especially in the GDR's final years. While the LP *Weihnachten in Familie* (*Family Christmas*) by Leipzig native Frank Schöbel and his wife, Aurora, became East German record company Amiga's bestselling recording of all time in 1985, with 1.4 million copies, new musical phenomena were always emerging—poppers, punks, rockers, skinheads, rappers—styles that subdivided into countless others. But who were the good guys and who were the bad guys? *Stasi*-bard Erich Mielke, over seventy years old, impressively articulated the political elite's ignorance and disorientation in a 1988 lecture on the country's subculture: "It is primarily a case of forces emerging patterned after western behavioral models, such as Punks, *Schihands* ["Ski-hands," instead of Skinheads], Heavy Metals, and their sympathizers. But also including the Kuffix [a nonsensical word, instead of *Grufties*, or Goths] most recently arriving on the scene." Phenomena that were limited, for the most part, to East German cities, with East Berlin leading the way, and Leipzig a close second.

The trade shows also shaped Leipzig's nightlife, with visitors flooding the city twice a year and thereby providing a seasonal effect, partly due to the huge increase in prices at fair time. Though Leipzig's nightlife offered a significantly large range of offerings by East German standards, standing in line was also a part of the trade-show experience, as with food service in general. Bouncers and hosts decided who came in, and decisions were often influenced by hard currency. A legend in this regard was Dicke Heinz (Fat Heinz), host for the equally legendary "Schorschl" Club in Connewitz, who

Music

Name	Established	Born
Butlers	1958	
Frank Schöbel		1942
Karussell	1976	
Inka Bause		1968
Die Art	1986	
Die Prinzen	1987	
Tom/Bill Kaulitz Tokio Hotel		1989

seated male and female guests at the tables in such a way that nothing could go wrong. The fact that the new building on the same spot still bears the name of its predecessor, due to its far-reaching fame, is not especially unusual, though now the building is an assisted-living facility. Most bars were located in the city center, however, and approaching them was not all that complicated. Entertainment was usually provided by dance bands or, less often, SPUs (those East German DJs), and alcohol was never a scarce commodity, but today all traces of Femina, Intermezzo, Sachsenquell, and Eden (East German beverage names) have disappeared.

Admission to the Moritzbastei required a student ID or a companion who had one. Once the venue was completely open, about four hundred events were held there annually, in the club's various rooms. There were particularly intense discussions there in fall 1989, even before October 9. Mrs. Merkel was not in attendance, however, but by then she had been living in Berlin for ten years anyway. Another, equally internationally famous woman, visited the establishment in 2000—a scantily clad and very tipsy Britney Spears. She did not have a student ID, but the Moritzbastei had dropped that requirement ages ago.

Mondays

"Powerful Affirmation of the Vitality of Socialism," was the top story of the *Aktuelle Kamera* (*Current Camera,* GDR news show) on May 1, 1989, which devoted half an hour to Mayday rallies all over the nation. About three hundred thousand people took part in the four-hour rally in Leipzig, under the motto "Everything with the people, through the people, for the people." A Socialist ritual practiced each year. The word *people* was not yet an explosive one, although it just so happened that it would be yet another Monday when the word would be so powerfully commandeered.

Just as after every May 1, GDR local elections were held on the following Sunday, though this time voter turnout and approval of the proposed coalition list was unusually low, at barely 99 percent. The worst result was in Leipzig, with 97.7 percent, where civil rights activists were able to document votes at nearly every polling place in the city's Mitte (central) district. The undeniable discrepancies between the official results and documented counts did not fit with the GDR's projected image but with reality. The first (free?) Miss Leipzig contest that took place several weeks later did little to relieve the tension, and on the day of her corona-

Mondays on Goerdelerring in fall 1989

tion on June 10, 1989, new discontent was provoked. Though it had been prohibited, Leipzig's musical street festival took place in the city center, and was attended by musicians from all over the country. When security forces put a rough stop to the festival around noon, loading participants and bystanders into trucks, protests broke out. The initiators did not simply give up. They found new places to sing and dance and be arrested, late into the evening.

Outside the country, there were even stronger indications. In Beijing, a battle in Tiananmen Square resulted in thousands of fatalities—which GDR leaders applauded. But a different wind had begun to blow in Eastern Europe. Mikhail Gorbachev's Glasnost and Perestroika did not affect only the Soviet Union. In the June elections in Poland, voters could vote for the opposition for the first time, and in July, Hungary worked to simplify its border installations to Austria. The latter caused many GDR citizens to change their vacation plans. Others occupied the West German embassies in Budapest, Berlin, Prague, and Warsaw, demanding their right to leave the country.

In face of the abundance of significant events at that time, the one in Leipzig on September 4 seemed relatively unimportant. It was a Monday during the fall trade show. Like every other Monday for the last seven years, people gathered in St. Nicholas Church to pray for peace, an event initiated and led by pastors Christian Führer and Christoph Wonneberger. On that Monday, however, the protest spilled out into the streets and banners were hung around the St. Nicholas Churchyard. "For an open country with free people," one of them read. People wanting to leave the country demanded, "We want out," while others shouted, "We're staying here." State Security forces tore down the banners but made no arrests, because of a camera crew that later broadcast the scene on Western television that reached large sections of the East German Republic.

On the following Monday, state forces were better prepared. Leipzig was declared off-limits to West German media, and the number of State Security forces was increased. But there were also far more demonstrators that day than there had been the week before. The police force met the group of about eight thousands with billy sticks and nearly one hundred arrests. Katrin Hattenhauer, one of the instigators the previous week, was arrested and not released until October 13. The movement, however, was just gathering speed. Despite harassment and government violence, thousands gathered at 5:00 p.m. on every Monday in the following weeks. At that time of day, most people had left work, and shops in the city center were still open, so their presence in the vicinity of the event did not raise suspicion.

On October 2, there were twenty thousand people on hand. State Security forces reported an "unlawful riotous assembly of large groups of people, who were disturbing the peace and public safety and impeding traffic in the city center." Once again, the demonstrators were met with violence. The outcome for the situation in Prague was different, where four thousand GDR citizens were holed up in the embassy. Several days earlier, West German Foreign Minister Hans-Dietrich Genscher brought that to an end with the words, "Dear fellow citizens, we have come to tell you that today your exit..." The event caused an exceptionally huge media storm and had direct consequences. The special West German trains coming from Prague and Warsaw through East German territory unleashed protests in Dresden and Plauen. These were events that did not fit at all with the pending celebration of the GDR's fortieth anniversary. But no one dreamed that the GDR would not be around to celebrate its forty-first. There was no stopping the demonstrations that accompanied the celebrations in many cities. But the regime was still in control—a situation the minister of propaganda made patently clear. The *Leipzig People's Newspaper* printed an editorial by brigade commander Günter Lutz on October 6, in which he wrote, "We are prepared and willing to actively protect that which we worked to create with our own hands, to actively put a stop to these counterrevolutionary acts once and for all. If necessary, with weapons in hand!" Three days later, it was Monday again.

It was clear that the SED had armed itself for this one. The government had mustered eight thousand security personnel in Leipzig—police, State Security, combat troops, soldiers with water cannons, and armored personnel carriers. In addition, hundreds of SED party members had occupied the seats in St. Nicholas Church since the early afternoon, and the mood in the city was getting more and more tense. That the day would bring about some kind of decision was perceptible everywhere, but

Personalities

Name	Born/Died	Role
Christian Führer	(1943–2014)	Lutheran minister, co-organizer of the peace prayers at St. Nicholas Church
Kurt Masur	(1927)	Gewandhaus choir director, read the "no violence" appeal
Bernd-Lutz Lange	(1944)	Cabaret performer, who with Masur, theologian Dr. Peter Zimmermann, and SED officials Kurt Meyer, Jochen Pommert, and Roland Wötzel, was one of the "Leipzig Six" that initiated the "no violence" appeal
Christoph Wonneberger	(1944)	Minister, initiator, and coordinator of Leipzig peace prayers, suffered a stroke on the morning of 10/30/1989, just hours before the Monday demonstration attended by 300,000, and was in a coma for months
Katrin Hattenhauer	(1968)	Civil rights activist, co-initiator of the first Monday demonstration on 9/4/1989
Jochen Lässig	(1961)	Co-founder of the "Justice" task force and of the New Forum, organized the "Freedom with Music" festival

it was unclear what that decision might be: Would it be the Chinese model, supported by rumors that stockpiles of banked blood and medical personnel had arrived in the city, or would the government yield to its people? To prevent violence, the Leipzig Six had drafted an appeal, read by Gewandhaus director Kurt Masur and broadcast on local radio that afternoon. Leaflets with the same text printed by Christoph Wonneberger in St. Luke's Church were also distributed, while more and more people flowed into the city center. Seventy thousand had come, many more than expected. Filled with courage and fear, they finally made their way to the Ring. Amazingly, there were no notable incidents.

1945–1989

Turning Point & Transformation
1990 to 2030

New Ground

Erich Honecker appeared before the SED's Central Committee on October 18, 1989, and gave a speech written by Egon Krenz in which he announced he was resigning from all of his positions effective immediately. He might have thought for a moment about Napoleon, the French emperor whose political career had also suffered a huge setback on October 18, in which Leipzig had also played a role. Honecker was ultimately stripped of power in the Politbüro, though, where a revolt against the seventy-six-year-old had been staged the day before. During the preceding weeks, however, he had exuded a great deal of optimism. "Neither ox nor ass can hold Socialism back," he proclaimed in August 1989 in conjunction with the announcement of a 32-bit microprocessor developed by the Mikroelektronik industrial combine in Erfurt. On the German Democratic Republic's fortieth anniversary, Honecker declared, "Ever forward, never backward." When he resigned just eleven days later, it was officially for health reasons, though the constitution of most of the other SED-bigwigs was not great either, as the subsequent weeks would show.

View from the university's high platform. Photo 2012

Building and Trabant cemetery on Edlichstrasse in Leipzig-Volkmarsdorf. Photo 1990

The disbandment of the old guard was by far not the only thing on East German minds at the time. More was happening within the span of a few weeks than had occurred in the decades before. There was much and intense discussion before and especially after October 9, when the crucial stand for change was taken. Where would the revolution lead? Should the GDR continue as an independent country with Socialist reforms, or was German reunification the answer? Everything seemed possible. Especially when the Berlin Wall unexpectedly fell on November 9 and the exhilaration that dominated everything at the time reached new heights. In the days that followed, all of East Germany first made pilgrimage to West Berlin or West German border regions. In just two months, nearly 3 million people flocked to the West German border town of Hof alone—fifty thousand per day, equivalent to the city's entire population. It was their first contact with capitalism abroad, including welcome payments. Sales tax income in Hof rose to unprecedented levels.

The Monday demonstrations in Leipzig, meanwhile, were drawing crowds of hundreds of thousands. Some 120,000 demonstrated on October 16, 300,000 on October 30, and, through mid-January, 200,000 took part each week. Demonstrators forced their way into the Round Corner on December 4 and into other state-security sites. The demands at the time went far beyond dissolving the intelligence agencies or simply changing Socialism. Demonstrators in Leipzig and around the entire GDR began shouting not only "Gorbi, Gorbi!" but also "Helmut, Helmut!" with increasing frequency, and "Wir sind das Volk!" (We are the people) became "Wir sind ein Volk!" (We are one people). After the Wall opened, many GDR citizens took matters of private reunification with the Federal Republic into their own hands, by moving to West Germany. The number of Leipzigers who officially emigrated in 1989/90 was 57,000, many of whom even left their children behind. By February 1990, city officials recorded 136 incidents of abandoned girls and boys. The desire to leave the country was strong. But that was not the only reason Leipzig struggled with mass emigration. The number of people immigrating to Leipzig was only about 24,000 and the death rate surpassed the birthrate. The reasons for why Leipzig's population sank so drastically during the first ten years after reunification were many.

Unlike the time of the actual *Wende* (turning point) itself, sharply declining birthrates in the years that followed had a negative impact. On the one hand, this was because so many young people were leaving, but even more importantly, because family planning ideas quickly changed with the new system. The average age of first-time mothers in the GDR was the early twenties, but in Leipzig under the Federal Republic, that age quickly shifted to the late twenties, creating a gap. The number of births in eastern Germany in 1994 was just 40 percent of the number of births in the GDR in 1988.

In 1994, Erich Honecker died. His political successor, Egon Krenz, took over in mid-October 1989, but stepped down by early December. Honecker functioned as political leader for almost twenty years, but Krenz lasted only one and a half months—evidence of just how fast things were changing. Hans Modrow's government, composed of various political initiatives, took over, with Leipzig native Manfred Gerlach at the helm of the state council. He went down in history as the last state council leader in the GDR, after which the office was eliminated by constitutional amendment. Even more important, however, were the first free People's Parliament elections on March 18, 1990.

In the weeks leading up to election day, the Monday demonstrations had already lost a great deal of steam. On March 12, just 30,000 people protested, though ten times that many gathered in Karl Marx Square just two days later, where federal chancellor Helmut Kohl campaigned in person. He was the guide on the path of least resistance, D-mark guarantor, and organizer of prosperity, who campaigned for the German Alliance, which along with the CDU and DSU, belonged to the Democratic *Aufbruch* (Awakening), whose frontrunner Wolfgang Schnur was revealed as Stasi confidential informant "Torsten" just four days before the elec-

Leipzig Population

Year	Population
1988	545,307
1990	511,037
1998	437,000
2000	493,208*

(* after incorporation of surrounding area)

tion. Later it would be discovered that CDU candidate Lothar de Maizière (confidential informant "Czerny") and SPD chief Ibrahim Böhme (confidential informant "Paul Bonkartz") had similar careers—a coalition eventually controlled by the SED's successor party, PDS, would not stand in its way, though support declined dramatically from 99 to 16 percent. The Bündnis 90 (Confederation 90) civil rights movement fared much worse, with just 2.9 percent, composed of children of the revolution rejected by the revolution. The results of local elections in Leipzig in early May 1991, however, were much different. Hinrich Lehmann-Grube, a Social Democrat and former Hannover city manager, was named Leipzig's first post-*Wende* mayor.

With the results of the East German elections, the course had changed to quick currency reform and many West German carpetbaggers made their way to the Saale, Pleisse, and/or Oder Rivers. Finally, the lack of obligatory bananas, dual-cassette recorders, and sex-toy catalogs was remedied, though business was initially transacted mainly in the streets, due to a lack of space. West German rug salesmen in particular took over vast sections of Grimmaische Strasse. Tentlike constructions appeared shortly thereafter, followed by sheds resembling buildings, which eventually moved from the central shopping district to green spaces. Meanwhile, GDR shopping centers remained empty, at least as long as they stocked only Eastern products. But because most Western products were expensive, that did not change much in the months to come. The countless used-car lots, filled with all kinds of Western cars, which popped up on the fairgrounds or at the Monument to the Battle of All Nations, seemed completely exotic by comparison. "When they rust, take them East," was a popular saying at the time. One result of this new market was that preorders were no longer needed to purchase Trabants, as announced in Zwickau on March 16, 1990. Very few people were interested in this East German brand of car anymore, and "Trabi"-carcasses littered many a roadside. The abrupt increase in motorization was reflected in accident statistics. In the first half of 1989, only 41 deaths occurred in Leipzig traffic, but during the same period in 1990, the number nearly tripled, to 114. West German traffic regulations were also adopted at that time: nearly all of the 145 green arrows were removed from city traffic lights—if only temporarily—resulting in traffic jams at intersections that had never seen them before, generating the motto, "Fast car—slow traffic."

Besides the colorful car bodies, impressive advertising measures made for some interesting contrasts in the otherwise gray cityscape and trendy changes resulting from these new influences were quickly visible. On March 2, the first jeans shop opened in Leipzig, on Stötteritzer Strasse, which offered leading American brands. The first video store opened one week later on Ernst-Thälmann-Strasse (called Eisenbahnstrasse today). New discos sprouted up like mushrooms in outlying towns, throwing the big-city youth and the local rural population together, which often led to conflict. The new era of freedom also quickly led to extreme political positions. The German Alliance's election showing in Leipzig in March 1990 led to violent confrontations between the Left and Right—a prob-

Comparative Election Results

National GDR People's Parliament Election in 1990		Local Elections in 1990	
CDU (Christian Democratic Union)	40.8%	SPD	35.3%
SPD (Social Democratic Party)	21.9%	CDU	26.9%
PDS (Democratic Socialist Party)	16.4%	PDS	13.0%
DSU (German Social Union)	6.3%	DSU	4.2%
BFD (Association of Free Democrats, Liberals)	5.5%	BFD	4.5%
Bündnis 90 (Confederation 90)	2.9%	Bündnis 90	7.5%
Grüne (Green Party)	2.0%	Grüne	3.7%

lem that came to the forefront in the 1990s. While Connewitz would emerge as an alternative center, partly because buildings abandoned for demolition could now be occupied by permission of the GWL (later the LWB), Grünau became a rightwing stronghold. The rightwing especially coopted soccer. Crime rates generally increased with the *Wende*, partly due to the fact that the old national structures were being dissolved, with no new ones established yet to replace them.

With regard to the parliament, reunification was easy to achieve. On October 2, 1990, all four hundred (East German) People's Parliament delegates resigned their seats and woke up the next day as (Federal) Bundestag delegates. Yet as the GDR was officially relegated to the history books, it was already clear that the process of reunification would be marked by more than just euphoria. The tasks at hand were not only huge and difficult, but also represented a historic first.

From Treuhand to the Extended Work Bench

"A state-owned East German printing machinery company has bought a marketing concern in the United States in what is believed to be the first such deal with a Western company," the *New York Times* reported on January 12, 1990. The East German combine VEB Polygraph Werner Lamberz really did take over the Royal Zenith Corporation in the motherland of capitalism, in order to boost its business in the United States. General Manager Thomas Schneider explained, "We're proud to be the first East German company to buy an American one—more will follow." The Leipzig combine that emerged from the Karl Krause and Brehmer Brothers companies employed about 16,000 people, had developed many innovative printing machines, and had exported them not only to the United States, but to over sixty countries. The takeover, however, was followed that same year by the company's liquidation, and individual units were also taken over. The branches located in Leipzig were bought by Heidelberger Druckmaschinen AG, which shut down most of the former East German facilities a short time later.

Shutdowns were a part of everyday life in Leipzig at that time, when continuing with existing structures was more of an exception. Of 118,000 industrial jobs in the municipal area, only 20,000 were left five years later. The reasons varied. Some of the existing facilities had worn out in recent decades or were full of outdated technology, capital coverage for starting up in the market economy was markedly lean, and the East German people had little experience with market practices. The somewhat desolate continuation of existing structures through the Treuhand state holding agency and/or Western "receivership" resulted in the unprecedented deindustrialization that was especially obvious in Leipzig, where thirty of 122 GDR industrial combines were headquartered and the industrial rate was over 35 percent. The currency reform of June 1, 1990, constituted a break. Though the official conversion rate from East to West marks was a little more than 4:1, all regular payments were made at a rate of 1:1, meaning costs were suddenly quadrupled and traditional markets like Eastern Europe could no longer be managed at reasonable prices. In the meantime, local consumers sated their voracious appetite for Western products, which was forty years in the making. The book industry concentrated in Leipzig was hit particularly hard, suddenly competing with colorful, shiny, nonideologically loaded products and hardly playing any continuing role at all. Socialist nonsellers sat in large containers, like the ones in front of the international bookshop on Petersstrasse on August 23, 1990, waiting to be hauled off to the recycling facility. Approximately 50,000 tons of East German books were destroyed in the early 1990s. Sales were not the only problem. Industry subsidies disappeared, soon giving rise to economic crises that could not be resolved without foreign investors.

Reclam Leipzig, one of thirty-three publishing houses operating under the same name in the East and West until 1990, suffered that fate. Unlike most of the other publishers that had already embarked on the path to the West with the Americans, publisher Ernst Reclam first headed for Stuttgart in 1950, and later to Ditzingen. There still was a Reclam Publishing in Leipzig, too, though under the aegis of the GDR's planned economy. The relationship between the capitalist original and its socialist counterpart was profoundly disturbed. After initial rapprochement, discord between the two continued in 1990, because the Leipzig publishing house tried to maintain its independence. Ultimately, Reclam Ditzingen took over Reclam Leipzig in May 1991. Sixteen employees retained their jobs, producing about fifty titles per year. One of those was the novel *Schlafes Bruder* (*Brother of Sleep*) by Robert Schneider, which became an international hit after initial resistance in Stuttgart in 1992. Ten years later, Reclam celebrated its 175th anniversary under the motto "Zukunft braucht Herkunft" (The future requires a past). Three years later, it became clear that the past was not so relevant after all. Reclam in Leipzig—then with just four employees—was closed, a fate shared by many historic publishing houses in the city.

— Swiderski industrial factory, prior to rehabilitation

It was not just the old established publishers that disappeared, however. The city lost its presence in nearly every economic sector. This was particularly evident in the immigration rates and sharp increases in unemployment, which reached 21.3 percent in 2005, higher than almost everywhere else in Germany. At the same time, the number of full-time jobs fell to 156,000, half as high as in 1989. Since reaching that low point, much has happened. Within eight years, about 40,000 new jobs were added, and unemployment fell below 10 percent. This was partially due to the number of large corporations that moved there.

Beginning in 2002, Porsche has been in production in Leipzig's northern district, and three years later, BMW moved into new digs there, designed by Zaha Hadid. The logistics sector developed just as fast in Leipzig as the automobile industry. Though the Leipzig/Halle airport plays a minor role in passenger transport, its significance as a freight hub has increased considerably since undergoing expansion and modernization in 2007, and it now ranks fifth in Europe, after Frankfurt, London, Paris, and Amsterdam. Additional cornerstones are the bio- and health technology sector, growing tourism, creative industries, and media. Film and television now play a much more important role in Leipzig than the book trade, which after the downfall of the traditional publishers barely has any economic relevance any more. Yet numerous new independent micropublishers encourage all kinds of creative potential, so the former city of books no longer ranks twenty-fifth, as it did in the mid-1990s, but tenth in terms of books published throughout Germany.

The existence of educational institutions in Leipzig also plays a role, like the Gutenberg School or the Academy of Graphic Design and Book Arts (HGG), but also indirectly the Literary Institute, the only poets' workshop of its kind in Germany. Furthermore, the city's relatively low rents leave more room for new establishments and old buildings from closed industries often become home to new creative endeavors. Especially in Leipzig's formerly densely industrial west, in the Plagwitz and Lindenau districts, industrial buildings have been transformed into office complexes or lofts, studios, galleries, or clubs.

The most prominent example is a former cotton-spinning mill, built in the late nineteenth century and once the largest on the European continent. The building is no longer home to the textile industry, but besides offices, an art-house cinema, an artists' superstore, and a bicycle workshop, about fifteen galleries; more than one hundred artists have moved in, including Neo Rauch, Tilo Baumgärtel, and papal portraitist Michael Triegel. Most of the resident artists reject the moniker "New Leipzig School," but it does figure pretty well in the international art market. At the beginning of the millennium, the Leipzig scene was still so completely fresh that so many potential buyers showed up for exhibition openings that they had trouble finding places to park their private jets at Leipzig airports. While the hype has died down somewhat, art has claimed and built up its place in the city. A wide range of creative talent has taken up residence in the *Tapetenwerk* (wallpaper factory), *Westwerk* (westwork factory), and many other former industrial facilities—open space from abandoned property. However, not all the industrial tracts, which once covered over 320 acres—more than half the size of the Markkleeberg Sea— have been reutilized.

Buntgarnwerke (yarn factory) on the White Elster

De-grayification

"I had a dream: the banks had the money for it."
—Dr. Jürgen Schneider

In the midst of the *Wende*-chaos, Dr. Jürgen Schneider, born in 1934, crossed Leipzig's inner city and saw palaces everywhere. The fact that they were completely derelict and in desperate need of rehabilitation did not bother him much, because he was a building tycoon. He was just working on a 215,278 square foot office building on Frankfurt's Zeil Street, or at least that's what his bank thought. It was actually only 96,875 square feet, according to the construction sign, but still. In Leipzig it would be a little more. Beginning in 1991, he or his real estate company acquired one old building after another. He eventually owned more than twenty properties in downtown Leipzig and over half of all the passages. Other investors were making their way to the eastern boomtown as well. The spirit of optimism pushed Leipzig real estate prices as high as Frankfurt's for a time—Frankfurt am Main in the West, that is.

In reality, the quality of buildings in Leipzig shortly after the *Wende* was not up to the standards of even Frankfurt an der Oder in the East. The building stock on the Pleisse River was considerably older and more rundown. So the burning question at the time (and the title of a television documentary)

Debris with a hint of Baroque—the belvedere on the Romanushaus dominates the rest of the prefabricated buildings on the Brühl

was *"Ist Leipzig noch zu retten?"* ("Can Leipzig still be saved?," which can also be interpreted as: "Do they still have all their marbles in Leipzig?"). Over decades, the city's many old neighborhoods had turned into a monochromatic gray landscape characterized by crumbling plaster, damaged windows, torn gutters, and leaky roofs. About twenty-five thousand apartments were inhabitable and stood empty, some cleared to make room for modern prefabricated buildings. The dilemma was first publicly discussed on January 6 and 7, 1990, at a Leipzig building conference. More than one thousand participants agreed that building preservation must be a priority. Of the 258,000 apartments in Leipzig, 196,000 needed rehabilitation—in the broadest of terms. Like one hundred years earlier, coal-burning furnaces were still standard in old buildings, and sixty thousand apartments still had "toilets on the landing" and no private bathrooms. In addition to the buildings' technical obsolescence, they were deteriorated, falling apart, and plagued by spreading flora, including mold and pigeon ticks. In areas of new construction, where there was little space available, rents were relatively high in the mid-1990s. A three-bedroom apartment would cost about 1,600 marks in average. In today's money, that would be close to 2,000 dollars.

Schneider Buildings

Royal Court	Golden Ball
Thieme's Courtyard	Wünschmann's Courtyard
House Romanus	Blue and Gold Star
Hunters Courtyard	Barthel's Courtyard
Weavers Courtyard	Big Joachimsthal
Barfussgasse 11, 13, and 15	11 St. Thomas Churchyard "Tea House"
Mädler Passage	Central Trade Show Palace
Bamberger & Hertz	Steib's Courtyard
Hainspitze	

Because the write-off potential made building in the East lucrative, more apartments were built in Leipzig than at any other time in the city's history, despite its continuing decline in population. In 1997 alone, there were nearly ten thousand new constructions, and almost twice as many renovations. What began as an attractive gap in supply soon turned into a vacancy problem (in 2001, 22 percent stood empty). Real estate and rent prices

fell quickly. And because this was happening all over East Germany, policy in the Urban Renewal East program changed in 2002 from building to tearing down apartments. Prefabricated buildings were especially targeted for removal from the market, but many a protected old building also disappeared, thanks to demolition premiums.

One such old building torn down was Thieme's Courtyard, which was on the eastern outskirts of town, whose future seemed bright in 1991, because it had been acquired by Dr. Jürgen Schneider. Rehabilitation never got off the ground, however, primarily because at Easter 1994, the building tycoon moved to America and went into hiding. At first, Schneider's disappearance was problematic for the contractors he had hired. There were more than two hundred of such companies working on renovation projects well underway, like Barthel's Courtyard, paying costs out of their own pockets. The damages

Aerial view of Leipzig, 2013

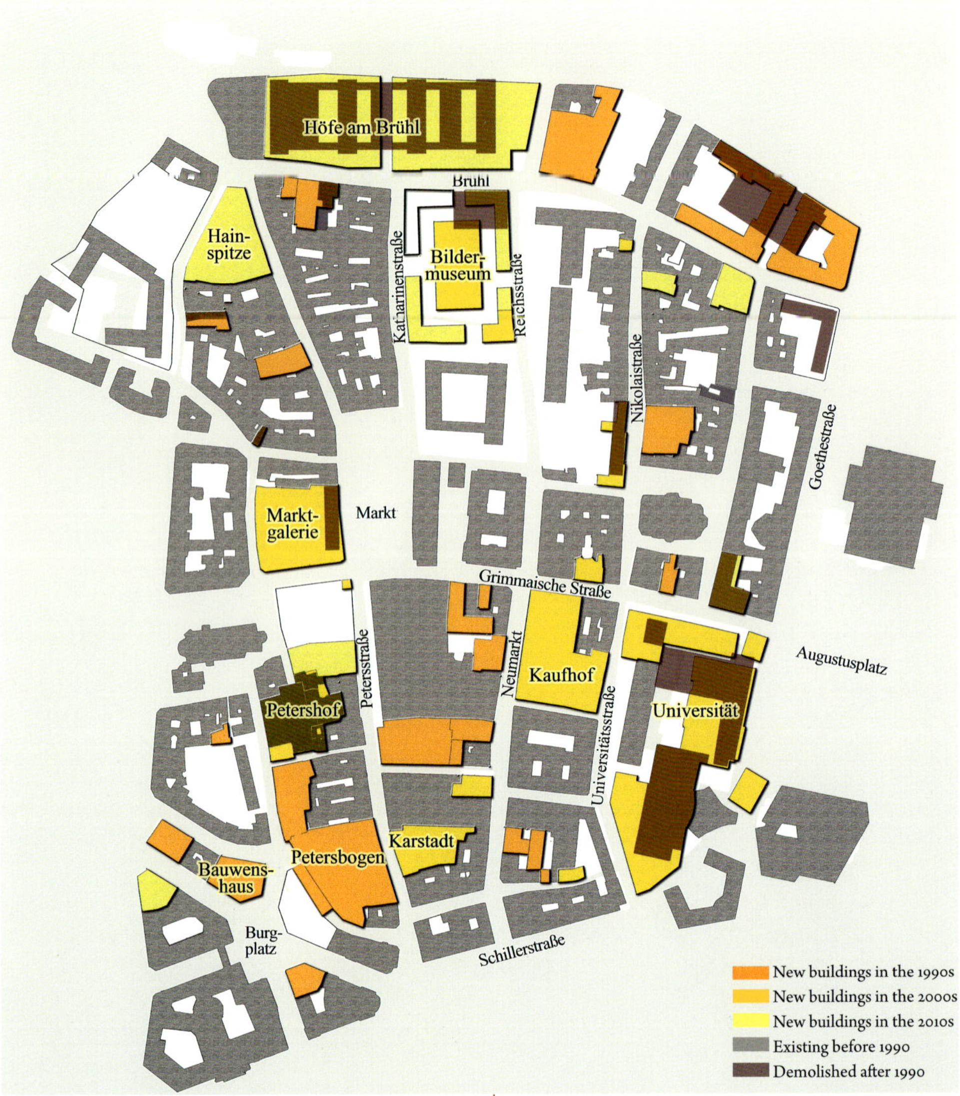

Construction in the city center since 1990

were huge, although renovation of most of Schneider's properties did not begin until after he went bankrupt and some of them were undertaken and paid for by his creditors. Nevertheless, Schneider's involvement probably saved some treasures, like Barthel's Courtyard, from demolition. He set the impetus and the standards for the entire city center's rehabilitation quality, which is easier, of course, when others are footing the bill.

Schneider was not the only fallen building contractor in Leipzig's post-*Wende* era, by far. Bavarian Manfred Rübesam's plans, for example, were much more spectacular. He acquired numerous industrial areas in Plagwitz from the Treuhand state holding agency, where he planned to build thirty skyscrapers up to nearly six hundred feet tall. The scenario never made it past the envisioning stage—surprisingly—and Rübesam declared bankruptcy. One Russian Ilyushin plane "parked" on Karl-Heine-Strasse, which belonged to the Da Capo Museum's classic collection, is reminiscent of his high-flying plans.

Meanwhile, it is not only visions like those which are a thing of the past, but most of the gray cityscape as well. Nearly 90 percent of the old buildings have been rehabilitated in the last quarter-century, though there are still a few left to do on the main streets and in the eastern part of the city. The Waldstrassen District, meanwhile, is not just a model for rehabilitation, but because there are no gaps in the old buildings, it is considered to be a mecca for historicism. Old buildings shape the cityscape—most in a positive way. With 15,600 buildings protected by landmark law, Leipzig has more cultural buildings than any other German city. Leipzig also holds the German record for demolished cultural icons, with most of the swaths emerging during the period of declining population.

In the city center, most of the gaps left by World War II have been closed. The architectural quality of the new constructions is a matter of taste. City Hall also made sure that traffic in the city center would slow down. This is rarely criticized nowadays, because it and the variety of the center's functions contribute to the great vitality of the downtown. Even parts of the university are still located in the middle of the city, though the campus got a complete facelift over the years. The building in Augustus Square designed by Erick van Egeraat is one of the most spectacular of Leipzig's new constructions from the last twenty-five years.

Gondwanaland is another, the largest tropical facility in Europe and one of many projects that arose during renovation of the zoo. Its fame and popularity have increased dramatically in recent years, and its service to the city as a cultural destination continues to increase. The same is true for the network of passages in the city center, which was not only renovated but also expanded to include many new passages as well. The Leipzig of today is characterized primarily by its refurbished past. Some of the things deemed positive today had negative origins, however. The abundance of green is just one sign of the city's former urban planning deficit. It could stay in those dimensions because the city did not grow any bigger after 1930. The idyllic lakes in the south are the result of a gigantic land grab, and the continued existence of Leipzig's many old buildings is partially due to the GDR's economy of scarcity.

Schneider's methods—sprucing up baroque gems by cooking the books—fits well within this succession, but his conduct was not without consequence. When he suddenly withdrew from the public eye in April 1994—reportedly for health reasons—it did not end well. His recovery in Florida led to his arrest, extradition, and trial on the duration of his "rehabilitation efforts." The Frankfurt state court assessed that the banks lost 6.7 billion D-marks altogether. Schneider was sentenced to six years and nine months in prison, two-thirds of which the building tycoon actually served. Representatives from over fifty banking establishments involved were read the riot act for their unscrupulous behavior but emerged unscathed. Deutscher Bank chief Hilmar Kopper added fuel to the fire by describing the financial losses for the contractors, about 50 million marks altogether, as "peanuts" on television (as opposed to the billions owed to the banks), which did not necessarily paint the banking industry or banking establishments in the best light. Subsequently, those falsely certified loan credits led to a general financial crisis for the banking industry. Real estate values rose especially high in Schneider's getaway location of Miami, by more than 300 percent in less than ten years. Coincidentally, of course. Probably.

Old Flagship—New Trade Show

"The trade show is Leipzig, and if you delete it, you delete Leipzig."
—Kurt Schoop

Seventy thousand people in Leipzig assembled for the Monday demonstration on March 18, 1991. The topic, meanwhile, had switched from the SED-government's policies to those of it successor, including the ever-increasing rate of inflation in particular. Unlike in GDR times, the new system's response to the rallies was not repressive, but not to react at all. Though political VIPs were on site. Two days earlier, Federal Commerce Secretary Jürgen Möllemann attended the opening of the spring trade show, after having also attended Munich's handicraft fair that same day. It would be the city's last general trade show, yet the end of the long-standing tradition was barely mentioned in the press. In the trade show's 826th year, which was also year one after fifty years of heteronomy, Leipzig's future as a supraregional trade-show city was uncertain. Leipzig had been brought back down to earth and was suddenly one city among many. There was no longer any need for a gateway to the East—and the trade shows of fall 1989 and spring 1991 were worlds apart.

On the new open market, Leipzig had no advantage except one—good contacts with Eastern Europe. That was much too little in comparison with the deficits that characterized the city and trade show. The Western side of the inter-Ger-

The new trade show in northern Leipzig

man competition had much more than a forty-five-year market-based head-start; it had also swapped out general trade shows for various specialized fairs decades before. By 1990, claims for those exhibitions had long been staked out, so there was basically no need for yet another trade-show city. The fact that a future for Leipzig's trade show was being forged at all was solely due to its historic past and probably to the fact that it was impossible for Leipzigers to imagine the city without the trade show. So in 1991, not only was the long overdue end of the old trade-show principle decided upon, but two additional decisions were made that pointed the way forward. The Leipziger Messe GmbH (Leipzig Trade Show Company Ltd.) was established and construction of new exhibition halls planned. The planners chose a new location for the fairgrounds and gave up the trade-show buildings in the city center and former site on Prager Strasse.

The decision did not necessarily favor nostalgia, as it physically distanced the trade show from the city and its own history, but it did allow for a much more systematic course to be set for the future, as the new area—the former Mockau airport north of the city—offered much better opportunities for development and access. The old personnel manager was also let go after ten years—as damage control. In November 1990, trade-show director Siegfried Fischer, acting alone, leased the shop areas in all of the inner-city trade-show buildings, including the Mädlerpassage, to a Mannheim real estate company for twenty-five years, for an extremely low price. It was a relatively common scandal at the time, which cost Fischer his job and Leipzig millions of marks in a subsequent settlement.

Specialty Trade Shows at the Leipzig Trade Show

Hochzeit Feste Feiern (Celebrate Weddings)
Baby plus Kids
Motorradmesse (Motorcycle Show)
Haus-Garten-Freizeit (Home, Garden, Leisure Time)
mitteldeutsche handwerksmesse (central German craftsmen's show)
Beach & Boat – Wassersportmesse Leipzig (Leipzig Watersports Show)
Leipziger Buchmesse/Leipziger Antiquariatsmesse/ Manga-Comic-Convention (Leipzig Book Fair/ Leipzig Antiquities Fair/Manga Comic Convention)
AMI Auto Mobil International/AMITEC (AMI international auto show)
Hund & Katz (Dog and Cat)
modell-hobby-spiel (models, hobbies, games)
Designers' Open
Touristik & Caravaning International Leipzig (International Tourism and Caravanning, eastern Germany's largest travel show)

"New guy" Kurt Schoop was an old hand in the trade-show industry. He modernized the exhibition content. In 1991, the book fair, while still located in the city center, was scheduled for the first time as an independent, subject-specific trade show. Nearly twenty-five thousand people visited both of the fair buildings in the market square. That was nothing compared to Frankfurt, where spaces fifteen times larger hosted 260,000 visitors in the fall. The editors at the *ZEIT* newspaper were not the only ones thinking that "Leipzig cannot be an alternative to Frankfurt, or even compete." That would change, partly because the "Leipzig Reads" literary festival was held concurrently with the trade show for the first time in 1992. Yet until 1996, the Leipzig trade show was considered to be an underdog at best, but at least then it was one with a glitzy dog house. After three years of construction and at a cost of 1.335 billion D-marks (about $850 million), the new trade show was inaugurated and not only caught up with the competition structurally but left it in the dust.

As one of the most modern complexes in Europe, it could be used by all trades and enjoyed great success, evidenced by the fact that the exhibition spaces have already had to be expanded. The Games Convention, which rose from nothing to Europe's market leader within five years, exploded at the seams in 2008. It became clear that the mother of all trade shows was still just a lightweight compared to Cologne, Düsseldorf, Frankfurt, and Hannover, despite a few successes, because it could not keep that first successful foster child from moving to the Rhine. In 2013, the Leipzig trade show has risen to eighth place in Germany in terms of sales and size of exhibition spaces—not bad for a new beginning. But today's trade show is no match for its historic counterpart (yet). The same is true of its status as a convention site, where Leipzig has also reached the German top 10, enough to place it in the top 100 internationally. Development and potential promise even better rankings, especially once renovations are complete at the convention center by the zoo.

New Shores

Leipzig's surroundings have long been considered as lacking in appeal. No Swiss landscape, be it Saxon or Franconian, and definitely not a real one, was ever in sight. Nor were there any other graceful or quaint geographical features coming to its rescue. When travel journalist Joseph Roth visited the city in 1931, he concluded that Leipzig "was devoid of even the least geographic grace and was not even situated on a decent river, but on several laughable little rivers instead, called Parthe, Elster, Rödel, and the like." And because large parts of its surroundings flooded regularly in the past, Leipzig has long been mocked as a big town by the sea.

While alpine attractions are still difficult to find in the city's environs, there are many reasons why Leipzig might have earned the right to be called a city by the sea in the meantime, though not because of the surrounding swampy terrain. Lakes dotted with sailboats, fishing grounds, and nude beaches make up for its lack of cliffs, and the water in the Elster and Pleisse Rivers can once again be defined as such. Casting a line from a riverbank in the 1980s might have been considered a subversive act or a sure sign of questionable mental health, but today the perch, pike, carp, and fishers are back. However, the water does have a brownish tint to it, due

Cospuden Lake in its best light

to nontoxic levels of iron and sulfate leaching out as the groundwater level rises. Berlin's Spree River is wrestling with the same problem, for which there is currently no solution.

Improved water quality and new political and economic conditions after 1989 have also led to efforts to raise the Pleisse and Elster millraces back out from underground. Even in the later 1980s, artists and architects brought the matter to public attention with the slogan "Pleisse ans Licht" (Uncover the Pleisse), and environmental topics also played significant roles in early Monday demonstrations. River recovery of the Pleisse millrace itself is proceeding rather slowly. In 2014, about one third of its nearly 2.5 miles has been recovered, and the section along Lampestrasse is in the planning stages. The Elster millrace, of which about 4,265 feet was covered, should flow completely above ground by 2018, and construction has resumed on the Karl Heine Canal. The canal is expected to extend to the Lindenau Harbor by fall 2015, and to finally accommodate watercraft—though no ocean liners will be among them. An additional small harbor, the *Stadthafen* (municipal harbor) will also be added at the site of the former Blüthner factory near the *Schreberbad* (garden pool). It will function primarily as an access point connecting Neuseenland with the city center, which can be reached from the city center directly via paddleboat or the Leipzig public boat.

Leipzig's Neuseenland forms the southern part of the central German lake district created by the flooded holes left by surface mining in the central German brown-coal fields. Nearly sixty lakes have formed in the area around Halle and Bitterfeld, covering about fifty-eight square miles—about one quarter of the Mecklenburg lake district. Nearly one-third of them are in Leipzig's Neuseenland, which extends from the southern edge of Leipzig twelve miles south to Borna. Just a few decades ago, the area looked like a lunar landscape—a comparison insulting to the earth's moon. Since then, the area has transformed into a local recreational destination. When the weather is nice, it feels a little like the Baltic Sea coast. Except that the 558-foot-tall Lippendorf brown-coal-fired power plant is constantly nosing into the pseudo-Mecklenburgian view, where it really does not fit. Yet that power plant acts as a signpost, as the water compound's sudden appearance against an unnatural background is similarly

Mendelssohn Bank—score-readers have the advantage

out of place. The process of transformation came in the wake of vigorous brown-coal mining in the area, described in the section "Lunar Landscape."

Surface mines still operate south of Leipzig, but their capacity has decreased by about 80 percent, because brown coal lost its ubiquitous dominance with the demise of the GDR. While East German planners had something in mind for reusing the crater landscape left behind by the brown-coal mines, mining in the GDR was expected to continue for the foreseeable future, so those plans were not likely to have been realized until the height of a climate disaster. Individual lakes, like Kulkwitzer Lake west of the city, or the Borna Reservoir, had already formed in the 1950s and 1970s, respectively. Most of the rest of the craters were not filled until the 1990s, after reunification. That was also when reforestation of areas above the groundwater level and the shaping of lakeshores began. Those around Cospuden Lake had already been reclaimed by nature, because the "Cossi" was dedicated as an Expo Project in the year 2000. The northern shore is just 4.3 miles from downtown Leipzig, so the lake has integrated very well with daily life in the big city, as it is accessible by bicycle as well as by boat. Unless the kingfishers are nesting!

Lakes around Leipzig

From the Olympics to Soccer

"The winner is Leipzig."
—Gerhard Schröder, former German Chancellor

When Ronald Reagan arrived in West Berlin in June 1987, no one had any idea that the city of Leipzig was about to enter the limelight. It was not just Reagan's line, "Mr. Gorbachev, tear down this wall," that caused a sensation, but also the American president's suggestion that Greater Berlin jointly host the 2000 Olympic Games. While West-Berlin politicians started working up feasibility studies, the SED's enthusiasm was held in check because it would be impossible to secure the borders in such a scenario. When Berlin mayor Walter Momper officially presented his plans to Erich Honecker in June 1989, the latter announced that the GDR had long had its own plans: Leipzig (far away from the border) already planned its candidacy for 2004. Though the proposal seemed less than promising, if only because such an undertaking could have been difficult to finance, Greater Berlin was off the table, despite the feasibility studies.

When it came to the Olympic Games, the GDR's policy was usually extremely success-oriented. Little East Germany placed third in the medals count at its last Olympic Games in Seoul in 1988—for the

The kettle in the kettle—the old central stadium has had a new interior since 2004 third time, behind the Soviet Union and ahead of the United States. Though doping played a role, its specific nature was never verified, not least because its use was common practice among other nations as well. Leipzig native Kristin Otto, who also trained at Leipzig's DHfK Sport Club, was crowned as the best female athlete, with six gold medals. The club was one of the most successful in the history of sports, primarily because of it state-of-the-art training methods, and won ninety-three Olympic medals. So it was all the more incomprehensible for many Leipzigers when the entire DHfK was shut down under protest in December 1990. At that time, its athletic facilities were in extremely poor condition. The stands at the swimming stadium, which was used as an outdoor pool until 2000, were in just as much need of repair as those at the central stadium, where capacity had been reduced to 37,000 spectators. But the stadium rarely sold out anymore. Though the VfB Leipzig soccer team, formerly known as "Lok," made it to the premier German league in 1993, the club was ejected from the highest league after only three wins and from one league after another in the years that followed. The athletic downgrade was followed by bankruptcy, before the club was reestablished as the 1st FC Lokomotive Leipzig (Leipzig Locomotives 1st Soccer Club), which started out in the eleventh league, or the ninth division of the German league. Some 12,421 spectators attended the game of the year in 2004 against Eintracht Grossdeuben II at the new central stadium, which included streakers, VIPs, and set an attendance record for the lowest national division.

Besides that laudable occasion, however, many unlaudable ones grabbed headlines. Downtown Leipzig was vandalized several times after soccer matches in the early 1990s, first on September 2, 1990, after Lok Leipzig's game versus Bayern München, when even shots fired. When Sachsen Leipzig (formerly Chemie) played against FC Berlin, the situation escalated completely. An estimated four hundred hooligans from the capital rioted at the Leutzsch train station, faced by tweny-five People's Policemen. When the latter fired their weapons, several were severely wounded, and one eighteen-year-old was killed. Though the violence decreased in subsequent years, it remained a part of East German soccer, as did the club's disastrous management. In 2011, FC Sachsen also declared bankruptcy and started over. Which is why it seemed inconceivable that one of Leipzig's traditional clubs would ever lead Leipzig to the national German soccer league before the city's twothousandth anniversary.

Dietrich Mateschitz, aka Red Bull, filled the bill in the soccer-hungry city. In 2009, he took over fifth-leaguer team SSV Markranstädt, who in the meantime (2014) became RB Leipzig and made it to the second German league and impressed many locals. They played in the central stadium, which has been renamed Red Bull Arena. Since it was renovated, it holds 45,000 spectators, though sporting events did not draw capacity crowds until the World Championship Soccer Tournament in 2006. Big sporting events— including track and field, indoor hockey, and volleyball—also took place in the neighboring arena, which was completed in 2002. The arena is also home to the HCL women's handball team, which, unlike the soccer teams, is particularly successful and has already won many German championships. Other Leipzig sports teams have had some success as well. In addition, the former DHfK facilities are used for Olympic training once again, but despite every attempt, not yet for the official games. Even though the city was temporarily seized by yet another vision of Olympia once more.

When then-mayor Wolfgang Tiefensee got out his cello during bidding for the National Olympic Committee for Germany (NOK) at the Hilton in Munich on March 13, 2003, no could have guessed that it would show Leipzig in a completely new perspective. Yet a short time later, the Saxon city really did prevail against Stuttgart, Frankfurt, Düsseldorf, and Hamburg in the national competition to host the 2012 Olympic Games. Lindenau Harbor was to function as the Olympic Village, Markkleeberger Lake as the site for water sports, and the Sportforum was to be the hub for the Games. Total costs were estimated to be $2.29 billion, but suddenly the tide turned and London, not Leipzig, won the bid.

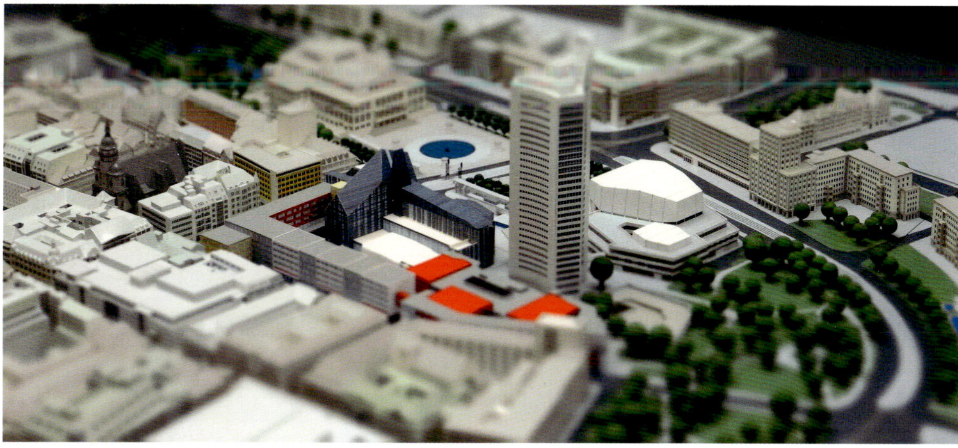

Visions

The year is 2030. Time has flown by. Leipzig is now two thousand years old. In 1965, the metropolis on the Pleisse River celebrated its eight hundredth anniversary, and its thousandth in 2015. But now it is already time for its two thousandth? Does time pass more quickly in this Saxon municipality? The basis for celebrating another anniversary so soon was found in the Vatican's secret archives, the surprising release of which has revealed numerous ancient travel descriptions. According to documents, a Roman penal colony named *Leipopolis* was established in the middle of Germania in 30 CE, where subjects of the Empire who had escaped crucifixion were settled. The report got the whole planet's attention. In the years that followed, an army of international archaeologists dug through Leipzig's entire central area and discovered not just two-thousand-year-old latrines, but the Amber Room as well—*Stern* has the exclusive.

This scenario or something similar might well happen in the future, even if admittedly more realistic assumptions exist. That reality can depart from even scientifically founded prognoses has already been shown by population projections in the past that seemed most reliable for Leipzig but then turned out completely differently. The latest projections from the Saxon State Statistics Agency in 2011 predicts a population of 538,600 in 2025, which means Leipzig's population, which already topped 540,000 by the end of 2014, would have to decline again. To be sure, the city does not exactly make it easy for statisticians. Population levels have seen extreme shifts for the last two hundred years, both upward and down.

City-planning priorities have also shifted many times in the past, and not just in Leipzig. Especially during the twentieth century, completely opposing views have prevailed at various times. Current trends advocate for a return of the European-style city. Many of Leipzig's current urban planning projects reflect this, which means more than just rehabilitation work, but also reinforcing and concentrating the urban core. One premise for increasing the quality of residence in the city center is further limiting through traffic. This approach has already strongly increased the vitality of the city core. In addition, the already generally dense network of passages is to be expanded, especially in areas where passages and through court-

Detail of Leipzig city model

yards already existed in the past. That will only be possible in the areas of Reichsstrasse, on the Brühl, Burgplatz, and at St. Matthew Church, including already existing brown fields or the location of future new construction in the city center. In years to come, focus will shift to Leuschner Square in particular. Besides a Catholic church already under construction, which happens to be located on Martin-Luther-Ring, of all places, there are plans for a new indoor market on the foundations of the old buildings. It might well be that there will even be a memorial to freedom and unity on the square someday, though the outlook is highly speculative at this point.

Meanwhile, plans for Leipzig's waterways are much more concrete. The completion of the Karl Heine Canal through to Lindenau Harbor and the uncovering of the last tiled sections of the Elster millrace were both already underway in 2014. Uncovering the Pleisse millrace is also a sure thing, though conversion will not be complete until 2030. To improve the city's flood protection, the Old Elster will be coaxed back into its former channel. The Elster Basin would only be used during floods then, would not permanently fill up with sand and, because it would be supplied with groundwater, could serve as a bathing destination close to the city center, provided the industrial sludge from past decades is removed. Last but not least, the Parthe River has also been mentioned, which does still flow above ground, but whose lifeless banks are to be reconfigured. Progress on that project has been sporadic, however, probably due to the fact that the "beautification" of the river's overflow is a luxury issue and much less important than other projects. Because of the steep increase in birthrates, expanding the educational infrastructure is also a current priority, but with increasing population numbers, the financial feasibility of existing housing and increased traffic will also play a role. Integrating this in ways that do not further impair the city infrastructure will not be easy, especially because the

View of St. Thomas Church from the Promenadenring, 2013

financial means required typically flow even slower than rush-hour traffic.

What the future might bring is beyond what this author can predict—source material is considerably lacking. It might be safe to say that Leipzig's erratic history will remain erratic, and that the city will benefit from its past. But not only that. The most fascinating thing about Leipzig in 2015 is the interplay of old and new, tradition and innovation, the St. Thomas Choir and Wave Gothic Festival just as naturally reconciled as elegant passages and modern trade fairgrounds or the hubbub of downtown and the silence of the alluvial forest. One can only hope that it is still just like that on the occasion of Leipzig's two thousandth anniversary, whenever that might occur.

Picture Credits

© 2015 Sebastian Ringel, 16, 60, 112, 120, 168, 185, 212, 218
© PUNCTUM/Peter Franke, 196, 216 • akg-images, front cover, 36, 58 • BArch, Bild 183-1990-0713-021/Waltraud Grubitzsch (geb. Raphael), 190 • BArch, Bild 183-L0902-114/ Ulrich Häßler, 192 • BArch, Bild 183-S0727-121/ Peter Koard, 179 • BArch, Bild 183-X0311-0022-001/Heinz Koch, 182 • BArch, Bild 102-02362/ Georg Pahl, 181 • BArch, Bild 183-1982-0905-103/ Waltraud Grubitzsch (geb. Raphael), 188 • BArch, Bild 183-H1114-0011-001/Wolfgang Kluge, 184 • photo: Rössing, Roger & Rössing, Renate, 1949, 175 • photo: Rössing, Roger & Rössing, Renate, 1952, 176 • from: Saxonia. Museum für sächsische Vaterlandskunde, Dresden: Eduard Pietzsch 1834/1835, vol. 1, 75 • Harald Kirschner/ transit, 172/173 • Julia Stöhr, Leipzig, 200/201, back cover • photo: Rössing, Roger & Rössing, Renate, 1950, 166 • photo: Sebastian Ringel, 15 l., center, r., 100, 206, 208, 209, 210, 214, 217, 219, 222 • picture alliance/zb, 202 • picture-alliance/dpa, 174 • picture-alliance/epd, 187 • publisher's and author's archive, 8/9, 12, 21, 66, 70/71, 72, 76, 78, 78/79, 81, 85, 96, 102, 103, 105, 118, 119, 123, 128, 137, 150, 152, 158, 170, 186 • publisher's and author's archive, postcard, 28, 82, 83, 88, 89, 104, 126, 131, 132, 147, 151, 156 • Stadt Leipzig, 5, 221 • Stadt Leipzig, Amt für Geoinformation und Bodenordnung, 211 • Stadtgeschichtliches Museum Leipzig, 10, 18, 24, 27, 30, 32, 34/35, 39, 40, 42, 45, 46, 48, 50, 53, 55, 61, 62, 64, 67, 68, 84, 86, 90, 91, 92, 95, 97, 98/99, 106, 107, 109, 110, 111, 114, 116, 121, 125, 129, 134, 136, 138, 140/141, 142, 145, 146, 154, 162, 164, 178

Every effort has been made to trace and contact copyright holders. If there are any inadvertent omissions we apologise to the concerned, and ask that you contact us so that we can correct any oversight as soon as possible.

Imprint

With kind support from Stadt Leipzig

Bibliographic information published by the Deutsche Nationalbibliothek
The Deutsche Nationalbibliothek lists this publication in the Deutsche Nationalbibliografie; detailed bibliographic data are available on the internet at http://dnb.dnb.de.

ISBN 978-3-361-00710-9

Front cover: "Leipzig's Petersstrasse at Trade-show Time," advertisement with stuffed camel from the Margarete Steiff company, postcard image, undated (around 1920)

Cover Design Phillip Hofmeister, Hofmeister Stauder. Büchermacher, Berlin
Project Management Kirsten Witte-Hofmann, Eva Schweitzer
Translation Cindy Optitz
Editing Patricia Nicolescu
Production Sabine Artner
Design and Typesetting Phillip Hofmeister Hofmeister Stauder. Büchermacher, Berlin
Reproduction Photographs Medien Profis GmbH, Leipzig
Printed and Bound by Westermann Druck Zwickau GmbH

Printed in Germany